Routledge Revivals

The Social Context of Literacy

First published in 1986, this book looks at the impact of mass literacy on everyday life, discussing the fundamental differences between traditional oral cultures and contemporary industrialised societies where most people rely on complex combinations of oral and literate communication. There is also a detailed examination of the problems of the sub-literate minority with recommendations for future programmes of assistance. This book also provides a historical survey of the spread of literacy in British society from the Roman occupation onwards. In conclusion, the author discusses the impact of information technologies on people with limited basic skills.

The Social Context of Literacy

Kenneth Levine

Routledge
Taylor & Francis Group
Routledge Revivals

First published in 1986
by Routledge & Kegan Paul

This edition first published in 2017 by Routledge
2 Park Square, Milton Park, Abingdon, Oxon, OX14 4RN
and by Routledge
711 Third Avenue, New York, NY 10017

Routledge is an imprint of the Taylor & Francis Group, an informa business

A Library of Congress record exists under LC control number: 8510839

ISBN 13: 978-1-138-24203-6 (hbk)
ISBN 13: 978-1-315-27929-9 (ebk)
ISBN 13: 978-1-138-24206-7 (pbk)

The social context of literacy

Routledge & Kegan Paul
London, Boston and Henley

First published in 1986
by Routledge & Kegan Paul plc

14 Leicester Square, London WC2H 7PH, England

9 Park Street, Boston, Mass. 02108, USA and

Broadway House, Newtown Road,
Henley on Thames, Oxon RG9 1EN, England

Set in 10 on 12 pt Times
by Inforum Ltd, Portsmouth
and printed in Great Britain
by T J Press (Padstow) Ltd
Padstow, Cornwall

Library of Congress Cataloging in Publication Data

Levine, Kenneth, 1945–

The social context of literacy.
(Language, education, and society)
Bibliography: p.
Includes index.
1. Literacy—England—Nottingham (Nottinghamshire)—Case studies. 2. Reading (Adult education)—England—Nottingham (Nottinghamshire)—Case studies. 3. Literacy—Great Britain—History. 4. Literacy—Economic aspects—England—Nottingham (Nottinghamshire)—Case studies.
I. Title. II. Series.
LC156.G7L39 1986 374'.9425'2 85–10839

British Library CIP data available

ISBN 0–7100–9745–X

'My honest friend,' said the gentleman, 'I perceive you are well acquainted with Scripture.'
[The shepherd replies]
'Yes, sir, pretty well, blessed be God! Through his mercy I learned to read when I was a little boy; though reading was not so common when I was a child, as I am told, through the goodness of Providence and the generosity of the rich, it is likely to become now-a-days . . .'

Hannah More's Cheap Repository Tract,
The Shepherd of Salisbury Plain (1830)

You see, when I first had this trouble with my reading and writing, this tax form, I had to fill them in but the girl friend did them for me. We'd been courting eight years; she knew. Cos I asked her straight away as soon as I went out with her, I says, I'm going to ask you sommat, now serious, I'm not very good at reading and writing. I says, I'm willing to work at anything and I says I promise you we'll have a house and a car, and we can go for four weeks holiday a year, although I'm as thick as two planks up here. And I says, I mean that, that wasn't bribing so as I could marry her. I just told her straight, John Bull, and she never said her Mam was against it all at the time. She wanted her to marry a doctor or somebody, you know how they are. That's why I call her the 'outlaw' . . .

'Bob' (1980)

Contents

Charts and Tables

Charts

Tables

Editor's preface

Simply a list of some of the questions implied by the phrase *Language, Education and Society* gives an immediate idea of the complexity, and also the fascination, of the area.

How is language related to learning? Or to intelligence? How should a teacher react to non-standard dialect in the classroom? Do regional and social accents and dialects matter? What is meant by standard English? Does it make sense to talk of 'declining standards' in language or in education? Or to talk of some children's language as 'restricted'? Do immigrant children require special language provision? How can their native language be used as a valuable resource in schools? Can 'literacy' be equated with 'education'? Why are there so many adult illiterates in Britain and the USA? What effect has growing up with no easy access to language: for example, because a child is profoundly deaf? Why is there so much prejudice against people whose language background is odd in some way: because they are handicapped, or speak a non-standard dialect or foreign language? Why do linguistic differences lead to political violence, in Belgium, India, Wales and other parts of the world?

These are all real questions, of the kind which worry parents, teachers and policy-makers, and the answer to them is complex and not at all obvious. It is such questions that authors in this series discuss.

Language plays a central part in education. This is probably generally agreed, but there is considerable debate and confusion about the exact relationship between language and learning. Even though the importance of language is generally recognised, we still have a lot to learn about how language is related to either educational success or to intelligence and thinking. Language is also a central fact in everyone's social life. People's attitudes and most deeply held beliefs are at stake, for it is through language that personal and social identities are maintained and recognised. People are judged, whether justly or not, by the language they speak.

Language, Education and Society is therefore an area where scholars have a responsibility to write clearly and persuasively, in order to communicate the best in recent research to as wide an audience as possible. This means not only other researchers, but also all those who are involved in educational, social and political policy-making, from individual teachers to government. It is an area where value judgements cannot be avoided. Any action that we take – or, of course, avoidance of action – has moral, social and political consequences. It is vital, therefore, that practice is informed by the best knowledge available, and that decisions affecting the futures of individual children or whole social groups are not taken merely on the basis of the all too widespread folk myths about language in society.

Linguistics, psychology and sociology are often rejected by non-specialists as jargon-ridden; or regarded as fascinating, but of no relevance to educational or social practice. But this is superficial and short-sighted: we are dealing with complex issues, which require an understanding of the general principles involved. It is bad theory to make statements about language in use which cannot be related to educational and social reality. But it is equally unsound to base beliefs and action on anecdote, received myths and unsystematic or idiosyncratic observations.

All knowledge is value-laden: it suggests action and changes our beliefs. Change is difficult and slow, but possible nevertheless. When language in education and society is seriously and systematically studied, it becomes clear how awesomely complex is the linguistic and social knowledge of all children and adults. And with such an understanding, it becomes impossible to maintain a position of linguistic prejudice and intolerance. This may be the most important implication of a serious study of language in our linguistically diverse modern world.

In this book, *Social Context of Literacy*, Ken Levine points out that literacy is usually taken for granted in so-called advanced countries such as Britain. The literate majority regard literacy as 'natural': for them there is no perceivable distinction between seeing a notice and reading it, they cannot remember how they learned to read, and they cannot imagine what it is like not to be able to read. It is widely assumed in a vague and misleading way that 'educated' equals 'literate', that everyone receives compulsory education, and that everyone therefore can and does read. But they can't and don't. Levine provides a historical perspective on the place of literacy in different societies and a useful conceptual analysis of what is meant by functional literacy. How much literacy do you need in order to function in different societies?

However, having criticised both everyday myths about literacy, and also much social scientific work, for being based on crude generalisations unsupported by evidence, the main part of the book is then a case study based on his own fieldwork in Nottingham. He discusses the local social, economic and industrial situation in the city, and discusses an adult literacy scheme, its organisation and what literacy and illiteracy mean to the students involved in it. If our understanding of such a complex phenomenon as literacy is to advance, it will not be by bland, armchair generalisations, but by the combination of careful conceptual analysis and observational and ethnographic fieldwork on what it means for individuals and groups to be literate or illiterate in different societies.

Michael Stubbs

Acknowledgments

My first and principal debt is to the men and women, tutors, students and others who agreed to be interviewed. Researchers sometimes take the cooperation of their respondents too much for granted, perhaps because they have been granted an indulgence they barely deserve. In recording my special gratitude to the literacy students, I would like to hope that they would find in the following pages an occasional item of interest and relevance to their problems and aspirations.

The empirical investigation that features particularly in Chapters 4 and 5 was supported by a grant from the Social Science Research Council (HR 5546). Throughout the period of the inquiry, I was assisted by the staff of the Nottingham Literacy Scheme to an extent that went beyond and far above any call of duty. As well as the organising staff, Peter Beynon, Jean Coates, Hilary, Patsy Jackson, Margaret Purdy, Terry Riley and Heather Roberts, there were many helpful tutors and group leaders too numerous to list.

Various individuals and agencies supplied information and contacts. Eric Galvin, formerly manager of the Central Nottingham (Broadmarsh) Jobcentre, George Mann of the Nottingham Housing Department, Dr Richard Madeley of the University Medical School, Nottingham Inter-Community Trust, Family First, all assisted in material ways. The personnel and training managers of the Nottingham firms surveyed must remain anonymous but I am grateful for their participation.

More recently, information has been supplied by The Bible Society, The Letter-Writing Bureau and The Post Office Public Relations Department. David Young and his colleagues in the University Library have tracked down many elusive references and sources.

I would like to thank my colleagues, Helen Meller, who read and commented very fully on a draft of the historical material, Michael Stubbs, the series editor, and Michael King for helpful suggestions. All the usual disclaimers apply absolving them from any guilt by association for the contents.

In a substantially similar thesis form, this work was accepted by the University of Nottingham for a PhD degree. A version of parts of Chapter 2 appeared in the *Harvard Educational Review*, Volume 52, Number 3, 1982.

Pauline O'Connor, Lynda Miller, Pennie Alfrey and Debbie Roberts all wrestled purposefully with the manuscript. I have also experimented with an unusually (and unprofitably) large number of different and incompatible word processors, spelling checkers and bibliographic databases.

1
Approaching literacy

Introduction

Most people can read and write fluently and are daily immersed in tides of print in the language they speak. What could be more natural, more taken-for-granted for this competent majority, than literacy? For them, there is usually no distinction between seeing a notice and reading it, and probably less effort expended in writing down an item on a shopping-list than calling it to mind in the first place. Moreover, there are few occasions in which competent adults are confronted with the limits of their reading and writing skills. Even if minor mistakes or failures occur, the repetition and redundancy built into written communication is capable of making the practical consequences unimportant. Should serious misunderstanding arise, it is often possible to save a situation simply by switching to speech and asking for spoken clarification.

There are other respects, too, in which individual and collective literacy tends to camouflage its own existence and makes itself 'transparent'. On the individual level, most people quickly forget the details of the learning process and cannot remember the time before they could read or write. Although powers acquired during childhood expand and contract during adult life, only a few people become conscious of their extent and fewer still are compelled to make any active response to the changes. On the social level, every community in Britain has been thoroughly permeated by writing for several generations and the recollection of entirely oral communications has vanished for all but a handful of very old people.

When everyday circumstances which bring literacy under scrutiny do arise, the explanatory ideas lay people will probably find to hand are a set of unsophisticated, common-sense assumptions which have filtered down from the thousands of hours of schooling earmarked for acquiring and utilising literacy. Even those who leave school without the ability to read and write fluently are acutely aware of the prevailing expectations regarding these skills. They will have witnessed the rewards bestowed on academic high achievers; their teachers will have stressed literacy's vocational importance and devoted much effort to inspiring interest in imaginative literature. There can be little doubt in the mind of any school leaver about the high 'official' valuation placed on literacy, and the endless assessments will have long since established his or her own position in the prestige ranking. While the results of the evaluation process are signalled in the clearest manner, precisely what it is that pupils have succeeded in or failed at often remains obscure to them. The vague and exaggerated notions many people take away from school about the extent of their capacities and incapacities can be compounded by an inability to carry out any self-diagnosis and the parallel belief that self-help is impossible. This induced helplessness turns out, in the long run, to be as much of a handicap as the absence of the basic skills themselves, and it leaves a great many of those who finally make their way to adult literacy schemes able to say in their initial interview nothing more explicit about their difficulties than, 'I need help with my reading and writing'.

The superficial nature of popular beliefs about literacy also expresses itself in the widely held conviction that everybody who has attended school can (or at least should be able to) manage any written communication. An instance of this attitude is the confident statement with which Q.D. Leavis opened *Fiction and the Reading Public*: 'In twentieth century England, not only every one can read, but it is safe to add that every one does read' (1932, 3). Such misconceived views are sustained by more than the individual smugness of the academically successful. There is a corporate complacency about literacy in Britain that reflects the huge economic and political investments that have been made in schooling, and also the comparatively early historical appearance of 'mass' literacy. This helps to close off many of the more searching questions that could be posed concerning the social functions and significance of literacy and illiteracy, and contributes directly to the social obstacle course that faces those who cannot read and write.[1]

There is no specific academic or technical specialism entirely devoted to literacy that is able to disturb this complacency, and the published material is slighter and more scattered than the social importance of the topic deserves. Aspects of literacy and its problems are taken up at the margins of several disciplines, with the result that studies tend to deal, often unsystematically, only with selected aspects. In the editorial introduction to *Literacy in Traditional Societies* (1968, 1), Jack Goody remarks that recently developed media of communication have attracted much greater scholarly attention than the massive and cumulative impact on humankind of five millennia of reading and writing. By exactly how much, if at all, this imbalance has now been corrected is a question for keyword analysis and citation indexes to quantify, but a large measure of the credit for any discernible shift of emphasis should go to the pioneering and wide-ranging essay, 'The consequences of literacy', written by Goody himself and Ian Watt in 1963 and republished in his collection. The importance of this contribution lay in its willingness to cross academic boundaries and to relate general issues in a way that fostered mutual recognition among different explanatory traditions.

It is worth considering briefly the way in which some of these traditions have approached the topic of literacy. Goody's lament for its academic neglect applies particularly to media and communication studies and also to the sociology of literature. Apparently sophisticated socio-historical theories of literary genres and printed media have been developed in these areas without, in the main, sufficient empirical attention having been given to the forms and levels of literacy they implicitly or explicitly assume readers to have possessed. Many of the conceptual skyscrapers dominating communications theory are thus totally lacking in foundations. In a variety of distinctive blends, the *histoire du livre*[2] and semiotic and structuralist analyses[3] have promised a dismantling of the written text and/or an account of the social institutions in which it came to be produced, but they have done so without any special consideration of, for instance, differences in the character and level of the author's and the readers' literacies. With some honorable exceptions, such as the work of Walter J. Ong and the group known as the 'Toronto school', to whom we will return, the capacity of readers in contemporary societies to understand written discourse is generally taken for granted.

Literary criticism, too, has on the whole been unconcerned with literacy. According to Eagleton's characterisation of critical theories (1983, 74), the Romantic critics of the nineteenth century were preoccupied with authors and authorship, while English criticism in the aftermath of Leavis and the American New Criticism was exclusively interested in the text itself. Only with the arrival from the continent of 'reception theory' did English-speaking critics possess a unified framework in which to deal with the imaginative role and interpretive capacities readers bring to literary texts. Reception theory argues that even the most explicit text contains ambiguities which force readers to resort to methods and conventions of interpretation brought from beyond the text itself.[4]

Those who turn to linguistics for insights into literacy are immediately confronted by a great deal of technical expertise and empirical research experience, most of which remains uncodified. The reason for this lies in the belief among many linguists, inherited from nineteenth-century theorists and reaffirmed by important twentieth-century figures such as Saussure, Jakobson and Bloomfield, that spoken language has a historical and explanatory primacy. Although a shift of emphasis is probably under way with the rise of such specialisms as discourse analysis,[5] literacy is still widely regarded as an applied field that raises few issues of theoretical significance.

Allusions to the importance of literacy in the development of social and political institutions are common in works of social theory, but the treatment is often cursory. In older works, the historical advent of literacy was significant mainly as marking the point at which historians were able to take over from archaeologists. It sometimes also served as the basis of quite arbitrary judgements about the threshold of 'civilisation'.[6] In recent works, literacy commonly functions as a convenient empirical measure of the level of economic and social development in a society, by-passing a variety of unresolved theoretical issues. Of the more considered socio-historical contributions, two examples must suffice. In a short work published in 1966, Talcott Parsons, the distinguished social theorist who dominated American sociology for more than twenty years, made sweeping claims for the role of literacy in human history. The argument of *Societies: Evolutionary and Comparative Perspectives* is that there are three 'very broad evolutionary levels' in the emergence of human societies and that innovations in literacy are directly involved in the transition from one to another. The invention of writing systems marks the end of the 'primitive', oral stage of societal development and the dawn of the 'intermediate' stage. In the 'archaic' sub-type of intermediate societies, writing remains a craft specialisation confined to elite groups, often for religious or magical purposes. In the 'advanced intermediate' sub-type, literacy is available for all the adult males of an upper social class. The final, 'modern' stage is marked by the institutionalisation of literacy among the entire adult population.

Exactly what explanatory role this evolutionary scheme fulfills is never made entirely clear by Parsons. Examples are given of the various social types (the Aztecs are placed in the 'archaic intermediate', and post-Confucian China in the 'advanced intermediate' categories) but there is no supporting empirical analysis and there is little reference to literacy in the rest of his voluminous writings.[7] What Parsons does provide, however, is the suggestive idea that writing is crucial to the differentiation of the cultural from the social sphere because it permits 'explicit cultural legitimation', that is to say, it transforms oral myths and belief systems (which tend to have only a local significance) into a broadcastable, public form in which they can function as justifications for the increasing differentiation of social power, wealth and prestige.

Largely because of its abstract and fragmentary character, Parsons's scheme for describing the stages in the evolution of mass literacy has not encouraged successors to apply or to elaborate it. The work of the economic historian of the Toronto school, Harold A. Innis, presents an interesting contrast in style and method. In *Empire and Communications* (1972) and *The Bias of Communication* (1951), Innis set out to document the role played by developments in the transmission of the written word in the creation and maintenance of monarchies and empires in Egypt, Babylonia, Greece and Rome. Departing from established historical methods which tended to explain major shifts between media by fluctuations in levels of circulation or the size of audiences, Innis employed a distinctive set of figure-ground analogies which permitted him to move freely across different periods and settings. As Marshall McLuhan, who inherited Innis's approach and pushed it to (and perhaps beyond) its limits, remarks in a foreword:

> He saw that the figure-ground relation between written and oral is everywhere in a state of perpetual change. Material conditions can quickly reverse the relationships between written and oral so that, where literacy may be the ground of a culture in one phase, a sudden loss or access of written materials, for example, may cause the literate ground suddenly to dwindle to mere figure. (Innis, 1972, viii–ix)

When Innis turned to the twentieth-century competition between oral and literate modes, the figure-ground analogies could result in striking but oracular interpretations:

> The clash between traditions based on the book and the newspaper contributed to the outbreak of war. The Treaty of Versailles emphasized self-determination as a governing principle and recognized the significance of language in the printing press. Consequently, it rapidly became outdated with the mechanization of the spoken word in the radio. Governmental influence over the press was extended to the radio. The loud speaker had decisive significance for the election of the Nazis. . . . The Second World War became to an important extent the result of a clash between the newspaper and the radio. (1972, 165)

Innis is a source of many suggestive and intriguing insights that are not always easy for others to use or develop. His acute sensitivity to the nuances of the oral mode is one of the more accessible aspects of his work, and it can be seen at its best unravelling the connections between trade, political institutions and philosophical ideas in the setting of classical Greece and Rome (1972). In contrast to Parsons, who promised a systematic, evolutionary theory of an orthodox kind that never actually materialised, Innis's choice of explanatory style was too experimental and impressionistic for the majority of interested scholars outside Toronto. In the event, neither of their contributions attracted a lasting following nor provided the basis for empirical research programmes into literacy or orality.

This very selective survey suggests that the study of what Goody and Watt term 'the technology of the intellect' has been seriously hampered by its lack of fit with the prevailing academic division of labour. The topic's sprawl across several disciplines results in identical issues being discussed in quite separate contexts with different vocabularies. On the other hand, not everyone that adopts (for example) a psychological perspective on literacy is seeking an answer to the same kind of question. The simple classification that follows attempts to introduce some preliminary order into the muddle. It sets out, firstly, to distinguish clearly the several different types of questions that can be posed in research devoted to literacy. Secondly, it maps the intellectual contexts in which each broad approach has developed. Thirdly, some of the more obvious constraints and limitations of each approach are outlined, and finally, some indication is given of the assumptions and commitments that distinguish the present work.

Competence studies

In the first of the three types of approach comes what may be termed 'competence' studies since they address the cognitive, linguistic and physiological foundations on which the individual builds reading and writing skills. Competence studies revolve around the question of how any individual is able to communicate via written symbols. From the various answers that are given to this question, an extensive instructional literature is derived made up of basal readers, reading schemes and exercises to improve reading speed, together with the fruits of 'applied' research on the readability of prose, the legibility of typefaces and layouts, and treatments of other technical aspects of producing and understanding texts.

The demand for reading instruction from within the school syllabus underlies, of course, much research and publication on literacy skills as such. The bulk of this work is carried out on behalf of teachers by investigators who have academic backgrounds in psychology or linguistics, and define their field of study as 'reading research'. In common with other types of competence study, the principal objective in reading research remains the development of explanatory models of the encoding and decoding of texts. In order to arrive at a general understanding of the many complex processes involved, the implicit starting point for researchers is not this particular seven-year-old with poor vision in one eye who is attempting to read a timetable, but an abstract and idealised person operating with a 'typical' text, possibly in experimental conditions. Questions about the source of the text, how and why it has the form and contents it does, the significance of its information for the reader, the interests that its publication serves, why writers are trying to express themselves on a particular topic, all these are considerations that fall outside the 'competence' frame of analysis.

Now these points should not be interpreted as criticisms of reading research for not being something else, or as a veiled attack on theorising and experimentation. However, it is as well always to bear in mind, firstly, that theoretical explanations introduce and refer back to artificial entities (like 'model' readers), and secondly, that they concentrate on selected attributes of the models and necessarily leave a great deal unexplained. This can best be illustrated by examining the role played by readability formulas in reading research. Such formulas are widely used to quantify the difficulty a text will present to readers by calculating average word or sentence length, or assessing the simplicity of the vocabulary used. Most formulas rest on the premiss that it is possible to judge the difficulty of a text in an entirely generalised fashion so that comprehension is measured in a way that ignores, among other factors, the importance of the text content to the subject. This has the curious and anomalous result that while these formulas are routinely employed to make evaluations of pupil progress and school performance, they are actually counter-productive when it comes to creating comprehensible texts. As Davison and Kantor's (1982) research indicates, adapting a text in a way that improves its readability score (by, for example, splitting complex sentences or simplifying vocabulary) may make the text harder rather than easier to understand. This is mainly because the classic measures of readability ignore several factors (logical ordering of ideas, background knowledge required of the reader) that are relevant to the practical difficulties encountered by real readers.

Although 'competence studies' employing school pupils as subjects have contributed much to the understanding of reading and reading difficulties, they embody a serious methodological limitation. In school, literacy skills are being exercised against a very specific backdrop of expectations and evaluations quite different to those that attend the average adult transaction entailing reading and writing. When children in school are asked by their teachers to read aloud from the blackboard or silently from a textbook, or to complete a worksheet, they are employing their literacy to satisfy a very specific and artificial demand, whereas when adults spontaneously wish (or find themselves in a situation that requires them) to exchange information, they are much more likely to be in a position to choose the medium and select the precise message. It is consequently hazardous to make unqualified inferences from children's literacy to adults' and there are studies of reading and writing in the classroom which themselves demonstrate vividly the extent to which school is a complex and specialised linguistic arena.[8]

A final point about the competence perspective is that it embodies a technological, 'how to' outlook and it is not primarily concerned with the conceptual or definitional aspects of literacy. It is perfectly true that there are frequent debates about, for example, whether a specific aspect of comprehension should be included in a particular definition of reading, but the competence literature is mainly preoccupied with the problems of applying and measuring existing conceptions of literacy rather than innovation.

Contextual studies

Whereas studies of competence concentrate on the individual, 'internal' dimensions of reading and writing, the second category, 'contextual' studies, takes the psychological and linguistic mechanics of literacy for granted and seeks instead to describe its relationships with the institutions and social structures in which it is embedded. Such descriptions are complicated by the fact that many of the causal relations operate in both directions.

The typical contextual study seeks to throw light on the way literacy serves, and is served by, particular historical or social situations. As most of the work discussed in this book falls into this category, very brief illustrations will suffice. With the implications for educational policy directly in mind, economists have considered the scale of returns to social investments in training in basic skills,[9] while sociologists and political scientists have argued over the significance of a literate electorate for the stability of both well-established democracies and developing states.[10] A similar, broadly functionalist logic is also detectable throughout the considerable volume of historical research devoted to understanding the development of Western literacy from the origins of the alphabet onwards, some of which is reviewed in Chapter 3.

Critical-cultural studies

The line between contextual studies and this final category is not so clear-cut as the other boundary. As its title suggests, the critical-cultural perspective on literacy embraces two central concerns which, though related, are not always equally developed in the same piece. The critical component is concerned with the way in which the distribution of literacy skills affects the information available to individuals and groups, and the influence this has in turn on the relationships between social classes, and between the individual and agencies of the state. In other words, it deals with the politics of literacy which are inevitably a combination of both dispassionate analysis and persuasive and 'interested' argument. Claims may be advanced or contested, for instance, about the extent to which the skills and information available to the citizens of a nation are adequate for the full exercise of their civil and political rights. A critical study may set out to document the fact that certain kinds of information or tools for thinking are available only in a particular format or medium that favours an identifiable group of consumers, or it might possibly attack their unavailability within the public domain. Another 'critical' issue might be raised by the claim that all newspaper readers need to be able to recognise the persuasive techniques at work in daily news coverage, picture captions and advertisements, that these skills should be taught as a matter of course to all children and adults, and that such a capacity is arguably a much more relevant measure of adult achievement than existing conceptions of functional literacy.[11]

The second, 'cultural' element reflects an interest in the connections between literacy and the kind of intellectual activities and products characteristic of a particular culture. Studies by A.R. Luria, Goody and Cole, and others try to demonstrate that the modes of thought available within a society are constrained by the way in which literacy has been institutionalised.[12] It has been argued, for instance, that certain intellectual operations of a rational and critical kind can only be performed (or only routinely performed) with the presence and assistance of writing. Less obviously, field research among 'tribal' groups shows that the uses to which literacy is put can be highly restricted in comparison to its apparently total integration into industrial societies. This is an important reminder that not all forms of illiteracy need have their origins in individual deficiencies. The point in history at which literacy is institutionalised, the political and social setting in which it takes root, the language in which an orthography first becomes available, these factors can permanently shape and limit not only individual capacities but also the systems of thought and the methods of analysis that exist (or are capable of being created).

I have already referred to the idea that literacy is essentially a technology for transmitting information, and although it will become apparent below that this view oversimplifies in several respects, it now receives wide acceptance. There are those whose philosophy of technology makes them keen to maintain a sharp demarcation between the means of communication and its content, and thus reluctant to admit the distribution of knowledge and information under the rubric of literacy. Hard though many of these sceptics may be to convince, a conceptual framework that attempts to keep in simultaneous focus both literacy skills and the content of the texts and documents on which they are exercised is precisely what distinguishes the critical-cultural approach from the other two, and it is what the remainder of this book seeks to develop.

Dimensions of literacy and illiteracy

The three approaches outlined above asked quite different kinds of questions of a subject matter that is itself highly diverse: for many purposes, literacy cannot usefully or manageably be treated as a unity, and while the next chapter tackles the thorny problem of an overall working definition for literacy, the present task is to distinguish five major component dimensions.

Writing originates as a system of visible signs for representing some of the features of a spoken language. Its relation with the spoken language tends to become less direct as, over time, it acquires distinctive and autonomous forms and functions, but it is clear that literacy has an irreducible linguistic core and this linguistic dimension is the first we shall consider. For present purposes, three key aspects can be distinguished. Firstly, there is the question of whether or not a community or society has access to a system of writing (an orthography); secondly, there is the matter of which vernacular language(s) this system happens to transcribe (with the proviso that the transcription of speech is only one capacity among many); finally, there are a variety of principles by which the orthographic system can operate (Chart 1.1).

The first two aspects need to be dealt with together for the following reason. It is certain that viable writing systems were independently invented several times in human history, and cases where writing developed from 'scratch' for the prevailing vernacular are relatively straightforward (even though little by way of direct historical evidence on the process of invention can be expected to survive). In fact, most pre-literate societies have probably made their initial contact with writing in more complex ways; in some instances long-term trading links enabled pre-existing writing systems or alphabets to be adapted to fit new languages; alternatively, military conquest by outsiders, followed by settlement or a colonial regime, introduced or imposed both literacy and a new language at

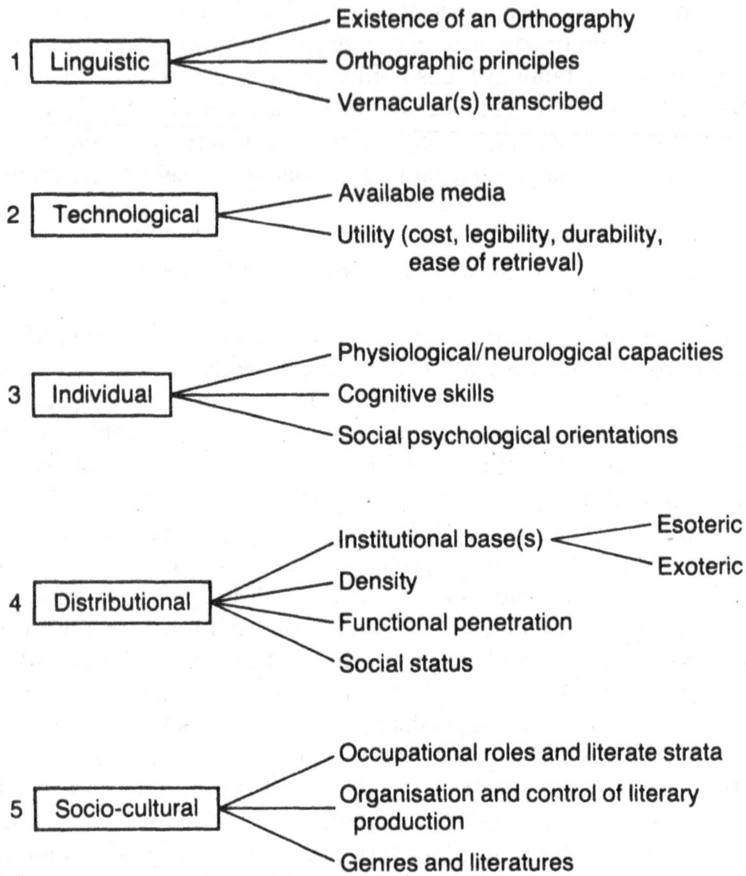

Chart 1.1: *Dimensions of literacy*

the same time. This creates a very intricate linguistic environment in which it is particularly hard to distinguish, after the event, the results of contact with a foreign language and culture from those due to the impact of literacy. For example, the spread through the ancient Western world of the three great written languages, Greek, Latin and, subsequently, Arabic, each associated with the political domination of major empires, produced extremely diverse effects. In some regions, the local vernaculars survived with modest accretions; in others they quickly collapsed under the weight of external influences, but practically every recognised kind of hybrid that can be created through the interaction of different languages, including bilingualism, pidgins and diglossia, resulted.[13] The existence of alternative orthographies and the social distribution of literacy were probably contributory, if not decisive, factors in determining local outcomes.

The English language itself bears the signs of having passed through a similar phase of interaction between several languages and literacies. The conversion of Anglo-Saxon kings to Christianity brought with it the possibility of a vernacular literacy as an alternative to Latin, using a modification of the Roman alphabet originating in Ireland (Leigh, 1983, 20). Following an extended period of depredation and settlement by Norwegians and Danes whose cultures were essentially oral, a literacy and literature based on Anglo-Saxon survived mainly in Wessex, only to be overlaid after the Norman Conquest by spoken and written French which, for a period, became the language of law and administration. Up until late in the fourteenth century, French, Latin and Middle English coexisted and competed, each providing specialised communicative functions for different social groups.

The third linguistic aspect, namely which system of representation an orthography employs, is important in relation to its ease of use and learning. The earliest innovation, pictographs, used stylised but ultimately realistic drawings, but had insurmountable disadvantages (for example, consider the difficulties of unambiguously signifying negation and counterfactual situations). A developed writing system, rather than attempting to represent ideas directly, will set up correspondences between visible marks and a linguistic intermediary. In pure phonological systems, the correspondence is between a written or inscribed character and a unit of sound, that is, a syllable or a phoneme; in pure logographic systems, the correspondence is with a word or a morpheme. In practice, most widely used systems depart from their basic principle and sacrifice consistency in order to achieve economy and completeness. Thus, while alphabetic writing based on a character-phoneme connection might appear to be superior (if only because the number of phonemes in any language is less than either the number of syllables or the number of words), languages adhering to strict phonemic spelling are nevertheless exceptional (Stubbs, 1980, 46–9).

Any perspective on literacy or illiteracy is obliged, then, to make some presuppositions about the mechanics by which writing is able to facilitate linguistic communication. This is not, however, to concede to linguistic frameworks any ultimate priority over the explanation of the social character and functions of writing and print. Just as linguists have reasonably opposed the reduction of reading and writing to a collection of physiological and neurological operations on the grounds that this ignores the meaningful character of what is being processed, so a sociologist is entitled to resist the restriction of literacy to cover exclusively the rule systems that connect visual symbols to phonemes or morphemes. The case against such a reduction is, firstly, that written communication, by definition, transmits information that has a social significance, and in operating within any particular social system, it comes to have a socially organised as well as a linguistically organised form. Secondly, the channels such communication utilises rest on a dynamic technology that is itself under constant transformation by complex historical and cultural processes. For many linguists interested solely in the apparatus of language, it is not inappropriate to bracket off encoding and interpretive capacities from the social settings and materials in and on which they are exercised. This reflects the linguist's focus on the means at the expense of the objectives and consequences of written discourse, though there is a point at which materials and settings begin to determine what linguistic rules will apply and thus what skills are required. The aspects of literacy that are explored below should thus be regarded as complementary to those that are treated in orthodox linguistics.

The second dimension of literacy is technological and deals with the tools and materials available for making and bearing the written characters. The evolution of the material base for writing has a long history, related to, but partly independent of, the linguistic dimension. The main tool/material combinations in this history could be summarised by the following sequence: a chisel or stylus on stone, clay or woodblock, quill or pen with ink on papyrus or paper, fixed blocks or type on paper, movable type on paper, electronic transmission and display.[14] The criteria governing the relative success of any technological means of creating visible characters are largely self-evident; apart from cost, the main factors are legibility, durability, portability and ease of storage and retrieval.

The third dimension deals with human individuals and the capacities and general dispositions they bring to written communication. Both reading and writing involve the integration of many separate mental and motor processes. Roughly speaking, it is possible to distinguish, firstly, physiological and neuro-physiological requirements for the control of the eye and hand movements necessary to scan and pen (or type) written characters. Secondly, there is an overlay of cognitive skills involving an assortment of processes ranging from shape-matching to the detection of subtle semantic differences and relatively complex logical operations. Thirdly, there is the social psychological matter of motivation and personal 'set' to transactions involving writing. With the exception of the latter, which is covered in Chapter 5, psychological and physical mechanisms (and their pathologies) are not dealt with in this book, and the reader is referred to the extensive literature that is available.[15]

The fourth dimension could be termed 'distributional' since it is concerned with how the linguistic and technological core of literacy becomes available to a community and how it is harnessed and integrated with the latter's social organisation. Four aspects are fundamental; the institutional base, density, functional penetration and status.

Whatever the circumstances governing the introduction of literacy in a society, there is invariably some agency or organisation which initially establishes a monopoly over its use. The examples most common during the earliest literate eras were priestly ('clerical') groups responsible for protecting a religious orthodoxy which had been or was being enshrined in a holy book, or ruling elites and their bureaucratic agents who tended to be jealous guardians of an instrument of potential political control. More generally, agencies which have a vested interest in restricting the dissemination of reading and writing techniques and which therefore tightly regulate the admission of recruits can be said to have an 'esoteric' stance towards literacy. This is likely also where the provision of scribal services for payment becomes the basis of a specialised occupation.

It would be wrong to regard religious and political elites as intrinsically disposed to esoteric attitudes. Protestant denominations like the Lutherans, and agencies such as the Bible Society, have actively proselytised for literacy because private study of the Bible has been marked out as an important route to salvation. The Catholic faith, in contrast, has traditionally seen the priest as an indispensible interpreter of holy writ for his flock, so that its support for literacy has lacked a specific doctrinal impetus. The role of particular types of institutional base with respect to literacy is clearly both historically and culturally variable.

The stance of organisations that define their mission in terms of extending literacy or which are given a societal charter to do it can be termed 'exoteric'. State-funded systems of basic education and adult literacy campaigns represent the characteristic contemporary examples in both 'advanced' and 'developing' societies.

The esoteric/exoteric concern of the institutional base is by no means the only organisational feature that can have a long-term impact on the character of literacy. The intimate and continuous association over many centuries between religions, and especially of course the 'religions of the book', and the diffusion of literacy raises many interesting issues. Wormald (1977, 99) points out that the Western Church's strong commitment to Latin, in contrast to the Orthodox and Byzantine branches which for the most part looked favourably on the use of written vernaculars by converts, severely retarded the spread of vernacular literacy. The domination of almost all formal education by Latin stifled opportunities for those equipped only with the vernaculars and helped to contain literacy within the ranks of the clergy and aristocratic elites. A parallel situation arose in sub-Saharan Africa, as a result of the association between Arabic and Islam (Goody, 1968, 11). Comparison of these different religious systems suggests further questions about their connections with the diffusion of literacy. Is there, for instance, a fundamental contrast between the intellectual output from the static tradition of textual preservation and scribal excellence within Christian monasteries, and the dynamism of peripatetic, religious scholarship in Islam? (Goody, 1968; Wilks, 1968; Gellner, 1981.)

It is hard for people who live in a culture in which reading and writing are so ubiquitous to recognise that its diffusion is not everywhere as complete. 'Functional penetration' refers to the range of activities and transactions in which literacy is institutionalised for a human group, that is to say, routinely expected and preferred or required. This is the dimension that covers what, following Goody (1968, 11–20), is often referred to in the literature as 'restricted literacy', instances where the range of uses of literacy falls far short of what is technically feasible. The principal reason for learning to read may be to study sacred texts, and literate activities may themselves be viewed not as instrumental but as forms of religious observance. In the period immediately before Tibet fell under the influence of the People's Republic of China, literacy retained an almost exclusively religious significance with instruction in reading the scriptures, prayers and religious manuals given by Buddhist monks, with little secular printed matter in circulation. There are many other contemporary examples of literacy in a particular language being used for ritual or religious purposes only:

among the Vai of Liberia, a traditional education in Arabic survives among the Islamic self-help brotherhoods. Individuals learn phonetic equivalents for Arabic characters mainly to help with the rote-learning of the Koran; for all non-religious activities such as business within the community, Vai is used, while the language of school instruction and business with outsiders is English (Goody, Cole and Scribner, 1977). Extreme cases of limited functional penetration arise also from secular causes. The literacy based on the Minoan-Mycenean scripts of Crete appears to have been employed solely for administrative purposes within the palace complexes, and as far as is known, neither personal correspondence nor imaginative literature was ever composed in them (Dow, 1973, 583–5; Goody, 1977a, 153).

These examples point to the sense in which all types of literacy are more or less 'restricted'. There are transactions in any society in which writing is not used even though it is applicable (for instance, as Chapter 5 demonstrates, in a great deal of shop-floor communication in industry), and a specific combination of language and script can always be expected to have a limited functional, as well as geographical, scope. This reinforces the point that while writing is a technology, its spread and consequences are not simply a matter of technological determination.

When literacy is broadly and deeply established, that is, at the high end of the penetration variable, reading and writing can emerge as distinctive recreational and intellectual activities in their own right. However much pessimistic critics may bemoan the decline of a book-based literacy, recreational reading in public and private is a very widespread activity. There are very few situations in Western society in which one is called on to justify the presence of a book, and as an incidental result, this prop is useful to people who wish to avoid social scrutiny and interaction in public places (Goffman, 1968, 60–1).

While density of literacy has been widely seized upon as the most important explanatory aspect of literacy, especially in historical analysis, little significance can be attached to it in isolation. Its popularity undoubtedly derives from the relative ease with which investigators can produce an apparently 'hard' and general quantitative measure simply by calculating the number of readers (or reader/writers) as a percentage of the adult or other appropriate population, though without an additional, standard criterion of what is to count as minimal literacy, comparisons are not, in fact, straightforward. The level of overall literacy rates and the significance of the possible concentration of skills in a particular age-group, sex or other social stratum is discussed in the section on definitions below, and the significance of rates will figure prominently in Chapter 3.

The fourth aspect of the distributional dimension is the diffuse one of status. The processes of institutionalisation and transmission which have been discussed frame the extent to which individuals can earn social honour and shame through the exercise of literacy skills. A concern for conspicuous display and status management, as much as practical utility or intrinsic enjoyment, can underlie the cultivation of reading and writing. Positive or negative evaluations may be attached to the channel itself (witness the preferential treatment generally given to documentary evidence and sources in, for example, the legal sphere), or to individual performers (being a published author is prestigious, incompetence attracts stigma), or to particular pieces of writing which have been endowed with special personal significance (the letters between unhappy lovers may be ritually destroyed, unread books are frequently prized possessions). The sources for positive valuations of literacy and negative evaluations of illiteracy is a theme to which subsequent chapters will repeatedly return.

The socio-cultural dimension, the fifth and final one, covers the distinctive social groupings and their intellectual products that literacy makes possible. Precisely because literacy is the foundation for so much artistic, scientific and other intellectual activity (or to put it another way, because written language is a code of unrivalled flexibility in which most other symbolic systems in a culture can be translated or represented), the problem for the investigator soon becomes one of what areas of potential study can safely be left out rather than what deserves to be included.

One of the substantial fields of inquiry within this dimension that has already been touched upon is the analysis of the social formations that literacy sustains or brings into existence. At the simplest level, any fully institutionalised literacy generates a set of occupational roles that are directly dependent on reading and writing skills. Among the first to emerge are clerks, personal secretaries, tutors, schoolteachers, and professional scribes (whose counterparts, professional letter writers, still operate in some Third World countries). The scale of commercial investment in the production of printed matter tends to rise with the size of the potential readership, and enterprises devoted to printing and publication develop refined divisions of labour, providing a diverse range of employment both to 'creative' writers and to supporting auxiliaries and technicians who need to have basic literacy skills.

A further possibility is the emergence of an entire social stratum deriving its livelihood from a knowledge of texts and a capacity to create and criticise in writing, that is to say, an intelligentsia. An interesting set of questions suggest themselves concerning the development of this influential social formation. What degree of penetration and density of literacy are required to support a full-time intelligentsia? What are the steps by which intellectuals detach themselves from the religious and political bases referred to above to achieve a partly autonomous existence? What constraints on the spatial and temporal organisation of intellectual transactions are imposed by the linguistic and technological dimensions of literacy?

In societies with a high density and extensive penetration of literacy, a more or less sophisticated system of publication develops alongside an intelligentsia to perform the complex task of mediating between authors and readers. The selection of which authors and what material will be published in which formats inevitably conditions the general cultural significance of authorship and readership. The range of functions such a system of publication and distribution performs very much depends on the political and economic structures that prevail, but circulation to mass audiences is everywhere regulated to some extent by a combination of cost constraints, editorial gatekeepers and legal restrictions over content. Where regulation is achieved mainly through the operation of market forces, the character of literary production can be examined via the kinds of analyses of ownership and control familiar to students of mass communications. In other cases, the control over written material in general circulation is achieved principally by denying to heterodox authors and viewpoints access to the technology for the reproduction of print.[16] Highly centralised systems of literary production are, however, rarely able to prevent the circulation of '*samizdat*' publications and illicit imports, while the work of 'approved' authors may want for an actual readership.

The difficulty of policing the reading and writing of a large population of literate adults has been one of the traditional grounds of resistance to popular education by conservatives in many societies, but literacy training itself can have direct ideological implications. Almost any lengthy course of instruction in literacy places a child or adult in a relationship of (temporary) subordination to the trainers who may, if they wish, institute a regime of rewards and punishments designed to inculcate any values to which they or their sponsors are committed. In addition, there is the quite separate question of the training materials employed. Content analyses of children's textbooks and reading schemes have demonstrated many times over that no instructional literature, however neutrally intended, can avoid subtle social judgements and discriminations that can leave lasting impressions, especially on newcomers to print. At the opposite pole, the propaganda content of some reading programmes is designed by their authors with specific ideological objectives in mind that extend far beyond the achievement of fluency in reading and writing.

The ultimate cultural products of a developed literacy are imaginative and technical literatures. An analysis and evaluation of a literary tradition and its genres is, of course, the objective of literary criticism. The fairly recent convergence between the concerns of some schools of criticism and the study of literacies was mentioned in an earlier section, but a few additional comments concerning the conventional limits of what is counted as literature are in order. Genres and literacies are different facets of the same phenomenon. The emergence of a major new genre or sub-genre in, to take an obvious example, the novel, can be seen as a kind of co-production in which the exercise of the linguistic skills and sensibilities of innovative writers implicitly challenges readers and obliges them to respond with new ways of reading text, of integrating it with their own experience, and of extrapolating from it in fantasy and imagination. In the past, as we have noted, the discussion of what linguistic devices particular genres employ and appeal to has been very largely restricted to texts on whose behalf it has been possible to make out a claim for 'seriousness' and enduring merit, to such an extent that the tasks of analysis and evaluation have merged into a single, staple, critical activity. With the advent of critical theories which could broadly be termed structuralist, the connection between analysis and seriousness has been partially severed. Although the frameworks available are at an early stage of conceptual development and thus leave something to be desired in terms of precision and rigour, the principle has been firmly established that any and all written texts, however ephemeral or banal, can be subjected to a broadly similar kind of detailed scrutiny.

The capacity to take seriously and examine closely 'trash' like romantic novellas, advertisements and comics is essential to the understanding of popular culture, but mundane texts such as public notices, graffiti or memos are equally important to the student of literacy. All of the latter are, in a sense, the popular literature 'below' popular literature, the unattributed written material that everybody is confronted by daily and which the majority handle with ease. In the case of railway timetables, technical instructions and tax returns, however, we move into territory where the complexities are capable of defeating even highly educated and otherwise 'literate' individuals. Each type of document can usefully be regarded as a (neglected) genre, making use of its own distinctive linguistic and informational devices, and imposing varied demands on the reader that always go beyond simply decoding text. These documents are the tools, often the only tools, for achieving a host of practical objectives and projects, personal and collective. As with any tool, until things go wrong, the immediate interest of users is normally in the application and the results, rather than the construction of the tool itself or the sources of their own facility with it. Even so, the most trivial leaflet on the assembly of a household gadget is obliged to make a host of assumptions about its readers, their knowledge, resources, lifestyles, skills, domestic division of labour, motives in purchasing the product, etc., all of which can be expressed both in what is said and how it is said, and also in what is left unsaid. The same leaflet will almost certainly reflect the philosophy of manufacture and marketing that underlies the product, and will probably provide clues to the producer's attitude towards customers and their rights as consumers.[17] The point here is that, on inspection, apparently negligible and inconsequential documents entail statements about large tracts of the cultures of which they are a part. They invite, and are capable of sustaining, detailed analysis of their often complex structures and ambiguous purposes. Secondly, to the extent that they are based on misrepresentations or faulty premises, they deserve exposure and criticism.

Middlemarch and a bus ticket, to use the examples that have featured in acrimonious academic exchanges, may be at opposite ends of the continuum of written communication, but their similarities are no less important than their differences. Like fragments from a hologram, with the correct illumination, each can reveal the outlines of the systems to which they belong (though it is not unreasonable to expect that the analysis and criticism of the ticket will be concluded a little before that of *Middlemarch*).

2

Defining and measuring literacy and illiteracy

Defining literacy

In tackling the problem of a suitable definition for literacy and illiteracy, it is important not to start with unrealistic expectations about the possibility of achieving a simple formulation acceptable to all interested parties. On the contrary, what might appear to be an endless series of disagreements and controversies will be encountered which reflect the fact that we are dealing with a complex amalgam of psychological, linguistic and social processes layered one on top of another like a rich and indigestible gateau. Different varieties of academic specialists cut slices out of this cake with the conceptual equipment their disciplinary training has taught them to favour. Consumers of the cake (teachers, pupils, politicians, employers) have very different appetites and push and jostle each other to secure a wedge of a particular size and, if possible, try to get their preferred wedge defined as the standard helping for everybody else.

Dictionary-style definitions of literacy state that it is a capacity to read and write, and also the educated state that is achieved through the exercise of these skills. Laying aside for the moment the vagueness surrounding 'reading', 'writing' and 'capacity', it is remarkable that reading and writing are so often represented as a unified skill. Stubbs has noted some of the defects in the idea that they are simply a mirror image of each other (1980, 5). The average reader can sight-read many words that he or she could not spell from memory or use in an appropriate written context. There are many disabled people who can read fluently but lack the motor control to handle a pen effectively. If someone can write something they can generally also read it, but the reverse is not necessarily the case. Most people in societies with well-established literacy read very frequently but write less often; there is only a small minority that actually spend substantial periods of time writing, while noboby writes a great deal but reads nothing (unless the existence of a class of illiterate sign-writers is discovered).

Even if we restrict our attention specifically to reading, a great deal of definitional confusion is generated by the fact that different commentators are talking about very different kinds of readers and reading situations. Some have children in mind (who may still be learning their spoken language) as opposed to fluent adult readers with considerable general knowledge at their disposal. Some experts derive their inferences from laboratory reading tasks which deny to the reader the external cues to meaning normally present in everyday contexts. The emergence of a generally accepted definition of a standard reader and a standard reading task is unlikely, if for no other reason than it would presume a full understanding of the exceptionally complicated relations between types of spoken and types of written language. At present, considerable theoretical divergences exist about these relations, and they are ultimately translated into rival conceptions of what is happening in the reading process.

At the risk of some simplification, the literally enormous literature on reading can be classified into two polar categories. In the first, the authors believe reading to be basically a process of decoding from written symbols to symbols standing for spoken language (most often, from alphabetic characters to phonemes), so that the criterion of successful reading is a facility at translating writing into the appropriate speech, always allowing that the speech may remain 'internal' and silent. In the second, the emphasis is on writing as coded meaning and reading as a form of reasoning about and with the code, so that the ultimate criterion of success is comprehension of the sentence or passage (even if, for instance, the reader cannot articulate specific words in it). Each of these general positions deals more plausibly with particular kinds of reader and specific kinds of reading task, so each is obliged to make some concessions to the other, and while most of the instructional literature is recognisably closer to one or other pole, there is also a considerable amount of eclecticism (or, less elegantly, bet-hedging).

Writing is no less complex or problematic but much less research is devoted to writing and writing difficulties, partly because the perennial debate about the 'correct' way to teach beginning reading in schools occupies the centre of the stage. It is permitted to do so by the traditional presumption that writing is a higher-order skill which is easily acquired through practice providing that reading has been mastered. The historical origins of this picture of the 'natural' development process are outlined in Chapter 3, but there are also several intrinsic features of writing that render it intractable to orthodox research techniques, with the consequence that there are no widely accepted procedures for establishing fluency in writing. Despite superficial parallels, the transcription of speech (via dictation) is by no means directly symmetrical with reading a passage out loud. Writing is very much a proactive activity and for many writing situations an objective benchmark by which to assess whether the author's expression adequately conveys his or her own meaning to the reader is lacking; issues of authorial meaning cannot be 'postponed' as easily as they sometimes have been in the testing of reading.

Despite the technical disagreements about how the detailed mechanisms of reading and writing operate, and the problem of standards of fluency which we have yet to confront, there is no serious challenge to the idea that they constitute the core of literacy. Opinions differ again, however, on how much significance can be attached to these skills in isolation. Advocates of 'adult basic education' (ABE) have argued that if literacy is intended to signify a socially useful and economically relevant asset then it cannot be segregated from a set of closely related communications skills and 'know-how'. For an illustration, they point to the way in which school leavers need to know about the conventions of letter-writing, holding telephone conversations and form-filling, as they operate within the process of seeking employment. There is little advantage, the case continues, in a young person being able to read if he or she cannot also look up a number in a telephone directory, make the call and hold an intelligent conversation. Similarly, the ability to copy or compose a grammatical and accurately spelt letter of application is negated if the writers do not know the appropriate norms of polite address in organisations, or to whom an inquiry should be sent. The terminology used to label these capacities is beside the point; what does matter, from the ABE standpoint, is that the type of knowledge gained in 'English' lessons in school has for many adults to be supplemented by training in additional techniques of communication and practical guidance about the way social institutions function.

Similar considerations apply to literacy's capacity to exploit other bodies of knowledge, as reflected in terms like 'computer literacy' or 'political literacy'. Where precisely do comprehension skills end and substantive information begin in these cases? Political literacy, for instance, could roughly be said to be a certain degree of substantive information plus a parcel of assimilation skills and critical capacities that a citizen needs to have available in order to participate in a meaningful and rational way in political choice and discussion. It is clear that the constituents of the political literacy parcel will be both culture-specific and ideologically contestable. In many non-European societies, local politics are traditionally a matter for oral discussion and debate within the community, with little or no role for literacy, but in the cultural environment of Europe and North America, despite the increasing dependence of parties and the electorate on broadcasting, the established political science wisdom is that level of education is strongly correlated with degree of involvement in politics, and that anything more than the most passive participation makes extensive demands on the individual's literacy.[1]

Thus while linguistically it could be said that the medium is always analytically separate from the message, for many everyday purposes literacy is defined exclusively in relation to particular social roles, pre-existing institutions and transactions, and finite bodies of information. This tends to discourage sharp distinctions between substantive information on the one hand and information handling competences on the other, a fact reflected in the way 'knowledge' is used to cover both aspects in normal usage.

The concept of 'functional literacy' has been the major vehicle by means of which a utilitarian argument for a broad-based, socially 'relevant' literacy has been advanced. A slight detour to trace its emergence will provide an opportunity to explore some of the ramifications of enlarging the traditional scholastic connotations of literacy.

Functional literacy: a brief history

The original conjunction of the terms 'functional' and 'literacy' is hard to date or attribute with any certainty. The notion of a level of literacy less rudimentary than the capacity to provide a signature and read a simple message, but less than full fluency, appears to have gained currency in specialist circles during World War II. This intermediate level of attainment was assumed from the outset to be associated with employability and, in a loose and unclarified way, with the social 'integration' and 'adjustment' of its possessors.

As in World War I, mass mobilisation uncovered alarming shortcomings in standards of basic education. In 1942, President Roosevelt was obliged to report to Congress that 433,000 men graded 1–A (eligible and physically fit for immediate service) had been deferred because they could not meet the Army's literacy requirement (Cook, 1977, 49). The US Army defined as illiterates, 'persons who were incapable of understanding the kinds of written instructions that are needed for carrying out basic military functions or tasks' (quoted in Harman, 1970, 227).

In a 1947 survey, the US Bureau of the Census used the term 'functional illiterate' to refer to people who had completed fewer than five years of elementary school, on the assumption that this correlated with an inability to comprehend simple written instructions. The Census questionnaire also included a direct (self-report) question about the respondent's ability to read and write, so that replies could be formed into a four-cell matrix of literacy/schooling conditions: 20 per cent of those with no schooling were counted as literate, whereas 5 per cent of those who had completed four years of school were counted as illiterate (Cook, 1977, 50–2). In this exercise, the Bureau of the Census was attempting to measure the literacy levels of a large population using indicators simple enough for respondents and enumerators to use in the field, but its formulation unfortunately perpetuated the idea of a strict equivalence between set amounts of schooling and reading and writing attainments. As we shall see, many of those who subsequently picked up and employed the term 'functional literate/illiterate' used it to make fine and potentially misleading distinctions about individual abilities.

Soon after peace was declared, UNESCO assumed the role of the main institutional haven for international literacy activity. In a speech immediately following the signature of the document formally establishing it, Sir Alfred Zimmern, the acting Executive Secretary, pinpointed illiteracy as 'a subject which interests a large number of our member states . . . it interests a number of states which have very few illiterates among their metropolitan populations' (UNESCO, 1947, 2). At first, UNESCO placed literacy work in the context of 'fundamental education', the aim of which was to '. . . help people develop what is best in their own culture . . .' (UNESCO, 1949, 16). The core content of fundamental education embraced the skills of thinking, speaking, listening and calculating, as well as reading and writing (UNESCO, 1949, 11), and a need for it was recognised to exist in highly industrialised economies as well as in 'developing' societies (UNESCO, 1949, 29). In the earliest documentation, the references are to 'literacy' without qualification. It is portrayed as one of the conditions for the establishment and maintenance of humane and civilised values: 'The skills of reading, writing and counting are not, however, an end in themselves. Rather they are the essential means to the achievement of a fuller and more creative life.' (UNESCO, 1947, 15). Gradually, the parallel theme of literacy's presumed potential for inducing and accelerating economic and technological development came increasingly to the fore: 'Illiteracy is part of a tragic circle of underproduction, malnutrition and endemic disease. The circle cannot be broken by an attack on only one of these elements . . .' (UNESCO, 1951, 1).

The optimism and internationalism that prevailed following the end of World War II fuelled confidence in literacy as a universally effective agent of progress and postponed any systematic examination of either the evidence for such an assumption or the likely practical problems of translating high hopes into useful fieldwork. Up until the mid-1960s, an orthodoxy survived in official and diplomatic spheres that treated illiteracy on analogy with an epidemic disease like malaria; it was seen as a kind of cultural pathogen susceptible to complete eradication by the widespread administration of a standardised educational treatment. The preferred form of this treatment was general primary school enrolment. As the UNESCO survey, *World Illiteracy at Mid-Century* remarks:

> If all children of school age in any country attended school for a sufficient length of time, there would eventually be no adult illiterates in the population, except those mentally deficient and incapable of learning to read and write. It follows, therefore, that the best means of preventing illiteracy is to provide adequate education for all children. (1957, 165)

Adult tuition was widely thought to be merely an extension of formal schooling to a mature clientele, often employing the same personnel, techniques and materials (mainly because these were the resources that were available). It only slowly came to be acknowledged that tuition designed specifically for adults who had gained little from a limited schooling, or who had missed out on it completely, was an absolute necessity given the premium development plans placed on fast results.

In the highest circles of UNESCO, unrealistic and somewhat ethnocentric expectations held sway, captured clearly in the following, lofty sermon by Dr Julian Huxley, Executive Secretary of the Preparatory Commission of UNESCO:

> Literacy is not enough. . . . Certainly for some people literacy has meant merely new ways of filling time, new forms of escape from reality – in the shape of cheap newspapers and magazines . . . instead of sending them to the stored treasures of art and wisdom or promoting a fuller enjoyment of reality and a deeper understanding of nature and human life. (UNESCO, 1947, 9)

At this stage, few governments in developing countries acknowledged the scale of the task before them, let alone possessed the educational resources to establish a taste for the classics of world literature among their populations. The dangers of the cultural paternalism implicit in Huxley's kind of approach were soon to be appreciated. One pamphlet warned that:

> There is no place in fundamental education for the view that illiterate people are children who should be disciplined into progress either by force or by the cut and dried plans of well intentioned outsiders. The purpose of all fundamental education work is to obtain the active participation of the people themselves in shaping their own future. (UNESCO, 1949, 16)

The concept of 'functional literacy' made its debut before an international public only with the publication in 1956 of W.S. Gray's authoritative survey of reading and writing carried out for UNESCO. Gray remarked that it appeared to have evolved slowly out of a quarter century of reading research and field experience (Gray, 1956, 21), and he defined it as follows:

> a person is functionally literate when he [sic] has aquired the knowledge and skills in reading and writing which enable him to engage in all those activities in which literacy is normally assumed in his culture or group. (1956, 24)

This definition was intentionally relativistic, setting a different threshold of literacy for each community (although it left unspecified what standard could apply to wholly pre-literate cultures). Gray juxtaposed the variable (but, by implication, non-rudimentary) standards embodied in a functional approach with the fixed, 'minimum' level of orthodox approaches, conventionally identified with the '. . . ability to read an easy passage and to write one's name or a simple message', which had been proposed in 1948 as a working definition of literacy by the United Nations Population Commission (Gray, 1956, 20).

Gray's formulation did not associate functional literacy training with work or any other specific social setting. He merely emphasised that the content of training should reflect the needs and motivation of the groups served and should aim at a self-sustaining standard, that is, one which permits the pupil to make independent use of what he or she has learned without further help from an instructor (1956, 21–2). At this point in his discussion, possibly concerned with the abstractness of his definition, Gray shifted his ground and discussed various quantitative and qualitative criteria relating to the amount and the content of training necessary to reach a self-sustaining standard. He asserted, quoting British authorities,[2] that: 'A person may be considered functionally literate whose attainments in reading and writing are equivalent to those of a person who has successfully completed three years' schooling' (1956, 25). Gray did not explain how such a correspondence had been established, and he apparently overlooked the fact that any fixed criterion had to conflict with the relativistic definition he had previously formulated. Despite these weaknesses, school grade equivalences were subsequently widely used as handy indicators for levels of adult functional literacy. Completion of secondary school became a 'benchmark definition' of functional literacy in the United States, enshrined in later legislation such as the Adult Education Act of 1966 (Hunter with Harman, 1979, 27), while the UNESCO International Committee of Experts on Literacy proposed the adoption of a similar criterion in 1962 (UNESCO, 1965b).

Gray's survey was one element in a successful international effort to get the problem of world illiteracy into the limelight, and in 1961, the United Nations General Assembly passed a resolution giving UNESCO the task of studying the scale of world illiteracy and recommending solutions. UNESCO responded in the following year with a plan entitled 'The World Campaign for Universal

Literacy' which, after substantial revisions, was finally presented to the Secretary-General a year later. It contained, among other things, outline plans for a ten-year international drive designed to make 330 million people literate at an estimated total cost of nearly $2 billion. This global and unselective strategy was to mark the zenith of the 'humanist' strand of UNESCO's thinking about illiteracy. The plan remained consistent with the belief that a basic education was a fundamental human right, but it implicitly accepted a low level of literacy as the typical likely attainment. Furthermore, it rested on the implausible assumption that the utility of literacy was intrinsic, so that its desirability would be automatically and universally recognised for example, by peasants in subsistence economies lacking access to postal services, writing materials and vernacular reading matter.

Although the General Assembly of the United Nations passed a resolution in December 1963 appreciating the report and encouraging, in general terms, its implementation, the World Campaign was subsequently abandoned as politically and economically unrealistic. One of the many factors leading to its demise was the fact that it was gradually becoming apparent to educationalists that many of the schemes that had already been attempted by national governments (e.g. in India, Nigeria, the Gold Coast) had failed to inculcate a rudimentary but permanent literacy in even a modest percentage of their illiterate populations (Jeffries, 1967, 50–7). The wholesale rejection of the 'global' approach created an intellectual vacuum and provided the opportunity for a functional conception whose major merits were supposedly its more realistic aims and a more calculative approach to the practicalities of literacy instruction.

'Functional literacy' possessed an appeal that transcended any doubts over precisely what range and level of skills it connoted. At first, its use probably suggested to lay readers little more than a general level of attainment that enabled adults to 'fit in' and 'function' in their social environments. In the complex UNESCO world of delicate diplomatic negotiations, a slightly fuzzy term suggesting mid-range competences could be useful. On the one hand, a standard lower than 'functionality' was morally and pedagogically suspect; research had indicated relapse into illiteracy where only rudimentary levels of literacy were inculcated (Ahmed, 1958; Committee on Plan Projects of the Government of India, 1963). On the other hand, the goal of a high-level competence for all could appear to be unrealistic in a poor country seeking economic aid to fund its literacy programmes, and was now virtually discredited.

Functionality was given a radically new meaning as a result of the Thirteenth Session of the General Conference of UNESCO in 1964, which substituted a five-year Experimental World Literacy Programme (EWLP) for the original 'global' strategy. The EWLP very strongly emphasised the economic and development potential of literacy:

> Briefly stated, the essential elements of the new approach to literacy are the following: (a) literacy programmes should be incorporated into, and correlated with, economic and social development plans; (b) the eradication of illiteracy should start within the categories of population which are highly motivated and which need literacy for their own and country's benefit; (c) literacy programmes should preferably be linked with economic priorities and carried out in areas undergoing rapid economic expansion; (d) literacy programmes must impart not only reading and writing, but also professional and technical knowledge, thereby leading to a fuller participation of adults in economic and civil life; (e) literacy must be an integral part of the overall educational system of each country; (f) the financial needs of functional literacy should be met out of various resources, public and private, as well as provided for in economic investments; (g) the literacy programmes of this new kind should aid in achieving main economic objectives, i.e. the increase in labour productivity, food production, industrialization, social and professional mobility, creation of new manpower, diversification of the economy. (UNESCO, 1966, 97)

The final report of the 1965 Tehran World Conference of Ministers of Education on the Eradication of Illiteracy explicitly identified the new thinking with functionality though at the same time it harked back to the much older notion that literacy gives people access to their own cultures:

> Rather than an end, in itself, (functional) literacy should be regarded as a way of preparing man for a social, civic and economic role that goes far beyond the limits of rudimentary literacy training consisting merely in the teaching of reading and writing. The very process of learning to read and write should be made an opportunity for acquiring information that can immediately be used to improve living standards; reading and

> writing should lead not only to elementary general knowledge but to training for work, increased productivity, a greater participation in civil [sic] life and a better understanding of the surrounding world, and should ultimately open the way to basic human culture. (UNESCO, 1976, 10)

It is difficult, so long after, to reconstruct the process by which functional literacy became synonymous with literacy for work. After the disappointment and failures of previous literacy schemes, the new literacy thinking – adult, selective, developmental, participative – required a label that suggested the economic benefits that could be expected from investment in literacy, and 'functional' carried appropriate overtones. While the public pronouncements continued to locate functional literacy as only the first step in a staircase of continuing education that led to personal and cultural enrichment in the noblest and widest senses, by the time the EWLP pilot schemes were operating, its operational meaning had shifted even further from Gray's original definition. A pamphlet published in 1970 frankly stated the work-orientated character of the pilot projects:

> Functional literacy work should be taken to mean any literacy operation conceived as a component of economic and social development projects . . . the teaching of reading and writing and occupational training cannot be conducted separately or disassociated in time – they are integrated activities. (UNESCO, 1970a, 9)

The literacy content of the eleven pilot projects supported by the United Nations Development Programme was therefore linked to training in technological skills varying from weaving to automobile repair, although since the projects mainly had rural settings, tuition associated with agricultural development predominated (such as the introduction of high-yield crop varieties). The training for 'fuller participation in civic life', if it took place at all, seems to have been given little emphasis. The *Practical Guide to Functional Literacy*, published by UNESCO in 1973, provides no examples of EWLP materials or strategies in this area.

The UNESCO review of the EWLP that appeared in 1976 acknowledged that its results were generally disappointing and it uncovered shortcomings in the management of projects, the numbers of learners recruited, the competences achieved, and the drop-out and probable relapse into illiteracy rates. The statistics of the EWLP, such as they are, claim that a million illiterate people were 'reached' by the entire programme at an approximate total cost of $32 million. However, less than 125,000 people appear to have demonstrably reached the criterion standard of functional literacy as defined and measured in those five participating countries with projects that produced analysable data on success rates (UNESCO, 1976, 174 and 184). The eventual consensus among the EWLP's evaluating experts was nevertheless that functional literacy:

> brings about a change for the better on condition that it is associated with a process of genuine innovation (of a political, social or technical nature) in which participants are themselves involved . . . the more the content of the course takes into account the workers' cultural environment, the more effective the functional literacy programme . . . (quoted in UNESCO, 1976, 160)

Presumably anxious to dispel the major doubts that were generated in many quarters about any further investment in literacy, the experts came up with an elaborately qualified and curiously circular hypothesis about its benefits. Far from triggering the take-off into a spiral of self-sustaining economic growth, they now suggested that its contribution was contingent upon the prior existence of just that network of institutions and media of communication that is normally regarded as its ultimate consequence:

> For literacy to be effective and lasting it must be sustained by an infrastructure that not only provides literates with abundant reading matter but also maintains their taste for learning and broadening their horizons: information media, stable and mobile libraries, means of producing and disseminating the written word, small museums, cultural clubs, not to mention the schooling of children (who ask questions of their parents) . . . (UNESCO, 1976, 192)

The Secretariat of UNESCO, in a paper presented to the International Symposium for Literacy held at Persepolis, Iran in 1975, was more forthright:

> The concept of functionality, in the broad sense of the term, comprises not only economic and productivist dimensions (which played too important a role in the operational plans and experimental projects, in order to meet the intervention criteria of the UNDP based on the notion of pre-investment), but also political, social and cultural dimensions. (quoted in Bataille, 1976, 40)

In finally rejecting a narrowly conceived, work-orientated literacy, international thinking had come full circle back to the 'humanist' position associated with the early days of 'fundamental education', but ironically, the vicissitudes of its career within UNESCO did not prevent 'functionality' from being taken up by the 'Right to Read' campaigns in the United States and Britain, which date from about 1962 and 1973 respectively. The versions of functionality employed in the United States literacy movement harked directly back to Gray's 1956 definition and, in various ways, wrestled with its circularity. The Economic Opportunity Act of 1964 enshrined functionality into legislation in a marvellously bureaucratic prose when it referred to adult basic education for those whose:

> inability to read and write the English language constitutes a substantial impairment of their ability to get or retain employment commensurate with their real ability, so as to help eliminate such inability and raise the level of education with a view to making them less likely to become dependent on others, to improving their ability to benefit from occupational training and otherwise increasing their opportunities for more productive and profitable employment . . . (quoted by Harman, 1970, 234–5)

The US Office of Education (USOE) produced the following definition of a literate person:

> one who has acquired the essential knowledge and skills in reading, writing and computation required for effective functioning in society, and whose attainment in such skills makes it possible for him [sic] to develop new aptitudes and to participate actively in the life of his times. (quoted in Nafziger *et al.*, 1975, 20)

Sticht defined functional literacy in the context of working life as 'a possession of those literary skills needed to successfully perform some reading task imposed by an external agent between a reader and a goal the reader wishes to obtain' (quoted in Nafziger *et al.*, 1975, 21). Much the same overall view of functionality was adopted in Britain where the literacy movement, as we shall see in Chapter 6, took its initiative from voluntary agencies. The early manifesto of the movement, *A Right To Read*, published in 1974, quoted with approval the US National Reading Center's (USNRC) definition:

> A person is functionally literate when he [sic] has command of reading skills that permit him to go about his daily activities successfully on the job, or to move about society normally with comprehension of the usual printed expressions and messages he encounters. (British Association of Settlements, 1974, 5)

Since recent definitions have entailed refinements of detail rather than revisions of substance, the point at which this history can be reviewed has been reached. It shows clearly the way in which functional literacy was at an early stage adopted by parties in a series of political arenas, military, educational and diplomatic, who needed a label for their convictions regarding the economic potential of, and justification for, mass training for adults in basic literacy skills. In the course of the extended battle for resources, 'How basic?' was converted into an economic rather than an educational issue, while the original idealism underpinning the quest for universal literacy was itself transformed into an ideology about the bases of cultural modernity and the contemporary prerequisites of citizenship and employability. In one sense, the belief that literacy could play a central role in social and economic development survived as an article of faith; little of the (admittedly scanty) linguistic and sociological evidence available at the time of the rise and fall of functionality unequivocally supported such a hypothesis, while many basic questions of technique and organisation remained unresearched. Nevertheless, 'functional' became the acceptable buzz-word, an essential ingredient every adult programme had to contain. It endured its setbacks and it flourishes still, largely because it promises substantial collective and personal returns from equipping individuals with an ill-defined but relatively modest level of competence.

Operationalising functional literacy

If a consensus among researchers in a field on basic definitions was required before fieldwork could be designed and executed, all research in the social sciences would quickly cease. As it is, although lip-service is paid to the ideals of consistency and comparability, they are freely ignored by each generation of researchers who discard established measures and pioneer new tools better-suited to their purposes. Empirical tests and indicators dealing with aspects of literacy and illiteracy are consequently legion, but most of them are derived from the reading syllabus and the demand generated for the assessment of performance within schools. The measurement of developmental literacy, which is concerned mainly with establishing age-related norms of progress, has very little bearing on the problems of adult learners, and need not detain us. In contrast, the basic aim in assessing functional literacy is to discover whether individuals are capable of meeting some kind of external social demand placed on them that entails handling written information and documents. In response to these different objectives, the general tendency is for developmental tests to be of a 'norm-referenced' type, but functional tests to be 'criterion-referenced'.[3]

Most measures of functional literacy contain three basic ingredients on which an endless set of variations can be worked. There is, firstly, some written input which constitutes the 'demand' side of the assessment procedure. The subjects are confronted with this input text(s) which they will be asked to read and to respond to in some way. The text may require completion or modification, oral or written answers related to its content may be sought, or the individual may have to carry out some physical or intellectual operation specified within it. The content of some tests is so closely related to a specific type of transaction (such as shopping) that the label 'functional' is strained, but the majority are wider in scope and impose tasks on subjects supposedly characteristic of those encountered by 'typical' people in 'everyday' circumstances.

The second element is what could be called the 'supply' side, the kinds and degrees of skill that the individual will be called upon to display as determined by the text and the problems it poses. By definition, functional tests are designed to tap spheres of practical competence, so many aspects of general knowledge, numeracy and 'life-skills' may be built in to the test content, as well as word recognition and comprehension skills.

The third element is the test designer's conception of a minimum level of literacy for 'survival' or adequate social functioning within a specific sphere of life. Some notion of a socially determined lower limit of competence is intrinsic to all functional measures and necessarily has an ideological character, reflecting a particular view of social rights, welfare and duties.

As far as the demand side is concerned, the problem is to select a single 'basket' of print-mediated activities that adequately reflects the immense diversity of ways the printed channel affects people in complex societies. It is not impossible to estimate the range of printed materials that a routine manual or clerical work role requires to be handled at a given point in time. It is a much more problematic task to carry out and defend a similar estimate on behalf of a proto-typical citizen in an 'average' occupation enjoying a 'standardised' lifestyle. Many tests adopt an over commonsensical approach and choose materials merely on the basis of convenience and their wide circulation. In this way, the USOE definition, quoted in the previous section, was linked to a list of everyday reading tasks, but there appears to be no systematic criterion of selection by virtue of which the USOE list of tasks should be preferred to the infinite number of rival lists that could be proposed.

Similar material selection problems restrict the generalisability of the results of major studies by Lou Harris and Associates (1970, 1971), and Northcutt, Kelso and Barron (1975), none of which produced a standard of functional literacy demonstrably applicable across the whole of (American) society. In the case of the Adult Performance Level Study (APL), carried out for the Office of Education, the demand side was made up of forty-two items covering knowledge of consumer economics, law and health. What emerged from this comprehensive study (the data were derived from 360 independent sub-samples representing the continental population of the United States) was not, however, a unified standard of functionality but three relative bands of performance ('least', 'marginally' and 'most' competent) which the researchers were satisfied correlated with three conveniently measurable variables: 'income', 'job status' and 'educational achievement'. Not surprisingly, a review of functional tests comes to the conclusion that the APL study was '. . . still arbitrary in assigning criterion levels of success' (Nafziger *et al.*, 1975, 18).

The construction of the demand side of functional literacy assessment procedures seems to present an even greater obstacle to crudely empiricist techniques. The problem is that print is an incidental and auxiliary feature of a great many social situations and settings. There are many substitutes for it and, for those that need them, strategies for circumventing it. It is very hard to identify a set of social transactions which can only be carried out via writing and which are absolutely necessary to adequate functioning, however this is defined. The priority that existing tests have assigned to, for example, acquiring a driving licence or reading a menu, is quite arbitrary. Many people have freely decided that driving and dining out are not essential for them, and we are not entitled to infer that a non-reader who does not drive or eat out is being handicapped by illiteracy. While it would be an overstatement to say that the material selection problem is insoluble, there does not seem to be any imminent prospect of a satisfactory solution.

Turning to the supply side, in attempting to characterise the minimum level of socially useful literacy, most established procedures specify only reading skills. Taking as examples the tests associated with the definitions mentioned above, the USOE list includes items like 'reading and comprehending a letter from a debtor or creditor' but not writing a similar business letter. The only item that does involve writing draws on its very circumscribed use in the completion of application forms. The USNRC and Sticht formulations are restricted exclusively to reading.

This neglect by the supply side of writing, and the heavy emphasis on the reading of texts dealing with regulations, instructions and guidance generally, raises some worrying and far-ranging questions about the interests underlying the enterprise of testing adult functional literacy. While it would be foolish to deny that even minimal reading skills are a desirable asset for any adult, a reading ceiling which can only cope with labels, instructions and application forms seems a very meagre basis for 'survival'. Subsequent chapters will show that despite the implications and claims to the contrary, equipping adults with rudimentary literacy will probably have a negligible capacity, in itself, to combat low pay, unemployment or general social deprivation. We will return to this issue at the end of this section.

The knowledge and skills elicited by the supply side of functional literacy tests can be extremely varied. The central, reading component is commonly associated, following the lead of the US Bureau of the Census, and Gray, with 'reading age' or school grade completion. Reading age is the average competence attained by a cohort of similarly aged school children. (Grade completion is the American equivalent but covers both reading and writing.) If a random statistical sample from the population of ten-year-old children scored an average of 115 points on a reading test, then anyone who achieves that particular score on that test has a reading age of ten years, irrespective of his or her chronological age. The 'raw' score from any test can thus be transformed, if the necessary group data exist, into a reading age, which merely indicates how an individual is maturing in relation to his or her peers. A similar link can be established with the scores obtained from readability measures.

Gray's initial definition suggested 'successful completion' of three years' schooling only (1956, 25) but he also referred to four- and five-year versions. UNESCO's adoption of fifth-grade level as the international criterion seems to have been based on a methodologically dubious study of literacy retention in Tagalog carried out in 1950 in the Philippines (Hunter with Harman, 1979, 16). The American Bureau of the Census regard as literate anyone fourteen years of age or older who has completed sixth grade (quoted by Harman, 1970, 227). In Britain, a reading age of nine years has been conventionally taken to be the threshold of functionality (e.g. British Association of Settlements, 1974, 3). The highest of these criteria would leave key written materials beyond the comprehension of the (barely) functionally literate adult. A study of thirty-six different leaflets issued by the Department of Health and Social Security in Britain, designed to explain eligibility for social welfare benefits, found a minimum reading age of 13.5 (using Dale-Chall) and an average slightly over 16.5 years (Hampson, 1978, 8–9). An evaluation of the difficulty of selected news items in British national daily newspapers (using FORCAST) indicates a range of required reading ages between 14 and 16.5 years (British Association of Settlements, 1974, 7).[4] Thus, 'functional literacy', as it is authoritatively defined, generally connotes a very low level of reading competence.

There are further and more fundamental objections to reading age and grade completion as measures of functional literacy. Firstly, the equivalence between a particular threshold of functional proficiency and a particular grade/reading age attainment, even if it can be validly established, exists only for a particular school system at a particular juncture and has no universality. Secondly, there are massive differences between school literacy, which largely consists of academic exercises imposed on pupils as a curricular end in itself, and adult literacy whose instrumental character naturally derives from its capacity to serve adult needs and projects. The use of grade completion and reading ages in adult contexts begs all the questions about the efficacy and relevance of school training as a route to competence that made the notion of functional literacy necessary in the first instance.

The final element, the 'survival' component, is perhaps the most problematic. It is not surprising that no genuinely empirical criterion for survival literacy is available. Other research programmes have foundered on just such a reef. Consider the similarities between 'functional literacy' and the notion of 'subsistence poverty' with which it has strong affinities. The tradition of reflection and enquiry about poverty that stretches back, among others, to Seerbohm Rowntree attempted to elevate the concept of poverty above the marshes of moral dispute and political prejudice by securing a scientific and impartial foundation for judgements about who are to count as the poor. This foundation was taken to lie in the formulation of the 'objective', minimum nutritional requirements for the healthy survival of an individual or household of specified composition. As Rein (1970, 60) has pointed out, every technical procedure that has been developed for rigorously measuring human material needs necessarily incorporates abstract, scientific ideas such as nutritional 'values', optimum levels of physical activity, ideally rational purchasing strategies. Any rigour and objectivity that the application of such concepts permits derives from their connections with the theoretical systems of, respectively, biochemistry, physiology and an idealised home economics.

A gulf necessarily exists between the 'scientific' notion of subsistence, defined (say) by a daily calorie intake, and the actual diet that any human group does or could follow. Some technical experts, faced with this gulf, have attempted to 'ground' their abstractions by collecting new or additional data on actual levels of consumption, real preferences and prevailing tastes. However, in order to identify relevant and representative samples of income groups from whom to infer levels, preferences and tastes, a prior criterion of poverty is needed. The subsistence research programme is thus trapped in an infinite regress; it requires a pre-existing concept of poverty in order to generate its own concept methodically.

Functional literacy is in exactly the same boat. Whether a researcher starts out from the actual reading and writing skills of samples of deprived people, or produces an abstract measure based on the average linguistic difficulty of a set of common print-mediated transactions, the standard of survival that results will be judgemental. However 'scientifically' and 'objectively' it is presented, it will necessarily be derived from prior assumptions about the nature and functions of literacy in society which, in turn, connect to contestable views on citizens' rights and the good life. The notion of survival or adequate functioning is irremediably a political and moral abstraction. This is not, of course, any kind of criticism, but a recognition that literacy needs, and thus survival standards, cannot be determined and settled solely through impartial, factual investigation.

The research programme that set out to create an objective, empirically precise, culture-wide standard of functional literacy hoped to identify a minimum level that would guarantee personal well-being in the same way as a subsistence diet was intended to maintain physical health. Such an idea was perpetuated not only by the way definitions of functional literacy have been formulated, but also by the propaganda and advertising that continues to issue from involved agencies and groups. But how, in practice, could a functional standard achieve so much? As it (or rather they) have been defined, they are adequate to deal only with a very restricted range of printed materials, especially instructions, labels, signs, application forms and form letters, which are all types of communication whose function is to elicit conforming behaviour (via prohibitions, warnings) or to institutionalise existing social arrangements further (via rules, guides, commands). Whether intentionally or not, functional competence has been defined in such a way that it is just sufficient to bring its possessor within the reach of bureaucratic modes of communication and authority. A literacy congruent with the USNRC's definition, for example, would undoubtedly be in the general interests of the state, employers, welfare agencies, authority generally, but it is reasonable to ask precisely in what respects it is beneficial to its possessors. Its net effect might well be to domesticate and subordinate the previously illiterate person further rather than to increase his or her autonomy and social standing.

The omission of writing in all but its most rudimentary forms is also relevant here. Writing is a powerful and distinctive medium of self-expression and self-reflection, and it has a great potential for recording and conveying innovation, dissent and criticism. It offers what is often the only channel of access to the decision-makers in bureaucratic organisations, and is virtually a necessary condition for effective participation in the organised political process in parliamentary democracies. Any survival standard that ignores the capacity to compose an intelligible letter or draw up an agenda is setting its sights dangerously low.

The overriding difficulty, then, with functional literacy remains the efficacy of the standards of ability it sets up as targets. There is little or no research available that demonstrates that fully illiterate and disadvantaged adults are assisted significantly by achieving functional levels of competence. Rather dated inquiries by Greenleigh Associates (1966) and Pattern and Clark (1968) found that basic education students rarely attribute a new job to increased literacy. The nagging suspicion therefore persists that low thresholds of functionality reflect a deliberate attempt in official quarters to minimise the embarrassing scale of the problem.

A sociological conception of literacy

The resilience of the concept of functional literacy suggests that it has been fulfilling, however imperfectly, a necessary role. Even so, its rehabilitation is no simple matter because its effects are the legacy of a great deal of rather blinkered thinking about the problems of literacy and illiteracy. At the heart of existing difficulties lies the fact that a concern with literacy has been the almost exclusive preserve of reading experts, psychologists and school teachers. Each of these groups has been preoccupied with evaluating the child's capacity to assimilate the written word. Occasionally, wider questions concerning the social distribution and utility of this capacity have been raised (e.g. Postman, 1970), but in such cases literacy is still often treated as a discrete individual practice, severed and abstracted from the social transactions and institutional activities in which, in adult life at least, it is normally an ingredient. Systematic analysis of the social context in which literate language use takes place has generally been outside the analyst's frame of reference. As we have seen, this is reflected in the rather cavalier assumption made by reading experts that any text whose 'difficulty' has been calibrated can serve to test and measure literacy since a text's informational content is deemed irrelevant to the notion of a generalised skill in reading and writing. While the idea of an autonomous, unified, purely linguistic literacy holds sway, it is difficult, for instance, to do justice to the complex competition between rival languages, dialects, channels and genres that exists in any culturally heterogeneous society.

Of course, it is easier to assert that literacy is a social practice to be viewed against the prevailing cultural and political realities than to deliver the finished, comprehensive analysis. A modest move in the right direction is to adopt definitions that will at least point the student in the right direction and encompass all the dimensions of literacy discussed previously. The first step is to discard an albatross of an idea – that literacy is a single, unified competence – and to begin to think wherever possible in terms of a multiplicity or hierarchy of literacies. However, a shorthand for the whole collection will still occasionally be needed and no great harm should follow from a general definition of literacy as the exercised capacity to acquire and exchange information via the written word. Functional literacy can be defined as the possession of, or access to, the competences and information required to accomplish transactions entailing reading and writing which an individual wishes – or is compelled – to engage.

In unpacking and defending these formulas, the most provocative elements, the multiplication of literacies and the integration of 'information' with literacy, can usefully be dealt with together. There are two main rationales for building information into our notion of literacy itself. The first is simply that the exchange of information is the end for which, with fairly minor exceptions, written communication is the means. The starting point for linguists and literacy practitioners alike has to be 'natural' attempts to transmit and receive some species of non-linguistic knowledge; technical attempts to assess the successes and failures of written communication are necessarily parasitic on everyday versions of these criteria. It is perhaps only the great complexity of the carrier systems that makes it seem worthwhile to 'hold constant' or 'bracket off' the information at the heart of particular exchanges; one of the associated costs is the idealisation of literate activities that has already been noted. This leads on to the second reason, the conceptual messiness of the alternative. Orthodox definitions presume an abstractly perfect competence as their base-line. This amounts to a belief in a set of linguistic skills that, once mastered, can be freely transferred across the entire corpus of written materials in a language. Faced with the massive diversity of types of text in circulation, each presenting the reader or composer with a distinctive set of communicative difficulties, the unified view strives to be comprehensive by adding more and more high-level cognitive skills to the already elaborate and unwieldy connotations of reading and writing. By far the more economical alternative is to accept that there is no clear demarcation between linguistic competences on the one hand, and common-sense knowledge and substantive information on the other. The competent interpretation of almost every text requires a combination of both, while comprehensible composition always requires accurate assessment of what the audience knows. The author of even the simplest domestic message like 'BUY COFFEE' trades on the recipient's ability to resolve the ever-present ambiguities (a jar from the supermarket, a sack from the importers, or market futures from a broker?) by knowledgeably invoking the appropriate context. Since different kinds of message invoke different kinds of social knowledge and employ different linguistic skills, literacy is clearly not all of a piece.

Having accepted that literacies are differentiated by the type of information they assume and transmit, a remaining task is to define information.[5] This could initially be understood, following a phrase of Berger and Luckmann's (1971, 26), as 'everything that passes for knowledge in society'. Such a monolith would subsequently have to be broken down in to manageable categories: although it is hard to propose relevant classifications independently of any particular objective or context of inquiry, since information is inherently organised by uses and users, it is unlikely that this will pose insuperable difficulties.

The broader national and international ramifications of literacy are brought into sharper focus by this perspective. The fluency with which an individual is capable of reading a newspaper need not be dealt with in isolation, but can be related to the character of the information being absorbed. How reliable are the sources on which the paper relies for news? How is the paper financed and what formal and informal kinds of censorship operate? Is the paper able to carry criticisms of the party in government? What influence do advertisers have on features and editorial matter? Such issues are directly germane to the skills that an understanding of the text will demand from the reader.

The definitions of literacy and functional literacy necessarily carry implications for our understanding of illiteracy. In this respect, they inherit an important feature from the broadly similar formulation by Bormuth (1978, 123): the property of applying symmetrically to the producers as well as the consumers of information. Authors become illiterate when, whether by design or incapacity, their written discourse misleads, mystifies or passes uncomprehended by potentially interested audiences. Illiteracy can therefore cover not only all instances of straightforward failure to transmit or receive information in a meaningful form, but also efforts to disguise and distort material being passed into a public domain. This broad illiteracy embraces some serious and perennial social irritants: the small print of legal agreements and professionalese generally, ambiguous or faulty advertising and labelling of consumer goods, the maze of welfare documentation and bureaucratic obfuscation as a whole.

By permitting access to needed information, as well as personal possession of literate skills, to count in the assessment of functional literacy, the denotation of (functionally) 'illiterate' is substantially altered. It is increased by the inclusion of people without printed material relevant to their information needs, but decreased by the exclusion of those who vicariously take advantage of the printed channel through another's mediation. In the first case, literacy is meaningless if it cannot be exercised or harnessed to the individual or the group's needs; the second case acknowledges that for many purposes, access to skills and information is a very effective substitute for personal possession, and that the individual is not literate or illiterate in isolation. This is well appreciated in countries with low literacy rates where the one literate member of a household or even village can disseminate vital knowledge and secure benefits for the entire community. These changes of emphasis carry important implications for adult literacy and library services which will be picked up in Chapter 6.

The proposed definition of functional literacy does not legislate for minimum norms or fixed societal standards, which presently generate a false sense of security for those who achieve them and inflict an unnecessary burden of failure on those who do not. It seeks to avoid applying the cultural tastes and standards of highly literate social strata on everyone in the community. It accepts that individuals are the final arbiters of their own information needs and thus their status as functionally literate or illiterate. It is, at the same time, hostile to arguments that treat literacy and illiteracy as logically alternative conditions and statuses. Everybody, however highly educated or polyglot, has finite and, in a real sense, inadequate linguistic resources at their disposal. Competence is in many respects a relative state, always affected by considerations of motivation and self-esteem. Most adult literacy tutors can, for example, cite instances of students who are able to master material that deals with their interests, but struggle with passages that are technically no more difficult but are felt to be alien and remote. To say everyone is illiterate in relation to particular bodies of information is not a rhetorical device intended to spare the feelings of those with severe incapacities. It is a frank response to the explosion not only of technical information, but the technical complexity of the modes of conveying it.

Finally, by linking literacy more intimately with information, these definitions direct our attention to the sociology of knowledge as a hitherto unexploited source of fruitful insights concerning literacy. The possession or lack of particular types of information constitutes a crucial component of the opportunities (or 'life-chances') available to a social class, and by the same token, the control of channels of dissemination is part of any apparatus of social domination. The social and political significance of literacy thus derives largely from its role in creating and reproducing – or failing to reproduce – the social distribution of knowledge. If this were not so, if literacy lacked this function, the inability to read would be a shortcoming on a par with tone-deafness, while an ability to write fluently would be as socially inconsequential as a facility for whistling in tune.

3
The historical perspective

Introduction

Although no comprehensive understanding of literacy in any society could be attained without an account of its origins and development, the construction of such an account is often problematic. For many regions and periods, the primary sources are unavailable or have yet to be properly exploited. More fundamentally, however, there is the unsettled question of what, in principle, a history of literacy should contain. Here, as Peter Laslett has suggested (1971, 207), there is a 'challenge to the historical and literary imagination'. The investigation of what proportion of a population can read at a particular juncture, an issue that Laslett himself has helped to locate at the centre of existing historical inquiry, has tended to throw up as many questions as it has resolved. In the introduction to a recent anthology of writing on the development of Western literacy, Graff (1981, 6) included among these emerging preoccupations 'the contexts of literacy, the needs for and uses of it, and the motivations that impel individuals to seek literacy and some to develop mass means for its transmission . . .' As well as trying to reflect some of these newer concerns (within the limits of space and a dependence on secondary sources), the following sections use the categories introduced in the last chapter in order to identify the shifting functions and evolving meaning of literacy and illiteracy in British society.

Literacy in classical Greece and Rome

A useful point at which to begin an account of the development of mass literacy within Western Europe is a consideration of the achievements of the Greek city states in antiquity. Although Gough (1968, 70) advances the rival claims of traditional India (the Mauryan Empire of the fourth and third centuries BC) and China (the Ch'in Empire of the third century BC) to be the first truely literate societies, it seems certain that an exceptionally widespread institutionalisation of literacy was attained in Athens by 500 BC, within only 200 years of the development of a phonemic (or morphophonemic) writing system for Greek.[1]

By formulating an alphabet consisting of 23–25 characters which, singly or in simple combinations, unambiguously represented all the phonemes in the spoken language, the Greeks made one of mankind's fundamental intellectual advances. The Semitic and Phoenician scripts immediately preceding either employed the same sign to record several different sounds, or multiplied the number of signs the user had to commit to memory. While syllabic writing systems (such as the Japanese hiragana and katakana scripts) and logographic scripts (such as Chinese) have demonstrated their viability as means of communication, they embody features which retard their diffusion throughout a linguistic community. Any writing system based on a large number of different characters, or one whose characters provide scope for auditory (and thus semantic) confusion, will rarely be mastered until well after the individual has completed the acquisition of oral language. Generally, the more complex the basis of an orthographic system, the more likely it is that fluency will be attained only by a minority of occupational specialists, though in general, religious and political factors can be as important as purely linguistic considerations in determining the 'success' of a system.

Whether or not the Greek city states were the first literate societies depends, of course, on the operative criterion of collective literacy. Havelock (1976, 2) puts the case for Greek primacy in the following, somewhat vague, terms:

> The civilisation created by the Greeks and Romans was the first on the earth's surface which was founded upon the activity of the common reader; the first to be able to place the inscribed work in general circulation; the first, in short, to become literate in the full meaning of that term, and to transmit its literacy to us.

Exactly what this 'full meaning' amounts to is, as we have seen, open to debate. Havelock ultimately defines societal literacy not by any orthographic development but by the existence of what he calls 'socialized readership' (1973, 343), consisting of a high (but unquantified) ratio of readers to speakers of the language. The implication is that once literacy reached this unknown but critical density (and Havelock's chronology sets the date this happened in Athens at about 500 BC), reading and writing skills could then be habitually and unself-consciously practised throughout the Greek-speaking world.

Some of the everyday uses of literacy in the city states do have a very contemporary ring. A wide variety of inscriptions on both stone and baked clay featured prominently in the Athenian urban environment. The Agora, the central place of assembly, definitely displayed public notices dealing, for example, with political meetings, forthcoming trials, military call-up. From the fifth century onwards, many public decrees were appended with the phrase 'so that anyone who wishes may read', indicating that some kind of general audience was anticipated (Harvey, 1966, 600).

The Greek term *grammatikos*, with the sense of 'a reader', appears to have come into use in the fourth century BC (Havelock, 1976, 3). In 403 BC, the form of the alphabet to be used in official records was finalised by decree. In the legal sphere, the plaintiff had to submit a written complaint to a magistrate, while a law of c.378/377 BC required that the evidence of witnesses be submitted in writing so that in their court appearances they could simply testify to their depositions (Harvey, 1966, 594). In the same period, some types of trading and personal service contracts were finalised in written form, as were selected types of loan, lease, will and dispositions of property.

Although the equivalent of account ledgers definitely existed, written receipts do not appear to have been in common use in this period and debts were settled before witnesses, while seals rather than signatures authenticated documents. Private letters were sent and personal memoranda recorded but how extensively it is difficult to assess. It is probable that many, if not most, households contained a few written documents or, at least, objects with writing, such as vases which commonly had painted captions and even cartoon-style comments coming from the mouths of the human figures depicted.

The important question of how common book-ownership and readership was is also hard to resolve. Attention has been attracted by the handful of great civic libraries like the one at Alexandria, and much has also been made of the occasional references in the works of playwrights such as Euripides and Aristophanes that imply the existence of a book-reading audience; the possibility that these writers were being ironic or sought to flatter cannot be discounted. Certainly, anything as elaborate as a private library would have been exceedingly rare in the fourth century BC (its 'books' would, of course, have been sheets of papyrus, gummed together in the case of longer texts to form scrolls). Since any lengthy text would take a considerable time to copy, it would have been expensive to purchase and it is probable that the majority of citizens did not own any. A contemporary source indicates that the cost of one papyrus roll in Athens in 407 BC was slightly more than a day's wages (Lewis, 1974, 132).

Although schools teaching the elements of reading and writing can be traced back to the fifth century, attendance was voluntary and, contrary to some suggestions, no statute making it compulsory was ever enacted in Athens. Harvey suggests that only the rich would have progressed beyond the basics (1966, 589), but the existence of informal instruction for adults cannot be ruled out.

The conventional portrait of Athens in the 'High Classical' era as the first instance of a society in which every social stratum had accesss to the written word is, in crucial respects, highly misleading. It is unlikely that the density of literacy in the city states will ever be established precisely, but it has been estimated that in the age of Pericles (c.495–429 BC) Athens contained up to 50,000 freemen in a total population, including slaves and aliens, of possibly 150,000 (quoted in Gough, 1968, 70, n.1). The literacy rate of citizens would certainly have been markedly higher than those of women, slaves or foreign residents. Literary references suggest that the education of women, for example, was not given a very high priority, and Harvey quotes a character in a fragment of a play by Menander (c.342–291 BC) who remarks,

> Teach a woman letters? A terrible mistake:
> Like feeding extra venom to a horrifying snake.

This could well caricature male hostility to literacy for women since Harvey quotes other references which suggest that women were expected to read, albeit only within their domestic roles. Even allowing for the minority whose duty was to keep state documents and the occasional individual taught to act as a personal secretary, the literacy rate among slaves would have been much lower than that of freemen.

There is little doubt, however, that Athens itself was well in advance of the rest of the Greek-speaking world in inculcating literacy: in the countryside and in other cities, rates in equivalent periods would certainly have been lower. Sparta is an interesting case in point since it earned a contemporary reputation, partly through slighting remarks by Plato, Isocrates and Plutarch, for indifference to education. Boring's detailed review of the evidence concludes that ordinary Spartans down to the second century BC could probably inscribe names and read practical messages, but little more (Boring, 1979, 96–7).

Another important qualification is that, by contemporary standards, levels of fluency would have been low generally, not just in Sparta. Several factors were involved in addition to the lower volume of printed materials in circulation. Rival versions of the alphabet persisted even after the standardisation decree of 403 BC, though the political and cultural dominance of Athens guaranteed the ultimate pre-eminence of the East Ionic form. Variation in the shapes of characters continued to reflect individual hands and the materials employed. Speed of interpretation was hampered by the absence of inter-word spaces and punctuation. The task of reference to a specific passage could not have been easy in long, unpaginated scrolls, many of which had to be unrolled to the end in order to discover the author and title (Kenyon, 1932, 66–7). For less permanent records, the erasable wax tablet was preferred despite its inferior legibility, and it was not until the first century BC that the Romans developed from it the parchment codex, the forerunner of the modern book.

In an important sense, then, only the highly visible, public face of Athens was fully or essentially literate. While functional penetration appears to have been reasonably extensive, the general impression remains that outside the legal sphere most transactions could be conducted orally if the participants so chose. Although the overall density of literacy among some sections of the population appears to have been comparatively high, the global picture obscures an underlying, sharply-defined, social stratification: the Athenian economy and social structure were dependant upon the contributions of under-classes whose social inferiority and powerlessness was reinforced by their illiteracy or semi-literacy. The severe inherent limitations of the media in use would have restricted the ordinary person's dependence on reading and writing and, in doing so, probably decreased the utilitarian connotations of literacy at the expense of its associations with intellectual life and the 'high culture' of a very small but influential social elite.

Turning now to the consequences of alphabetic literacy in the ancient world, it is necessary to be wary of the occasionally exaggerated claims made by specialists immersed in, and enthusiastic about, Hellenic culture. There are intractable difficulties in disentangling cause, effect and coincidence, and the result can be a tendency to implicate literacy indiscriminately in all the intellectual and social innovations that appeared during the critical two centuries after the advent of 'socialised readership'. While Goody and Watt are probably justified in identifying the passage of Ancient Greece from oral to predominantly literate institutions and sensibilities as a cultural transition of world-historical importance, they are given to sweeping judgements such as the statement that:

> The overwhelming debt of the whole of contemporary civilisation to Classical Greece must be regarded as in some measure the result not so much of the Greek genius, as of the intrinsic differences between non-literate (or protoliterate) and literate societies . . . (1968, 55)

In contrast, Havelock is careful to point out that many of the social characteristics now regarded as the basis of Greek civilisation were evident several hundred years before the onset of literacy. He challenges, for instance, the judgement of both Goody and Watt and Harvey that literacy was a necessary condition for the operation of Athenian democracy (1976, 6). Such a view appears to derive largely from an overestimation of the importance of the institution of ostracism, and an associated assumption that reading and writing were essential for political participation. The annual opportunity for citizens to cast a potsherd ballot inscribed with the name of the individual to be banished was infrequently exercised except during a seventy-year spell in the fifth century BC (Vanderpool, 1973, 217). The several thousand ballots that have been recovered point, in fact, to the existence of a restricted literacy. Many of the names are inscribed in crude characters and are misspelt or incomplete. Groups of ballots display similar styles of writing, probably indicating the hands of scribes or political activists who sold or gave them to illiterate voters (Vanderpool, 1973, 225).

While literacy made possible the thorough diffusion of Greek ideas and values throughout the Mediterranean world and their subsequent appropriation by Rome, the very sophisticated oral culture which preceded the alphabet was not immediately eclipsed. It was, after all, the corpus of oral poetry by Hesiod and Homer that featured in the earliest transcriptions, and the value that continued to be placed on oral teaching and debate was considerable. As Socrates tells Phaedrus in the *Seventh Letter*:

> Written words seem to talk to you as though they were intelligent, but if you ask them anything about what they say, from a desire to be instructed, they go on telling you just the same thing for ever. (quoted in Goody and Watt, 1968, p. 51)

Notwithstanding the preference for the oral dialectic and a fear that written documents would establish themselves too easily as popular dogma, Greek science and philosophy were major beneficiaries of the massive intellectual advantages conferred by written presentation. The capacities of written discourse were integral to at least two specific intellectual achievements: the emergence of impartial historical description, and the development of logic and epistemology.

Herodotus and Thucydides were arguably the first to recognise the task of the historian in anything like contemporary terms. Thucydides, in particular, made an explicit effort to distinguish between documentable events and the myths and imaginings with which they were inextricably bound up in pre-literate cultures.

Writing undoubtedly acted as a similar facilitator in Greek advances in the mapping and description of the physical world. The cumulative analysis and criticism of rival intellectual positions is often seriously hampered, if not made impossible, in the spontaneity of oral discussion with its rambling and repetitive patterns. In addition, Goody argues forcibly (1977a, 52–111) that written lists and classificatory tables introduce the possibility of associations and operations alien to orally based thinking. Graphic presentation simplifies oral discourse through selection and 'decontextualising' it (Goody, 1977a, 78), while manipulation of graphic schemas can focus the thinker's attention on the nature of implicit differences and oppositions. While the advent of the alphabet could not, in itself, provide ready-made solutions to problems of how best to describe and classify the natural world, it did offer a medium for cumulative attempts at refinement and improvement.

Progress in the empirical sciences was paralleled and assisted by the major developments in epistemology for which classical Greek philosophy is especially renowned. The analysis of the process of reasoning itself is an enterprise that it is particularly difficult to envisage being successfully accomplished in an entirely oral context. Without the ability to list statements, rearrange them and assign alphabetic labels to stand for their contents, it is difficult to believe that the crucial distinction between the factual truth of particular assertions and the validity of general forms of argument would have been achieved.

The case of Ancient Greek literacy provides two important lessons for students of literacy. It serves as a reminder that notwithstanding the possibility of intellectual innovation as a result of the advent of a script, it is well-established, pre-literate knowledge and cultural forms that are preserved in the earliest writings, thereby exemplifying McLuhan's adage that the initial content of a newly-created medium is transferred from an older one. Secondly, the idea of a 'restricted' literacy is unhelpful unless it can differentiate between the several kinds of limitation potentially involved, and it could be actively misleading if it is taken to imply that there is a final, presumably contemporary, stage of complete 'literacy'.

Rome assimilated Greek literacy early in its long phase of ascendancy over Southern Europe and the Mediterranean, and subsequently a complex process of elaboration in forms of publication and documentation, together with the diversification of audiences, took place.[2] This increase in the importance and functional penetration of literacy was associated partly with the legal and administrative apparatus of Rome's inter-continental political empire, and partly with the flowering of classical Roman literature. In many of the outlying regions of the Empire, such as the British Isles, the Roman occupation was the context which provides the earliest surviving evidence of literacy. The short-term linguistic impact of any occupation is generally on spoken language forms and a substantial Latin vocabulary can be detected in 'native' languages like Welsh, Celtic and Breton including, significantly, words relating to reading, such as *abecedarium, grammatica* and *littera* (Davies, 1973, 10). In the longer term, Latin was to survive as the language of educated written discourse well into the Early Modern period of European history. Even after Rome was sacked by the Visigoths in 410, its barbarian conquerors accepted and adopted Latin as the medium of written communication, though remoter areas of the former empire lapsed into near-total illiteracy.

Medieval manuscript literacy in Britain

Before considering the situation in Britain after the Norman Conquest, a comment on Anglo-Saxon literacy is appropriate. Much of the evidence about Anglo-Saxon literacy is linked to the reign and personality of King Alfred (b. 849). According to subsequent mythology, Alfred miraculously began to read and translate from Latin simultaneously on St Martin's Day, 887, although Asser's not entirely reliable life of him suggests that he began to learn at the age of twelve. Whatever the truth of the matter, in the process of becoming literate, he seems to have acquired a deep commitment to arresting the decline in learning that had resulted from the destruction by Danish raids of key monastic centres. Confronted with reports of the widespread ignorance of Latin among the clergy, Alfred completed a translation of Pope Gregory's *Pastoral Care* (also called *The Shepherd's Book*) and delivered a copy to all his bishops. Each copy was prefaced by a letter in which Alfred notes that prior to the recent decline in standards, 'many could read things written in English'. This could constitute confirmation of early vernacular literacy or it may simply be a reference to the difference between English characters and Roman letters (and an incidental reminder that literacy in Latin was not instantly or automatically transferable to other languages, and vice versa).

Alfred suggested to the bishops that they should follow his example and

> also turn into the language we can all understand some books which may be most necessary for all men to know, and bring it to pass . . . . that all the youth now in England, born of free men who have the means that they can apply to it, may be devoted to learning as long as they can read well what is written in English. One may then teach further in the Latin language those whom one wishes to teach further and to bring to holy orders. (Whitelock, 1955, 819)

Exactly what Alfred was promoting remains uncertain. The letter outlined a personal project and there is no evidence of a concerted organisation of schools for laymen or a detectable short-term rise in the literacy of the laity. There are, moreover, few references to 'ordinary' people owning or reading books, although because of their cost, ownership would tend to underestimate literacy. The written survivals from the Anglo-Saxon period as a whole are major literary productions such as the Anglo-Saxon Chronicles, versions of the scriptures and codes of 'law', about 2,000 writs and charters, miscellaneous ecclesiastical documents, and a small number of wills. What fraction these represent of the original number is hard to estimate since each type of document has a different likelihood of long-term conservation, and the authenticity of some of them has been severely questioned. This indirectly indicates the limited role that literacy probably played in commercial, legal and administrative affairs: self-authenticating documents are a prerequisite for any developed bureaucracy yet the sealing of writs can definitely be traced only as far back as Edward the Confessor's reign (Clanchy, 1979, 17). Whether a state archive existed during Alfred's reign is disputed among historians. C.P. Wormald argues that the notion of the statute is not yet fully established even at the end of the Anglo-Saxon period, so that although the wording of writs shows the beginning of drafting conventions, the written versions of the 'law' lack the force of the sovereign's verbal commands (1977, 111). The latter were apparently noted down largely for personal convenience by members of the royal court who happened to be present, or sometimes by scribes from a monastic scriptorium such as the one that operated in Westminster Abbey.

The Norman Conquest did little to breach the clerical/aristocratic monopoly of literacy which had been established. The introduction and spread of French as a major spoken language probably assisted the decline of written Old English which had already deviated considerably from the spoken form and acquired an archaic and learned quality. For the next 200 years, until a transformed English language re-established itself, French competed with Latin as the dominant medium for literary and legal communication, so that those below the stratum of the gentry faced two non-vernacular languages in any attempts they made to gain a mastery of reading and writing.

In these two centuries following the Conquest, a great variety of new forms of documentation were introduced and standardised for basic economic and legal transactions. This increasing and cumulative reliance on writing constituted a fundamental cultural transition that affected even those in English society who remained illiterate. In a far-ranging and detailed study of the period up until 1307, on which this section draws extensively, M.T. Clanchy demonstrates the slow and piecemeal displacement of oral procedures and sensibilities by written modes. Take, for example, the changes that took place in the way the transfer of property was documented. Land and property of value was traditionally conveyed by having persons of good social standing witness the transfer of a symbolic object which stood either for the property or the parties concerned – a piece of turf from the land or a knife belonging to the original owner. The new owner could produce or refer to these objects as some kind of title to the property, but if a dispute arose, the principal recourse was to find the witnesses and get them to swear that they recalled the ritual transfer. The same mechanism was at work where gifts to churches or monastic institutions were marked by the placing of the Holy Gospel upon the altar, an exceptional arrangement which would function as a mnemonic and assist those present to recall not only the fact of the donation, but its timing (Clanchy, 1979, 205).

As writing gradually emerged as the preferred medium of legal transactions, ritual transfers gave way to the charter. In essence a 'public letter issued by a donor recording a title to property' (Clanchy, 1979, 64), early charters are written accounts of a particular occasion designed to be read aloud to a specific, finite audience. Individuals and property are identified in a local, subjective way with a lack of awareness of the ambiguities being created for strangers and successors; some end with personalised greetings such as 'valete'. The disappearance of these features and the gradual introduction of the past tense for legally significant acts like 'giving' are tokens of the recognition that a record for perpetuity was being created. In the thirteenth century, the use of charters to record property transfers became commonplace and their format began to be standardised. The contents became progressively formulaic and distinct from other conventional written or oral modes. Thus, the donor starts by addressing 'all the faithful in Christ', and land is legally conveyed via such phrases as 'I have given and granted, released and quitclaimed'.

A similar change affected will making. In the twelfth century, making a will was still essentially an oral act in front of witnesses. In important bequests, the testators words might be recorded more or less verbatim by someone present, a practice that went back to the Anglo-Saxon era. Subsequently, the emphasis shifted to witnessing the testator's act of placing a seal on a pre-existing statement rather than being present when he dictated it. When wills were first officially listed or 'enrolled' (in London, from 1258), probate was based on the witnesses whose names were entered on the roll. By the end of that century, witnesses names were not entered separately on the roll and the will had become a self-contained, internally authenticated, closed and sealed legal document (Clanchy, 1979, 203).

The twelfth century also saw the setting up of the first permanent state offices for producing and storing documents. The royal chancery developed out of the Exchequer created by Henry I, and was later duplicated on a more modest scale by bishops and large religious houses. For the early Middle Ages, the roles and numbers of personnel in the state chancery are not entirely clear and its organisation was complicated by a peripatetic court. The average number of surviving letters from English kings rises steadily from about ten per year during the reign of William I to about 120 per year in the reign of Henry II. Papal correspondence shows a similar increase and slightly higher averages over a comparable period (Clanchy, 1979, 44). The surviving material is undoubtedly a small fraction of the original; the earliest extant exchequer (pipe) roll for 1130 refers to the issues of 300 writs in that year alone. Clanchy points to the nearly ninefold increase in the weight of sealing wax used by the English chancery between 1226 and 1271 as a rough index of the increasing significance of paperwork in the machinery of government (1979, 43). Innovation in bureaucratic procedures was also taking place. Triple chirographs or agreements between two parties with triplicated and separated texts (one copy being retained by the treasury archives) appear in Richard I's reign as part of the general tendency to enroll a wider and wider range of public and private material.

There is little doubt that these new and quintessentially literate procedures would appear to be alien and suspicious to many people and it was not unusual for an element of the pre-literate practice to be retained. A legal treatise from the first half of the thirteenth century warns that:

> a gift is not valid unless livery follows; for the thing given is transferred neither by homage, nor by the drawing up of charters and instruments, even though they be recited in public. . . . If livery is to be made of a house by itself, or of a messuage for an estate, it ought to be made by the door and its hasp or ring, by which it is understood that the donee possesses the whole of its boundaries. (quoted by Clanchy, 1979, 208)

The use of seals or unattached tokens like finger rings helped to give other types of documentation a substantial, concrete quality and such devices generally epitomise the later stages of manuscript literacy. The symbolic devices in the centre of the sealing-wax impression harked back to a proto-literate society since, among other advantages, they enabled even those who could not write themselves to produce a distinctive proof of authorship. By the same token, even a non-reader might recognise the authority underpinning a document via its large and imposing seal.

Seals were crucial to the era not only because they provided a bridge with a largely oral culture, but also because they anticipated the technology of printing by mechanically impressing a standardised image. Nevertheless, sealing was a very partial solution to the twin problems of a general suspicion of written procedures and the prevalence of forgery. Although some of this forgery reflects straightforwardly dishonest motivation, its extent points to the existence of problems in the transition from oral to literate culture. The possibilities for forgery were generated by the imperfection of dating procedures for documents and an underdeveloped and uncritical historical sense that was itself associated with the recency of written records. The fabrication of charters by monks, scholars and administrators commonly entailed creating documents consistent with existing oral traditions and was necessitated by the increasing reliance by courts on parchment evidence of titles to property. Even forgeries which entailed absurd anachronisms of form and content could on occasion pass as authentic simply because so few people had any idea what, for instance, an Anglo-Saxon charter would have looked like.

Another procedure that helped to connect oral and literate worlds was public proclamation; new regulations were commonly published in this manner, especially in cities, and even exemplary pieces of written legislation like Magna Carta were repeatedly read out in public, often in more than one language.

The primacy and enduring respect for the oral mode was clearly registered in the language itself. 'Writing', in the sense of composing a text, would have suggested dictation rather than the wielding of a pen. Although there were many individuals competent at both composition and inscription, literary creation was regarded as a verbal skill based on dictation with its roots in the discipline of rhetoric, whereas 'writing', in the sense of making fair copies, was the quite separate providence of the professional scribe. The distinction would have been easier to make in Latin where *scriptitare* = making a fair copy, and *dictitare* = composition. In the twelfth century, to 'record' meant to bear witness. Thus, the medieval reflex would have been to associate writing with speaking a text and reading with hearing a text read aloud. Silent, 'internalised' reading was extremely unusual in the Middle Ages and possibly all but unknown in antiquity, partly because it excluded interested non-readers, and partly because it requires a high level of fluency and an easily legible text.

The activities of reading and writing would not have appeared to be as intimately connected as they seem to us and would normally have been skills acquired separately (Clanchy, 1979, 218). The technology of writing, combined with the division of labour between literary creation and inscription mentioned above, gave texts much less consistency of appearance than is now the case. Drafts and memoranda were generally written on wax tablets or scraps of parchment, while larger parchments were employed for records, and vellum (calf skin) was used for the finest, illuminated manuscripts and books. Imported paper made its appearance early in the fourteenth century, though its use remained very restricted for several centuries. Ordinary grades of parchment were relatively cheap, but a finished manuscript consumed quantities of several rather more expensive commodities – ink, sealing wax and the scribe's time.

'Scribe' or 'scrivenor' refers to an occupational role that was highly differentiated. At one pole was the 'clerk', routinely transcribing correspondence, acting as a notary or compiling registers; at the other pole was a manual craftsman with close affinities to the visual arts whose artistic identity and reputation rested on calligraphic expertise and virtuosity at illumination. An elaborate Gospel or other illuminated book, involving several crafts for the binding, would constitute the culmination of a monastic scribe's career, and might stand scrutiny as an ornamental masterpiece, valued as a decorative and sacred object rather than just a copy of a text. Many more humble documents celebrated rather than simply reproduced their subject matter, so that legibility, accuracy and economy of effort were by no means always the dominant criteria in production. Some embellishments such as rubrics and underlining improved readability, but many documents display marginal illustrations and 'doodles' that are relevant mainly as expressions of the copyist's artistic individuality or simply boredom.

During the Middle Ages, popular notions concerning literacy and illiteracy were based on an idealised and antiquated framework of concepts. The terms *litteratus* and *illiteratus* came from Classical Latin and signified the presence or absence of literacy together with the overtones of 'educated' still borne today by 'lettered'. If there were no contextual qualifications, it would have been assumed that the reference was specifically to Latin. A parallel conceptual axis of *clericus/laicus* derived from Greek where the poles contrasted the elect, chosen by lot, with the mass. With the rise and spread of Christianity, it had come to refer to those specially consecrated to Christ, the clergy, as against the ordinary members of a congregation, the laity. Since it was churchmen who constituted the majority of those that could read Latin, *clericus* and *litteratus* became linked and their connotations converged. It is clear that by the twelfth century, any educated laymen could be described as *clericus* and also that in popular usage, *clericus* and *litteratus* were interchangeable. There was thus a definite linguistic predisposition for people to think in terms of a completely literate clergy and a uniformly illiterate laity, even though the reality was much less black and white.

Such a predisposition was reinforced by the institution of 'benefit of clergy'. After the separation of church and civil law courts following the Conquest, the ecclesiastical authorities struggled to retain jurisdiction over clerical offenders. Those claiming the right to a trial in church courts gradually included more and more officials with very limited duties and the tests of status required regular revision. The authorisation of a bishop and tonsure were used, amongst others, in the thirteenth century, but a reading test as proof of 'clerkship' came to take precedence by the fourteenth. The accused could plead clergy before or after conviction in a civil court and he was then required to read the 'neck-verse', a passage in Latin from the Bible – frequently the first verse of the fifty-first Psalm. The incentive to 'prove clergy' was the light and non-capital punishments of church courts and the low levels of security in bishops' prisons. Persistent abuse led to the privilege being progressively curtailed but a reading test was finally abolished only in 1705 (Davies, 1973, 164).

The enormous differences between medieval and modern conceptions of literacy make it exceptionally difficult to establish any medieval equivalent of a literacy rate. It has already been emphasised that reading and writing were in any case not linked as intimately as they are in contemporary basic education curricula. A facility at writing was much more sparsely distributed than the ability to read as a result of the restricted access to formal tuition and the difficulty presented by the writing materials themselves, both of which helped sustain the occupational role of the scribe and the belief that at least some forms of inscription required his expertise. To the extent that criteria of literacy did exist, they looked to upper thresholds of attainment, to literary and scribal excellence, in contrast to the contemporary preoccupation with minimal achievements and standards derived from concepts like 'functionality'.

Clanchy has suggested that the possession of a personal seal was the medieval equivalent of a 'functional' literacy competence since it was the device that permitted individuals to carry out socially significant transactions in writing, even though, as we have seen, it did not in itself guarantee any individual skill at all (Clanchy, 1979, 184). In the twelfth century seals had been the almost exclusive preserve of lords and bishops but by the fourteenth century their use had spread and become common among smallholders and even some serfs. In aristocratic circles, this development was regarded as a breach of a natural prerogative. A high official of Henry II is recorded 'putting down' a knight who had mentioned the use of his seal, with the cutting comment, 'It was not formerly the custom for every petty knight to have a seal, which befits only kings and important people' (quoted in Clanchy, 1979, 36). On the other hand, the statute of Exeter of 1285 required 'bondsmen' to use a seal on their written testimony in inquests, though whether the practice became standard has not been firmly established.

The increasing involvement of the nobility and gentry in transactions entailing written records not only generated an incentive to acquire and improve reading abilities throughout the upper stratum of medieval society but also helped to create an audience for literature as a leisure pursuit. Although military matters and the martial arts remained major preoccupations of the knightly class, the education of 'gentlemen' and the prevalent conceptions of their appropriate accomplishments began to incorporate literary knowledge and creativity. In addition to the evidence provided by fourteenth-century wills of noble magnates owning sizeable libraries, Orme (1973, 31–3) cites the example of the literary circle around Chaucer, consisting of men like Sir Lewis Clifford, Sir Richard Stury and Sir Philip la Vache, who owned books, patronised authors, and wrote and exchanged verse with each other.

A taste for romances, histories and lives of the saints can be traced among merchants, legal specialists, and prosperous craftsmen in the towns. There, too, it was the utilitarian need to master reading and writing for business accounts and correspondence (in French and English rather than Latin) that appears to have led to a subsequent cultivation of literary tastes. Merchants and other members of the middle strata must have been aware that bookishness was an effective way conspicuously to display the refinements increasingly associated with their noble social superiors and thus earn the kind of social approval that rarely derives from the possession of 'naked' wealth.

The evidence suggesting the use of literacy as a means of social climbing is necessarily indirect. Parkes notes (1973, 562) that manuscripts in the Bodleian Library such as Dunce 137 and 132 contain compilations of technical formularies and legal treatises bound together with miscellaneous 'entertainments' in French such as Robert Grosseteste's *Le Chasteau d'Amor*, the *Fables of Marie de France*, and a Bestiary. The collection and binding together of manuals of practical and moral instruction, together with the occasional romance, captures well the emphasis on self-improvement that characterises the contents of surviving fourteenth- and fifteenth-century secular libraries. There are indications, too, that at least some of these collections were transcribed by the compilers themselves in the same handwriting they used for business documents. The growing preference for cursive hands for all general writing purposes is important in itself as a mark of the greatly increased social utility of late medieval vernacular literacy. Vernacular longhands obviated the need for the drastic abbreviations used in Latin manuscripts and generally speeded up and cheapened the production of books (Parkes, 1973, 563).

The discussion of institutional instruction in reading and writing has been deliberately delayed to underline the point that the existence and routine use of a range of sophisticated written instruments of communication considerably pre-dated the development of an effective infrastructure of schooling. Medieval thinking, which took it to be quite natural for only a very small and selected part of the population to receive (and to anticipate their children receiving) formal teaching in literacy, contrasts starkly with the contemporary state of affairs, where an opportunity to become literate is generally regarded as a universal right, even within nations unable to implement policies that make this opportunity widely available.

The inherent complexity of medieval educational arrangements is exacerbated by the absence of surviving records for many localities and types of institution, frustrating attempts at broad generalisation or simple classification. As far as literacy is concerned, however, the historical process of central importance is the creation and gradual growth of a lay stratum of the population equipped with a relatively high level of competence in literacy. Prior to the end of the twelfth century, there are few references to a literate laity because, with the principal exception of a few 'places' located in the households of great noble families, most formal instruction took place under the auspices of monastic institutions and was provided primarily to prepare pupils for entry into them. The relatively high literacy of the clergy as a whole was necessitated by the obligation of priests to perform a daily mass and other sacraments as required, and unless the liturgy was committed to memory with the assistance of a competent reader, these duties required an ability to read, pronounce out loud, and understand Latin. In addition, both minor and major orders were expected to study the scriptures and the approved commentaries on them. Such was, in a manner of speaking, the official job-description; in reality, the linguistic skills of the clergy fell well short of the desired standard. Surviving diocesan correspondence indicates that the concern of scrupulous bishops with the inadequate learning of their clergy, their woefully inaccurate Latin grammar and their incapacity to sing or chant harmoniously abides well into the seventeenth century. In addition, bishops' registers in some dioceses record that candidates for ordination or appointment to a benefice were examined for fitness and learning and from time to time were rejected or given a conditional ordination only.

Fourteenth- and fifteenth-century sources suggest that younger candidates in the minor orders found the mastery of Latin especially taxing (Orme, 1973, 14–19). It is worth re-emphasising that these relatively advanced requirements for literacy applied only to the clergy. The Christian way of life in the Middle Ages did not permit, let alone require, ordinary people to study the Bible privately. After the Synod of Toulouse (1229), the Church proscribed vernacular versions of the complete Bible on the grounds that in untutored hands and heads it would promote heterodoxy and heresy.

In England it was not until the 1390s, when the Lollard Bibles produced by Wyclif and his associates began to circulate, that the full vernacular text was available to the laity. Henry IV's reign initiated a long period in which the vernacular Bible was prohibited and its publishers and possessors persecuted, though with little success in the face of the combined force of Lutheranism and increased literacy. Nevertheless, ecclesiastical and political opposition persisted until 1535 when Coverdale's Bible appeared with a dedication to Henry VIII (who subsequently authorised the distribution of a modified version to all churches).

The medieval church's initiatives in the educational sphere were made with its own internal needs and deficiencies very much in mind. An early milestone was the decision of the fourth Lateran Council of 1215 to authorise every church with sufficient funds to organise teaching in Latin. Pope Gregory IX (1227–41) reinforced this policy with a decree that priests should 'have a man to keep school' and encourage their parishioners to send their sons to him for an education in the faith (Davies, 1973, 22). Until after the Reformation, a training in literacy in England remained predominantly clerical in the twin respects that it was usually given by clerics and that its Latin-dominated content strongly emphasised scriptural and other religious materials. From the thirteenth century onwards, however, the teaching role was increasingly assumed by secular clerics and unordained persons, while the curriculum evolved beyond those topics and texts specifically required by a Christian way of life.

References to 'school' in medieval sources cover institutions of all levels from primary to university. Most writers qualified the term by indicating either the kind of curriculum followed or the character of the school's founding statutes. The closest approximation to the contemporary primary school was generally called a 'song school'. In the song schools attached to cathedrals, systematic instruction in music was provided for the choristers; elsewhere, pupils were probably taught principally to chant psalms and prayers (i.e. 'plainsong'). Although there are no absolutely clear-cut demarcations, song schools appear to have concentrated on rote learning and the sounds of letters and syllables, leaving Latin grammar, translation and probably writing generally, for subsequent study at a higher level institution. In this and other types of school, liturgical materials were prominent in the curriculum. In part, this followed from the prevalent assumption that the purpose of schooling was to prepare children for a vocation in the Church, or at least to give them a grounding in the faith, but it was also determined by the simple fact that texts like the Catechism, the Latin Psalter and Horae Beatae ('Book of the Hours') were the only ones of which there were likely to be several copies within the parish.

Even the form in which the alphabet was conventionally presented respected the religious context of education. Most books intended for teaching contained the distinctive 'criss-cross' or 'Christ-cross' rows which were an arrangement of the letters of the alphabet so-called after the initial, embellished symbol of the cross and the terminating Latin phrase 'est amen'. Instances of this device, usually printed in black-letter face, survive from the fourteenth through to the seventeenth century.

Some initial teaching of the alphabet was done using tablets of hardwood and other materials, incised or embossed with Christ-cross rows and other texts. From the sixteenth century, as paper became more widely available, the characters were printed in the form of 'horn-books' which protected the paper from grubby or clumsy hands by semi-transparent sheets of horn attached to a solid backing-board.

Printing also increased the variety of 'primers' available for initial and intermediate readers. These often included 'ABC' in their titles and were prefaced by the Christ-cross rows and sometimes a syllabary, followed by a selection from the Creed, the Lord's Prayer, psalms, hymns, the Catechism, the Ten Commandments, an Almanac, etc. Books of this sort became the initial preparation for grammar school. The Paston family purchased a manuscript primer in 1447 when it cost two shillings, a price that placed it out of the reach of poor parents (Davies, 1973, 102), but printed versions sold for threepence and sixpence in the sixteenth century.

Similar elementary instruction (and occasionally more advanced teaching) was offered in the chantry schools. Originally endowments to pay for priests or chaplains to conduct memorial masses, chantries began to support a variety of charitable institutions including hospitals and almshouses. The proportion of chantries providing specifically for schools or individual schoolmasters grew steadily from the end of the fourteenth century until 1548 when the link with schooling was statutorily severed in the Reformation. Well-heeled merchants, prelates and other prominent citizens, together with such collectivities as town corporations and guilds, were active in funding chantries which were an important source of free education for poor people. At Aldwinkle in Northamptonshire, a syllable school was founded in 1489 where 'the said chaplain . . . shall teach and instruct in spelling and reading six of the poorest of the town of Aldwinkle . . . freely without demanding or taking remuneration from their parents or friends' (quoted in Davies, 1973, 39). Arrangements sometimes allowed the master, who was invariably a cleric, to charge fees on a means-tested basis, as at Liverpool, where one John Grosse, a prosperous rector, supported a priest 'to keep a grammar school and take his advantage from all the children except those whose names be Grosse, and poor children that have no succour' (quoted in Orme, 1973, 196).

To the extent that they attempted to impose more or less strict qualifications for entry to exclude those lacking 'first letters', medieval and early modern grammar schools regarded themselves as second-level institutions. Their statutes sometimes specifically prevented the admission of non-readers as at St Paul's, Canterbury, Westminster and Merchant Taylor's (Davies, 1973, 41), while Winchester College and Eton expected their newly-arrived scholars to be already familiar with Donatus whose *Ars Minor* was the standard Latin primer (Orme, 1973, 69). Nevertheless, there was considerable popular demand for elementary education and it was not uncommon for fourteenth- and fifteenth-century grammar foundations to make special arrangements to teach 'petties' or infants. In some instances a special reading teacher was employed; in others, the petties sat alongside the grammarians and were taught either by the same masters or by ushers or even senior scholars. Basic literacy instruction was provided only with reluctance by some teachers who preferred to cultivate links with the universities.

The core of the grammar school curriculum was derived from the *trivium*, the classical study of grammar, rhetoric and logic. The objective was to give pupils a familiarity with the principles underlying the Latin language together with its literary heritage. This linguistic focus of teaching was severely academic. It was not, for example, until well into the fifteenth century that elementary grammars for English (as opposed to Latin) became generally available, subsequent versions of which became standard in Tudor schools.

Practical and occupationally useful areas of knowledge did not feature very prominently in the 'core curriculum'. French studies had faded from schools after 1400 following several decades of intense literary competition with English, despite a continued demand for fluency in French generated by its continued use in the common law, in diplomacy, and in commerce. This demand had to be satisfied largely by 'teach-yourself' publications, dialogues, narratives and primers like the delightfully titled *A Good Boke to Lerne to Speke French*, which were issued and re-issued frequently in the period 1480–1520. Generally, learning of an applied nature directly related to occupational roles in business and commerce was mainly conducted outside the grammar schools, principally in specialist institutions like the 'business schools' that grew up in Oxford from the thirteenth century, or through apprenticeships. Some schools did include a treatment of *dictamen*, the composition of letters and drafting of formal documents, but the references to this topic in the statutes of Thomas, Archbishop of York's grammar school at Rotherham (founded 1483), and Bishop Sherborne's grammar school at Rolleston (founded 1524), imply that its standing was lowly. Rotherham payed the master who dealt with writing £5 6s. 8d., while he gave the grammar master £10. Sherborne suggested that dull or lazy pupils were the ones that might benefit from being taught writing and accounts (Orme, 1973, 78).

In an era when access to schooling was restricted both geographically and socially, it is important not to neglect the possible contribution of informal tuition to the total numbers of readers and writers. Such tuition is prone to being overlooked since it leaves little by way of formal records to indicate its extent. After the advent of printing, introductory primers and beginning reading texts feature very prominently in publishers' and stationers' lists, and this may, it could be speculated, point to a demand from the general public beyond the classroom. Further, equally tenuous clues to the prevalence of informal scholars and autodidacts come from contemporary estimates of literacy/illiteracy. The oft-quoted remark by Sir Thomas More in his *Apologia* (1533) that 'far more than four parts of all the whole divided into ten could never read English yet' suggests a ceiling of about 50 per cent on literacy. It seems extremely unlikely that 50 per cent of the population could have completed a formal primary schooling in the first quarter of the sixteenth century, preserving the possibility that informal tuition was one important route to medieval literacy. Against this, the Bishop of Winchester reckoned readers as a minority of one in a hundred in roughly the same period as More. Such a large disparity may indicate nothing more than divergent conceptions of what constituted reading fluency, and it would certainly be optimistic to suppose that either figure was anything more than the most subjective of guesses, so new evidence will be needed both to establish the overall density of late medieval literacy and also the role of informal tuition.

The particularly inclusive periodisation of 'medieval' that has been used in this section presents difficulties in achieving a succinct summary. There is, nevertheless, a case for seeing the era of handwritten manuscripts as a unity despite the internal developments that have been noted. The absence of major technological innovations with a direct impact on literacy (apart from the introduction of paper) kept the inscription of the written word as expensive in terms of effort as it had been in classical times. A contemporary observer would be struck by the contrast in the way coding and decoding skills were parcelled up within social roles, by the range of practical tasks which could not be accomplished or even assisted by literacy (so that it would not, for the majority, have had much utilitarian significance), and by the many vivid manifestations of an autonomous oral culture.[3] The amount of written material in circulation was, by modern standards, infinitesimal, and the institutional apparatus for disseminating it embryonic. However, the period saw a definite shift in literacy's main institutional setting from an early monopolisation by the administration of government to a less esoteric religious base. The fact that the Christian Church remained less than totally committed to mass vernacular education (as well as ill-equipped to provide it), together with the existence of regional linguistic variations and the persistence of functional competition between English, French and Latin, all helped to keep literacy 'restricted' and density comparatively low. In an era in which a great deal of knowledge was uncritically reproduced from unknown classical sources and, in advance of the legal enforcement of authorial copyright, amended and expanded without acknowledgment or attribution, modern notions of authorship and publication are clearly inapplicable.

The advent of print

Manuscript book production was a small-scale but flourishing industry in several major European cities at least two centuries before Johann Gutenberg perfected a compatible combination of movable metal type, screw press, ink and paper, some time in the late 1440s

(Steinberg, 1979, 18). Although the monastic scriptoria continued to operate throughout the era of incunabula (that is, early books printed before 1501), their output was not adequate to serve the rising demand for printed matter. The rules of monastic orders often set limits on the number of hours during which monks were permitted to transcribe, leaving the monastries unable to respond to market forces. From what little is known about the operation of scriptoria, they appear to have been organised to facilitate multiple copying from dictation. This procedure led to the accumulation of errors and the circulation of inconsistent and badly corrupted texts. Such poor quality control provided commercial opportunities for the secular 'stationers', forerunners of the modern publisher, who set up in urban centres alongside existing booksellers and catered largely, but not exclusively, for institutional clients like law courts and universities. The latter exerted a great influence on publishing through the large volume of regular business they could guarantee, and institutions like Paris and Oxford licensed their own stationers and supervised their operations (Febvre and Martin, 1976, 20). The concern of the universities for accurate and authoritative copies led to the development of a system of out-work in which copyists reproduced only a section of a manuscript at a time (a *pecia* or quire of pages) from a carefully checked, exemplary copy, in return for a prearranged fee.

An organisational framework for commercial publication and retailing thus existed well in advance of the printing press. What the typographical technology added was the mass production of exactly similar copies with a drastic reduction in the manpower needed. Eisenstein (1968, 3) estimates that down to 1450, ten copyists were needed for each clerk producing original material; by 1500, the presses enabled one printer to serve twenty clerks. Editing and correcting in advance, partially pioneered by the *pecia* system, could now be fully exploited, eliminating the laborious checking and emendation of each manuscript copy. The initial manufacture of type became the labour-intensive stage of book production. Clapham (1957, 386–7) calculated that cutting the punches for a fount would have involved at least a year's work for two men; the same number could produce cast and dressed type at no more than 25 characters per hour, and although it was, of course, re-usable, a stock of tens of thousands of characters was required before composition would begin.

The idea of an edition of identical copies of an arguably definitive text which could be broadcast to an anonymous audience was a crucial innovation with enduring consequences for the character of all intellectual and literary activity. Equally significant, though perhaps more mundane, was the capacity of the presses to reproduce maps and diagrams from woodblocks or engravings. In the short term, it was these developments rather than the potential for very large print runs that proved important; the evidence suggests that incunables were generally published in modest editions of about 200 (Hay, 1967, XXII).

Historians of printing agree that occupational and organisational changes associated with the production of printed matter occurred rapidly in comparison with the impact on authorship. The range of titles of early printed books differed little from the body of writings which were already well-known and in circulation throughout the later Middle Ages (Goldschmidt, 1943, 2; Hay, 1957, 4). Manuscripts were widely copied from printed books as well as vice versa. Thus, Johannes Trithemius, Abbot of Sponheim, ironically had his *De Laude Scriptorium*, exhorting monks to continue their scribal craft, produced in a Mainz printshop (Eisenstein, 1979, 15).

Authorship continued to be dominated by monks, beneficed clerks and public officials. Patronage by noble sponsors continued to support a great deal of literary endeavour by writers who, in the absence of effective copyright legislation, had no control over pirated editions. The traditional roles of *glossator* and commentator were, however, rendered largely obsolete, to be replaced by bibliographic specialisms made possible by the new devices for the convenience of readers and scholars – title pages with date and place of publication, running heads, punctuation, footnotes and cross-references. The scriptures and devotional works like Books of the Hours and Thomas à Kempis's *Imitation of Christ* continued to be the most popular publications. The Vulgate Bible was printed at least forty-four times by 1500, and within another hundred years, vernacular editions existed for every major European language (Hay, 1967, xxii). Equally important and worthy of research in the future (though few instances, unfortunately, survive) was the vastly increased output and new variants of job printing, the production of ephemera such as bulletins, broadsheets, handbills and calendars. Such modest and everyday matter must have represented the first intrusion of print into the lives of many uneducated people. Another staple item for jobbing printers was the religious indulgence or printed pardon: Eisenstein notes that the earliest dated work of both Gutenberg and Caxton were indulgences (1968, 4–5).

The physical appearance of early printed books is a further reminder that print culture was an elaboration and extension of manuscript culture rather than a radical departure from it. Printers went out of their way to make founts that resembled established German and Italian styles of handwriting, even though the ligatures and ornamentation of the characters increased preparation time and reduced the legibility of the resulting page.

The links between the advent of print and rates and modes of literacy have been sadly neglected by scholars more anxious to examine print's connections with established fields of historical research such as the Reformation, the rise of empirical science, and the diffusion of humanist ideas. One of the prevailing assumptions seems to be that print and literacy 'naturally' reinforce each other:

> Nor can it confidently be argued that it needed printing to cure illiteracy. It is as clear that the invention of printing by movable type was the result of a rising demand for books as it is obvious that the greater quantity of books thus made available encouraged literacy still further. (Hay, 1957, 4)

The most important audience for printed materials was the vast public of Christian adherents and it was the powerful combination of print and increased literacy that was a major factor in the differentiation and factionalising of this public. Initially, Rome regarded print favourably as God's indication of the Western Church's superiority over the infidel (Eisenstein, 1979, 303), but it was the Protestant Reformation that first harnessed its unprecedented propaganda capacity. Luther's Ninety-Five Theses of 1517 were said to have spread the length of Germany in a fortnight and were circulating widely throughout Europe within a month (quoted by Eisenstein, 1979, 310). Anti-Papist cartoons and pamphlets aroused individuals who had never before had their opinions canvassed by vernacular literature (Eisenstein, 1979, 304).

Luther himself declared printing to be 'God's highest and extremist act of grace whereby the business of the Gospel is driven forward . . . [It is] the last flame before the extinction of the world' (Black, 1963, 432).

Attitudes to the circulation of the Scriptures were transformed almost immediately into doctrinal issues which helped further to characterise and polarise the Christian orthodoxies. Lutherans believed that the core of the Christian message could not be corrupted by the vehicle in which it was disseminated, and Protestantism as a whole came to be distinguished by its stress on Bible study as a route to personal salvation. In contrast, following the Council of Trent (1545–63), Rome fixed the Canon of Scripture in the Latin Vulgate, and Catholic thought emphasised the oral transmission of Christ's words to the Apostles as a precedent for face to face instruction of the laity by priests (Eisenstein, 1979, 319).

Literacy in early modern Britain

The sixteenth century saw a considerable expansion in both schools and universities. In a survey that covered ten English counties, W.K. Jordan could trace only thirty-four schools open to the laity in 1480. By 1660, a total of 410 new schools had been set up, to which must be added an unknown number of fee-charging institutions, schoolmasters and private tutors who fell outside Jordan's purview. He calculated that this represented one grammar school for every 4,400 population; throughout eight of the ten selected counties, there was a school offering free tuition within a radius of twelve miles (Jordan, 1961, 290–1). Statistics such as these have discredited the former view of historians that Henry VIII's dissolution of the monasteries inflicted permanent damage to educational provision. Most would probably now agree with Stone that the breaking of the clerical monopoly over instruction secured the foundations of a system that, in the long term, proved responsive to the requirements of administration, the professions and business (1964, 70). Not only were entrants to these enlarging occupational sectors increasingly drawn from grammar school alumni, but successful practitioners were notably generous with educational bequests and endowments. Even the landed gentry, as a class not traditionally in the vanguard of educational progress, began to foresee their sons benefiting socially from a knowledge of the classics and vocationally from attendance at an Inn of Court (Stone, 1964, 70). The expansion of the grammar schools had an inevitable 'roll-over' effect on demand for elementary instruction which, as indicated above, probably drew extensively on individual and informal efforts, as well as the petty schools.

By the middle of the seventeenth century, convictions about the proper approach and sequence of literacy teaching activities had hardened into a pedagogy disseminated through primers, catechisms, manuals and 'theoretical' publications. The initial stage was normally given over to teaching recognition of the letters of the alphabet and establishing their associated sounds through drills and oral repetitions. Horn books extended the repertoire to letter combinations and syllables. The teaching method that dominated the first stage was what Cressy (1980, 4) terms a 'secular catechism' – verbal interrogation by the teacher followed by verbal pupil responses; writing featured only peripherally, if at all. The second stage was marked by the transition from horn book to an intermediate text such as a primer or catechism where the longer words pupils encountered had to be broken down into constituent syllables and letter combinations. Reading fluency and accurate spelling were the main objectives of the second stage and most teachers appeared to have sought proficiency in reading aloud and spelling from memory before formally introducing pupils to writing. Writing, with the calligraphic aspects still largely displacing 'composition', together with reading practice from the Bible and other uplifting, adult texts, made up a third stage, at the end of which a pupil was considered ready to start Latin studies. Tudor and Stuart educationalists judged five to eight years of age to be the period in which these basic literacy skills should be acquired. This presumed the kind of continuous and skilled tuition that only the most fortunately placed children would have received. Evidence on actual rates of pupil progress is available for 1698–1715 from a register of Great Yarmouth Children's Hospital, where the attainments of children admitted and their progress were carefully documented (presumably because both the master and the pupils were given cash incentives for reaching various levels of literacy). Despite the fact that the children came largely from 'respectable working families' and were not foundlings, only 16 per cent of the sixty-one boys aged between six and eight were fully able to read, while girls were even less accomplished, so that only 13 per cent out of eighty-five were able to read testament or Bible by the age of fifteen (Cressy, 1980, 32–2).

In the countryside, children aged between five and six began to learn to read from their parents, or other, usually female, instructors such as school-dames. Those children who were able to attend school started at about seven and were expected to be reading up to Bible standard and writing legibly within a year. If a family's economic circumstances were pressing, a child would be taken away to work at this point. The fact that an eight-year-old became an important potential source of family income at roughly the stage he or she was mastering writing is one further reason for believing that reading was a skill much more widely diffused than writing (Spufford, 1979, 414).

Although much of the quantitative data available concerning literacy are fragmentary and derived from small, localised samples (see Appendix 2), recent historical research has permitted some preliminary assessments to be made about the literacy levels of different social groups. This work makes the earlier statement of Altick's (1957, 18) that the ability to read was more democratically distributed in Tudor and Stuart England than at any subsequent time before the end of the eighteenth century, particularly problematic. If by 'democratic', Altick meant only that no social stratum was formally denied access to 'primary' instruction, or was entirely illiterate, his assertion is unexceptionable. It would be quite wrong, on the other hand, to infer that there was little or no variation in literacy rates by social origin. Surveying collections of data derived from ecclesiastical depositions, marriage licences, wills, and loyalty oaths and covenants, Cressy (1980) is confident (despite chronological fluctuations, regional variations and statistical limitations) that literacy in Elizabethan and Stuart periods closely reflected social rank. Employing the capacity to append a signature to a document, as opposed to being able to make only a mark, as the criterion of literacy, Cressy identifies three broadly defined social clusters within each of which literacy attainments were very roughly comparable. The nobility, gentry, clergy and professions make up the cluster with the highest level of literacy, consistently over 90 per cent signing irrespective of the type of document involved. The intermediate cluster, consisting of tradesmen, craftsmen and yeomen, varied within the range 32–86 per cent literate, while husbandmen, labourers and servants made up the least literate cluster with rates generally below 27 per cent.

The uniformly high literacy of the 'gentle' cluster is to be expected. The clergy and the professionals were, of course, obliged to exercise reading and writing skills within their occupational roles, and the qualifications for entry imposed on them were more or less effective literacy 'screens' (see Chapter 5). Similarly, the titled aristocracy often discharged the kind of administrative and public commitments that directly entailed literacy. Even so, the philistinism of the English nobility was the subject of critical contemporary references in the works of humanist theorists of education like Ascham, Elyot and Mulcaster, and it is revealing that as late as 1547 it was considered necessary to draft a clause in a bill specifically to extend the benefit of clergy to peers unable to read (Stone, 1965, 675). Irrespective of its extent, however, illiteracy was no more incompatible with the rank of knight or esquire than the possession of literacy was capable, in itself, of making a craftsman the social equal of a knight.[4]

The variability in rates of literacy within the intermediate cluster largely reflects the real ambiguities that characterised the central regions of the social structure, and these are not always accurately captured in occupational designations. Those engaged in large-scale commercial and enterpreneurial activities, and those who worked with expensive commodities or merchandise, displayed high levels of literacy approaching that of the gentle-professional cluster. Merchants and wholesalers needed to handle correspondence, invoices and ledgers on a daily basis, though as with the gentry, there were occasional markers in their ranks. Tradesmen and independent craftsmen on a smaller scale, the blacksmiths, butchers and carpenters, a majority of whom operated in smaller towns and villages, had rates in the range 32–44 per cent. As Cressy noted (1980, 131) the extent to which reading and writing are integral to a craft or trade is not the only factor underlying variations in rates. In retailing, particularly, the level and character of the customer's literacy may be an important consideration. Cressy's figures for rural literacy, 1580–1700, (1980, 132–3) show that vintners, goldsmiths and saddlers, purveying luxury goods to a predominantly upper-class clientele, had a combined literacy rate of 84 per cent (N=50), while bakers, victuallers and butchers, presumably with more variable custom, had a combined rate of 48 per cent literate (N=219).

The lowest literacy cluster contained most outdoor and heavy manual trades including mining, fishing and agricultural husbandry. Building trades as a group contained many markers: only 34 per cent of the 412 slaters, thatchers, masons, bricklayers, carpenters, joiners and glaziers in Cressy's rural sample could sign.

Together with labourers and the somewhat vague category of 'husbandmen', it was women as a group that displayed the lowest rates of literacy. Even in the relatively affluent, urban dioceses of Norwich (1580–1700) and Exeter (1574–1688) only 13 per cent of Cressy's sample of 1,633 women could sign (1980, 119–20). In the primary sources on which Cressy relies, women are not differentiated by social standing, but it is clear that illiteracy of wives and daughters must have been common even in the strata and occupations where most men were fully competent, and this is in keeping with attitudes to the domestic and spiritual inferiority of women in the seventeenth century.[5]

By the accession of George I in 1714, Cressy estimates that the overall literacy rate in England was 45 per cent for men and 25 per cent for women, compared to 30 per cent and 10 per cent respectively at the time of the Civil War (1980, 176). The explanation both of this rise and the social differentials which it conceals, raises some difficult issues concerning the political and social significance of Early Modern literacy, issues which partly prefigure the debate over the relationship between the industrial revolution and literacy levels. In Cressy's view, the question comes down to the relative strength of ideological 'push' factors as against the effects of economic 'pull'. It is suggested that the ideological push came from the rhetoric and evangelism of moralists and reformers who stressed the spiritual and civic benefits of a literate populace.[6] Cressy maintains that the push was weaker than elsewhere in Europe since the propaganda on behalf of popular education was not translated into state-financed programmes, and private, local philanthropy remained the basis of provision. Indeed, there were serious political reservations in influential quarters about the wisdom of making the higher learning, if not basic literacy, available to those whose social station did not necessitate it.

Cressy interprets the occupational stratification of literacy levels as definite evidence that individuals were 'pulled' towards acquiring reading and writing skills by their utility and their economic value in particular trades and occupations. The 'push' and 'pull' analogy, apparently borrowed from theories of population migration, does very little to clarify matters. Neither the religiously inspired crusade, nor the opening up of occupational sectors to which literacy is relevant, could mechanically raise literacy rates unless these developments generated appropriate patterns of popular motivation and took place in a context of adequate opportunities for instruction. Any significant rise in rates must always entail both structural and motivational shifts, so a sharp division between push and pull factors is unrealistic.

The link between occupation and literacy rates remains much more ambiguous than Cressy allows. Crude economic pull could only have operated where reading and writing were widely known to be pre-conditions for entry into a trade or occupation. Outside the established professions and the clerical specialisms auxiliary to them, relatively few occupational roles in this period necessitated literacy. Most manual skills were transmitted entirely by demonstration and oral instruction on the job or in the workshop. Instructional texts and the certificates and credentials based upon them played a negligible role

If literacy was not yet primarily a vocational preparation, how then are we to explain the apparently clear occupational differences? Working environments provide differential access to written documents and varying amounts of contact with people already literate. Even though the work task itself may not entail literacy, work relationships can stimulate motivation and allow opportunities for instruction and self-instruction. The character of employer-employee-customer relationships, indoor or outdoor location, length of work-cycle, and the time-span of supervision, as well as the nature of the job skills themselves are all likely to have been implicated, and most of these factors retain their relevance to literacy in working life.

In other central areas of social life such as the purchase of household necessities, the discharge of family and kin obligations, travel and recreation, the written word would have been a background element unlikely to present a serious obstacle or a major inconvenience to the illiterate person. Although precise estimates are not possible, it cannot be doubted that a much smaller proportion of culturally available information of all kinds was disseminated through written channels. Many activities, events and experiences today recorded in handbooks, newspapers, periodicals, brochures and local ephemera like parish magazines and club newsletters, were not documented at all. The lower degree of differentiation and specialisation in written forms and genres combined with the relative expense of bound volumes meant that the ordinary household possessed little paper with print. A characteristic publication in mass circulation was the almanac, sales of which reached a peak of 400,000 annually in the 1680s, second only to the Bible (Capp, 1979, 44). Marvellously miscellaneous, almanacs typically contained a selection from the following: a calender with planetary motions and conjunctions, tables of legal terminology, charts of human anatomy indicating zones controlled by zodiacal influences, weather prospects, medical notes, weights and measures, omens and defences against witchcraft, data on farming and gardening related to the appropriate season, lists of fairs, road directions, tables of the dates of kings since the Conquest and events since the Creation, prophecies and prognostications for the year ahead. Both by their intermixture of practical information, entertainment and fiction, and by their confident assumption that they could encompass all practical knowledge on a sheet or in a small book, almanacs provide a rough measure of the contemporary uses and limitations of popular literacy.

Almanacs could only be accepted as popular encyclopaedias because they were complementary to the continuing vitality of oral cultures and sub-cultures. In rural areas especially, oral transmission covered the bulk of domestic skills, work technologies and leisure pursuits up until the coming of the railways. Historians, possibly blinkered by the emphasis of their professional training on documentary sources, have generally underestimated the importance of the oral channel and antedated its eclipse by the written word.

Important legal changes were taking place with respect to publishing. Since the spread of printing, the 'stationer' was the key entrepreneur who purchased a work from its author, commissioned its printing, and arranged for its distribution and sale. The Stationers' Company received various forms of protection from the Crown and in the middle of the sixteenth century it was granted a charter which amounted to a registration and licensing system for printed books (Cornish, 1981, 293–4). The Company's privileged position was preserved through most of the seventeenth century (with the Crown retaining rights over Bibles and prayer books) but finally lapsed through parliamentary opposition in 1694. The stationers, unprotected from outside and foreign competition, had to wait until the Copyright Act of 1709 to regain their monopoly. The Act gave the 'sole right and liberty of printing books' for fourteen years from publication to authors, providing the title was registered prior to publication with the Stationers' Company. Enforcement was backed up by powers of seizure and financial penalties (Cornish, 1981, 294–5). This statute provided a blueprint for a great deal of subsequent legislation which gradually extended the principle of creator's copyright to graphic work and other media.

The English Revolution of 1640–60 initiated a series of indirect, long-term, but nevertheless important, consequences for literacy. The development of an embryonic mass literacy was assisted by the period of freedom from censorship and centralised control of publication that followed the onset of the Revolution. Many works that had been actively suppressed, published abroad, or kept by their authors in manuscript, appeared in print and all kinds of heterodox, radical and directly heretical texts circulated freely. Levellers (briefly), Ranters, Quakers, poets, scientists, enthusiasts for polygamy and advocates of free love all had their day in print. Political broadsides that would have been considered unquestionably seditious in the 1630s were openly read aloud in taverns. The volume of topical literature in circulation rose dramatically. The number of pamphlets published in England increased from twenty-two in 1640 to 1,966 in 1642; 700 newspaper titles appeared in 1645 alone: between 1640 and 1660, a total of 22,000 items in both categories have been listed (Hill, 1980, 49; Stone, 1969, 99). The audience for political ideas and debate was greatly extended by this explosion of written polemic and propaganda, partly because many of the pamphleteers adopted an unprecedentedly plain, conversational style of prose appropriate to a mass readership containing many novice readers. It can thus be said that the Revolution politicised literacy in two distinct respects. Firstly, it demonstrated emphatically to radicals and conservatives alike that the written word carried an enormous potential for political persuasion. Secondly, some of the Puritan publications contained the demand for a universal, free, compulsory education as 'the main foundation of a reformed Commonwealth' (quoted in Stone, 1969, 79), and this proposal was mirrored in the enthusiasm with which the Puritans founded schools and distributed Bibles throughout England, Wales and Scotland. The creation of a state-financed and centrally controlled system of schooling was not destined to be an imminent achievement (except in the self-governing communities of immigrants to New England), but the ideal had established its currency and secured a place on the political agenda.

The period of free political comment and publication was short-lived and in 1660 comprehensive censorship returned. Only official newspapers were permitted to 'appeal to the people'; all books dealing with history or affairs of state had to be vetted by one of Charles II's Secretaries of State, while those concerned with theology, philosophy or science were scrutinised by the Archbishop of Canterbury, The Bishop of London or the Vice Chancellor of Oxford or Cambridge, as appropriate (Hill, 1980, 46).

Restoration censorship was associated with a predictable phase of intellectual conservatism and educational contraction (Wrightson, 1982, 186). The inference widely drawn by the propertied and powerful was that the overeducation of the lower orders corrupted the latter's natural obedience and incited disloyalty (Stone, 1969, 85). The presumption that reading and writing attainments were naturally determined by an individual's station in life was shared even by those who had struggled to educate themselves. Thomas Chubb, born in 1679, the son of a maltster from East Harnham, wrote in the introduction to a work on the scriptures that:

> The Author was taught to read English, to write an ordinary hand, and was further instructed in the common rules of arithmetic: this education being suitable to the circumstances of his family and to the time he had to be instructed in. (quoted in Spufford, 1979, 422)

Spufford also notes (1979, 418) that John Bunyan, the most famous of all seventeenth-century spiritual autobiographers, had a keen appreciation of how fortunate he was in his own educational experiences. His father, despite holding a cottage and nine acres in Bedfordshire, was obliged to travel as a tinker to keep the family in subsistence. Bunyan wrote that 'notwithstanding the meanness of . . . my Parents, it pleased God to put into their hearts to put me to school to learn both to read and write'.

The Early Modern Period is best seen as a transitional phase between a predominantly oral medieval culture and the extensive literacy of post-industrial Britain. Although literacy's density remained only in the mid-range throughout, the mass production of books (and, perhaps more importantly, ephemera) disseminated print sufficiently widely to alter profoundly even the oral cultures in which the totally illiterate participated. The institutional apparatus of publication begins to acquire some of its modern commercial characteristics, and a systematic preparation for vernacular literacy became available for a sizeable minority of children through a recognisable 'core curriculum'. The divergence between the way reading and writing were perceived and valued closes considerably, but their respective distribution remains unequal, and both lack their contemporary functional and occupational utility. The seventeenth century is the earliest period for which the diaries and autobiographies of poor people survive in any number, and the analysis of these re-emphasises the extent to which literacy remained harnessed to a religious base.[7] Just as most books in general circulation had an inspirational character, so most of the earliest pieces of autobiography are devoted to spiritual revelations and self-scrutiny.

The eighteenth and nineteenth centuries

Eighteenth-century debates between proponents and opponents of popular education were able to start from a substantial consensus that the general function of education was to preserve and reproduce existing social arrangements and distinctions. The recurrent theme amongst the opponents, even prior to the French Revolution, was the danger of an overeducated working class becoming disaffected. In Bernard Mandeville's *An Essay on Charity and Charity-Schools*, published in 1723 as an appendix to *The Fable of the Bees*, there is a mercantilist argument against diminishing the numbers of the 'Laborious Poor' that was to be reiterated in more or less equivalent terms for over a century throughout Europe:

> To make the society happy and people easy under the meanest Circumstances, it is requisite that great numbers of them should be ignorant as well as Poor. Knowledge both enlarges and multiplies our Desires, and the fewer things a Man wishes for, the more easily his Necessities may be supply'd. . . . Reading, Writing and Arithmetic are very necessary to those, whose Business require such Qualifications, but where Peoples Livelihood has no dependance on these Arts, they are very pernicious to the Poor, who are forced to get their Daily bread by their Daily Labour. (Mandeville, 1970, 294)

Writing in *Free Inquiry into the Nature and Origin of Evil* published in 1787, Soame Jenyns (quoted in Altick, 1957, 31–2) described ignorance as:

> the appointed lot of all born to poverty and the drudgeries of life . . . the only opiate capable of infusing that sensibility, which can enable them to endure the miseries of the one and the fatigues of the other . . . a cordial, administered by the gracious hand of providence, of which they ought never to be deprived by an ill-judged and improper education.

The events of 1789 in France confirmed many of the opposition's worst fears: in a Common's debate of 1807, Mr Davies Giddy MP made the following contribution:

> Giving education to the labouring classes of the poor . . . would be prejudicial to their morals and happiness; it would teach them to despise their lot in life, instead of making them good servants in agriculture and other laborious employments. Instead of teaching them subordination it would render them fractious and refractory. (quoted in Silver, 1965, 23)

On the other hand, advocates of popular education were motivated primarily by two allied convictions. The first was that individual Bible study could inculcate a desirable and necessary sense of morality and piety amongst those most susceptible to vice. The second was that the experience of basic schooling itself helped to instil self-control and prepared the way for the 'habit of industry'. It was 'industry, frugality, order and regularity' that were perceived as the objectives of Manchester charity schools (quoted in E.P. Thompson, 1967, 59). Basic literacy was for many teachers merely the opportunity to establish these norms, and expectations about levels of attainment were low. A great many schools set up at the end of the eighteenth century and the beginning of the nineteenth, for instance, by the National Society for the Education of the Poor, by the Wesleyan Methodists and by Hannah More (the force behind Cheap Repository Tracts) failed to provide any instruction in writing. Contemporary attitudes to teaching the children of the poor were concisely summarised by one James Hanway (quoted in Stone, 1969, 89) who remarked that, 'Reading will help to mend people's morals, but writing is not necessary'.

Although the period from 1700–60 has escaped the detailed, quantitative attention that historians of literacy have given to the subsequent eighty years (conventionally taken, in this field, to be the span of the Industrial Revolution), there is little dissent from Cipolla's judgement (1969, 62) that Britain was one of the world's most literate societies at the onset of the eighteenth century. It seems reasonably certain that at this time a majority of adult males possessed a rudimentary literacy (as measured by their capacity to sign documents), and that Britain had achieved the threshold of 30–40 per cent adult literacy, considered by Bowman and Anderson (1963) to be the requirement for 'take-off' into self-sustaining economic growth, well before the introduction of steam power or factory production.

The pre-industrial eighteenth century saw a variety of changes at first sight conducive to an improvement in levels of literacy. The number of institutions providing an introduction, however superficial, to basic literacy definitely increased over the course of the century; the Society for Promoting Christian Knowledge set up over a thousand of the charity schools of which Mandeville had so strongly disapproved, and a roughly similar number of endowed elementary schools were established (Altick, 1957, 34). New and modified genres of popular literature including, most notably, local newspapers, weekly reviews, chapbooks, ballads and religious tracts, commanded the increasing sales that financed further ventures in publishing and printing. In minor but telling respects, the urban environment began to expose every passer-by to print. Neuburg writes that:

> There was a considerable increase in the extent to which the printed word became part of the background of men and women who had not previously been exposed to it. The use of flysheets and tradesmen's handbills became more prevalent, as did the use of printed wrapping paper; and in 1762 the shopkeepers' signs which had for so long been a feature of London's streets were abolished, and their place taken by printed notices and announcements above the windows or doors of shops. (1977, 105)

Despite these developments apparently favourable to literacy, the quantitative data available for 1750–1800 reveal a plateau in the levels of male literacy for England as a whole, balanced by a steady, slight reduction in female illiteracy (see Appendix 2). Specific regions such as Lancashire experienced an absolute decline in literacy rates to a low of 43 per cent of men and 18 per cent of women able to sign at marriage in the 1810s (Laqueur, 1974, 99). The fact that the stabilisation of rates coincides with the initial phases of industrialisation proper, plus the evidence of decline originating from a locality massively transformed by the establishment of mills and factories, has greatly exercised historians (see particularly Altick, 1957; Bowman and Anderson, 1963; West, 1965, 1978; Stone, 1969; Sanderson, 1972, 1974; Schofield, 1973; Laqueur, 1974; D. Levine, 1980). Unfortunately, the vigour and extent of these discussions have not been translated into a clear picture of the part played by literacy in this crucial social transition. Several of the most central questions, such as the possible existence of a threshold level of aggregate literacy for national economic development, the relative strength of occupational, spiritual, political and recreational motivations to acquire literacy, the role of literacy in migration to towns and entry into urban labour markets, the precise literacy requirements of the new manufacturing technologies and modes of labour organisation, the impact on consumption patterns, the contribution of formal schooling as against informal adult learning, all remain unsettled.

This lack of resolution is, in part, due to genuine difficulties in interpreting literacy rates, complicated as they are by concomitant large-scale population increases and migration. In part, too, there has been an over-exclusive reliance on the crude rates derived from parish marriage registers, and a failure to compensate for the limitations of this form of evidence by the integration of complementary qualitative material. Finally, the intellectual context of the recent historical interest in literacy has not always encouraged analysis of the germane issues. Some scholars have collated literacy rates not for their intrinsic interest but because they are useful proxies for measuring the scale and effectiveness of schooling. Others have come to literacy data with pre-existing interpretations of industrialisation to confirm or demolish, so that literacy gets pushed from centre stage as soon as the desired effect has been demonstrated.

As a consequence of these problems, the goal of some historians to establish determinate relationships between increases in literacy and economic productivity, narrowly defined, or with even more complex indicators of structural change such as rates of social mobility, must be judged, in important respects, unfulfilled. The evidence from both nineteenty-century and contemporary Third World examples confirms that the initial launch of large-scale production of manufactured commodities is compatible with the employment of predominantly unskilled and sub-literate employees. Sanderson's view (1972, 89) is that some representative occupations created by the new technologies (such as powerloom weaving) demanded less skill and were characterised by lower literacy rates than the traditional textile trades. A broadly similar consideration is that the level of literacy represented by a capacity to produce a signature was not necessarily either a functionally or an economically significant skill. Contemporary research has claimed that in manufacturing it requires the equivalent of six years of elementary school instruction to produce a literate employee more productive than an illiterate counterpart,[8] but even by the late 1840s, only two years of school attendance was typical (Laqueur, 1976a, 269).

In general, the new manufacturing processes did not require literate operatives, but increased literacy unquestionably played a part in supplying personnel equipped to carry out supervisory, clerical and managerial roles. Laqueur quotes authoritative estimates (1974, 102) that between 1750 and 1850, the increase in service sector employment (25 per cent to 40 per cent of the total) outstripped the increase in manufacturing (30 per cent to 40 per cent). Obviously, not all service sector occupations necessitated literacy, but growth in this area is especially significant because it took place in an era prior to standardised educational qualifications. This strengthens the likelihood that reading and writing were productive skills with a value clearly recognisable to both buyers and sellers in service labour markets. Sanderson produces some evidence (1972, 92–3) that early manufacturing concerns were run with very small administrations, but it is in any case to be expected that the main growth in anciliary roles based on document-handling would be attendant on a subsequent stage of bureaucratisation in private and public enterprise. In the case of commercial clerks, for example, the 1851 Census counted a total of 43,741 as against 727,478 employees in manufacturing trades, and an 1871 survey found an average of only four clerks in Liverpool commercial offices (both quoted in Lockwood, 1966, 19): large offices developed after 1880 with the emergence of 'rational' techniques of costing and sales analysis designed to cope with the increased scale and complexity of transactions.

The failure to demonstrate convincingly the existence of economic growth directly generated by literacy throws into serious doubt all the frameworks that assign to it a major economic role in modernisation. In the refashioning that has taken place, what were originally secondary assumptions about the social side-effects of an increasing density of literacy have been brought to the centre of the stage. Literacy's contribution to modernisation is increasingly seen as socio-political rather than economic; in essence, literacy and schooling are portrayed as the combined agency through which a nascent proletariat was endowed with the values, disciplines and rationalities that legitimated the new work and domestic patterns of industrial capitalism. Such an interpretation usefully directs attention to the settings in which tuition took place and the materials on which it was based, both neglected in the narrow economic reading. It does, however, take both of these factors somewhat for granted, overlooking the heterogeneous kinds of provision that existed for basic education, and assuming within this provision a very high degree of ideological conformity.

Already articulated in part by Laqueur (1976a, 268–70; 1976b; 1976c), it is possible to sketch the outlines of an alternative approach more sensitive to the plentiful evidence of the cultural and political diversity of the educational institutions available to the working class. This thesis suggests that the character of the paths and the agencies leading to literacy, and the particular values and responses which they elicited from poor parents and children, were major elements in the long-term development and differentiation of working-class culture. The situation was not, however, simply one in which a schooled and literate 'aristocracy' of labour gradually placed a social distance between itself and an illiterate and disreputable 'rough' working class. A key period is 1785 to 1840 during which the effects of demographic and economic changes were felt, and in the middle decades overlaid, by the disruption of the Napoleonic Wars, but before the full impact on educational provision of institutionally-funded schooling. In this period, the working class separated into elements that assimilated 'respectable' cultural forms in school, work and worship, and those that embraced 'subterranean' traditions of autonomy, community solidarity and political dissent. At one, more institutionalised, pole lay the schools founded by the British and Foreign, the National, and the various infant societies, the Sunday schools and the factory schools. To greater or lesser degrees, these offered literacy embedded in syllabuses and regimes intended to inculcate piety, discipline and obedience, as these virtues were perceived by the predominantly middle-class sponsors and organisers. At the more informal pole lay the private venture schools, the corresponding societies, the ale and coffee house reading rooms, self-help and casual instruction from parents and friends, while in an ambiguous intermediate zone lay institutions like mechanics' institutes. Admittedly miscellaneous, the salient characteristics of the collection around the informal pole are the greater continuity they provided with the oral traditions and culture of the labouring stratum, and their fuller incorporation within, and control by, working-class communities. Unlike the formal agencies, these introduced literacy to the working classes on something approaching their own terms.

The detailed evidence to support this position cannot be assembled here, but the literature already contains useful pointers. Laqueur argues persuasively (1976b, 199) that the continuing success of relatively expensive, fee-charging schools in the face of competition from free or nearly free church schools stemmed precisely from the form and content of the education offered by the latter which was alien to working-class parents:

> schools provided by religious bodies – particularly those provided by the overwhelmingly dominant Anglican National School Society – were suspect as foreign, as strange to the community. The discipline they sought to impose was either noxious in itself, made compliance expensive, or was thought to be irrelevant to elementary education. Teachers were self-consciously above and outside the community they purportedly served and were often viewed, like charity workers, as agents of oppressive authority.

Many small, fee-charging schools (such as dame schools) were run by untrained teachers indifferent to pupils' irregular attendance and unkempt appearance. If they did not attempt to impose an elaborate disciplinary or moral regime, this was probably preferred by those parents anxious to purchase basic skills for their children rather than socialisation into the values of their social superiors. It is likely, for the same reasons, that informal teaching and self-help flourished, particularly in conditions of high geographical mobility and general social dislocation, when they could supplement an irregular or partial school attendance or even substitute for schooling entirely.

The widespread use of informal, decentralised, 'grass-roots' avenues to literacy that preceded the domination of mid- and late nineteenth-century education by the prototypes of the modern school had two principal consequences for popular culture. Firstly, the introduction of literacy via familiar channels and acceptable opinion leaders minimised resistance to the medium of print and permitted the steady conversion of rural areas from their near-total dependence on oral communications. The isolated, traditionalistic, oral sub-cultures depicted in Thomas Hardy's novels were already exceptional by the 1840s and were finally destroyed by the coming of the railways with their rapid distribution of newspapers and mail.

Secondly, becoming literate outside the classroom was, for a substantial minority, itself an act of political emancipation, an aspect of 'the march of the intellect', as a frequently used contemporary metaphor described the education of the working classes. Part of the success of radical publications like *The Rights of Man* or Cobbett's *Weekly Political Register* lay in the extent to which they created a political consciousness amongst novitiate readers. In a broader sense, however, their publication marks the culmination of a 150-year development in which the written channel ceased to be harnessed exclusively to the exercise of political authority and social control, and gradually came to be the principal means of political dialogue between geographically and socially segregated interests. The presses proved as suitable to the expression of social protest as they had long been to its suppression, and the anonymity and broadcastable character of many forms of publication opened up a new field of tactical threat and counter-threat. Even as early as 1747, the municipal authorities in Nottingham considered it worthwhile to print handbills rather than issue a proclamation forbidding disturbances at the elections (Laqueur, 1976a, 267). The 'infidel societies' were eventually able to retaliate, as the following example from London in 1800 illustrates:

> FELLOW COUNTRYMEN
>
> How long will ye quietly and cowardly suffer yourself to be imposed upon, and half-starved by a set of mercenary slaves and Government hierlings? Can you still suffer them to proceed in their extensive monopolies, while your children are crying for bread? No! let them exist not a day longer. We are the sovereignty, rise then from your lethargy. Be at the Corn Market on Monday. (quoted in E.P. Thompson, 1968, 516)

The style and spelling in these radical squibs reveals the frequently modest literacy of their authors, although literary limitations might not blunt the meaning of certain communications, as in this effectively menacing paper found in Chesterfield market:

> I Ham going to inform you that there is six thousand men coming to you in Apral and then we will go and Blow Parlement house up and Blow up all afour hus labring Peple cant stand it no longer/

> dam all such roges in England governes but never mind Ned lud when general nody and his harmey comes we will bring about the Revolution then all these greate mens heads gose of. (quoted in E.P. Thompson, 1968, 784)

The quotations from Thompson are a reminder that the close links between the spread of literacy and the organisation of proletarian protest is one of the subsidiary themes dealt with in *The Making of the English Working Class*. The political sophistication of the various radical movements and groups is clearly reflected in the degree to which they were able to exploit written media effectively. The continuum runs from conducting clandestine correspondence, through raids to hang flysheets and daub graffiti, to the sustained publication of radical journalism and the production of theoretical works.

During the 1820s and 1830s, commercial developments in publishing increased the range of popular genres intended largely for a working-class readership. At the beginning of the century, the cost of copyrighted books was extremely high: a three-volume novel averaged 16s. in 1815, while a leading author like Sir Walter Scott commanded 25s. for *The Lay of the Last Minstrel* (1805), 21s. for *Waverley* (1814), and 31s. 6d. for *Kenilworth* (1821), prices comparable with the skilled manual worker's weekly wage. High prices reflected production costs; imports of paper were disrupted by the hostilities with France on top of which it carried a 3d. per pound tax, while compositors were members of a skilled manual elite with wages of 36–48s. per week around 1815 (Altick, 1957, 262–3).

Circulating libraries helped to widen the audience for serious writing but elicited a safety-first pricing policy from publishers by guaranteeing in advance substantial sales of selected titles and editions. The breakthrough to cheaper literature came via reprints of the classics and series publications of works pirated or out of copyright, together with weekly or fortnightly part-works which sold for under 6d. Pocket novels, miniature classics and literary digests were pioneered by small publishers, eventually forcing the market leaders to respond. Even so, cheaper books mainly benefited the middle classes and they remained, in Altick's phrase, 'minor luxuries' in manual household budgets.

Despite a stamp duty of 4d. per copy and a massive tax on advertisements that stood, in 1830, at 3s. 6d. an item, the economics of publishing favoured large circulations for newspapers and periodicals rather than books. Many publishers, including some of the most politically committed, chose to circumvent the stamp duty and, by employing semi-secret networks of distribution, attained sizeable readerships for unstamped publications in the period 1830–6, despite an official policy of harassment and prosecutions (Wiener, 1969; Hollis, 1970). The decision taken in 1836 to reduce the newspaper stamp duty to 1d. reflected the protests of the legitimate publishers, but it was also symptomatic of a more general response by liberals, conservatives, educationalists and the established church to new, working-class modes of communication and organisation. This response adopted a regulatory strategy and embodied the belief that the insidious cultural tendencies already apparent had to be countered by encouraging institutions that disseminated civilising values rather than by direct opposition. These institutions – schools, libraries, museums – could now employ print as the basis of 'profitable' and 'rational' uses of leisure, a project on which it was possible for the respectable working class and the middle class to co-operate. The rhetoric of the philanthropists and sponsors of civic provision always emphasised the hoped-for moral benefits, that family visits and private study would displace the ale house and the brothel, but the political 'spin-offs' were by no means forgotten. Edward Edwards, in an open letter to the Earl of Ellesmore, Chairman of the Royal Commission on the British Museum, wrote that:

> To place good literature in everybody's reach is certainly the best way to counteract the empty frivolity, the crude scepticism, and the low morality of a portion . . . of the current popular literature of the day. And what can be more likely to defeat turbulent appeals to passion than calm appeals to reason? What can better be adapted to make man attached to what is good in existing institutions and contented to seek by peaceful means the improvement of what by chance may be defective? (quoted in Corrigan and Gillespie, 1978, 13)

The struggle for, and gradual emergence in the course of the nineteenth century of, a state-funded system of national education in Britain is ground too adequately covered in orthodox histories of schooling to warrant repetition here. Despite this coverage, an historian experienced in the Victorian period has recently noted the neglect of the relationship between schooling and literacy:

> Although useful statistical work has been done in this area, there is little systematic analysis (at least for the period after the 1830s) of literacy and reading matter, literacy and participation in social and political movements (e.g. the co-operative movement), literacy and the commercial press from the mid-1840s. (Silver, 1983, 22)

An important by-product of protective legislation for children, beginning with the Factory Acts and poor law reform, was the evolution of inspectorates and commissioners to ensure standards and efficiency (Midwinter, 1970, 33). Attention was necessarily focussed on the content of teaching and the idea of a minimum threshold of effective literacy begins to be articulated in detail. Robert Lowe's Revised Code, for example, first introduced in 1862 in response to the Newcastle Report's findings, is notorious for its crude payment-by-results provisions which had a deadening impact on elementary education (Simon, 1960, 356), but its codification of standards remains interesting. The highest (VI) of the 1882 standards were as follows:

> Reading
>
> A short ordinary paragraph in a newspaper, or other modern narrative.
>
> Writing
>
> Another short ordinary paragraph in a newspaper, or other modern narrative, slowly dictated once by a few words at a time.
>
> Arithmetic
>
> A sum in practice or bills of parcels.
>
> (Midwinter, 1970, 84)

This formulation is not too different to the early UNESCO standards of functional literacy described in Chapter 2. The newspaper narrative has come finally to replace the traditional Biblical narrative as a representative reading task, and the arithmetic tests mostly have a vocational flavour, though dictation as a measure of writing fluency has a continuity with the concerns of manuscript culture.

By the time the Elementary Education Act was passed in 1870, the literacy rate, as measured by signatures in the marriage registers, had already reached 80 per cent for men and 73 per cent for women (see Appendix 2). There can be little doubt that this and subsequent legislation which, in principle, secured compulsory, free, elementary education for all, pushed literacy, as measured by this minimal criterion, to its official, 'ceiling' levels of around 97 per cent for both men and women by the end of the century. Here, the point worthy of re-emphasis, however, is that an approximation to 'full' literacy was achieved in Britain before the creation of a full state school system, despite the fact that the latter is so often taken to be the only infrastructure capable of creating and sustaining mass literacy. Even if we look to the cultural dimension of literacy, we see a parallel process of anticipation. The extended ideological and political battles over the principle of an education for the working classes helped to form a full array of popular genres of literature and radical (or at least, independent) journalism a whole generation before elementary schooling received its final official approval in the form of state compulsion. Pre-modern types of schooling were generally much more concerned with controlling and directing the application of literacy than with measuring or maximising individual attainments. Thus, the Victorian era sees the origin of an administrative and political preoccupation with the statistics of minimum educational standards out of which the contemporary notion of functionality grew.

4
Tutors and students

Introduction

This chapter and the one that follows examine specific and more or less contemporary cases of illiteracy. They draw extensively on the findings of a research project conducted in Nottingham between 1978 and 1980. With the assistance of the Local Education Authority and the organisers of the Nottingham Adult Literacy Scheme (NALS), the author carried out interviews with a sample of adults who were receiving help from the scheme for severe and usually longstanding problems with reading and writing. In the interviews, which were tape-recorded, the students talked about their family backgrounds and their schooling, their work experiences, the problems they had faced as a result of illiteracy and their feelings about, and progress within, tuition. On separate occasions their volunteer tutors were also interviewed.

The research was prompted by the rapid growth of adult literacy activity in Britain during the 1970s, a development that raised several general questions that appeared to lend themselves to sociological analysis. To those not professionally involved in the basic education of adults, and possibly to many who were, the most puzzling feature was how it could be that such a large minority could remain illiterate despite having received a decade of schooling in one of the world's most sophisticated and well-established educational systems. And how, in a culture so heavily dependent on the use of writing, could the existence of this minority have passed unnoticed for so long?

The sudden appearance of tens of thousands of people anxious to act as volunteer tutors was itself remarkable. Many of them had never previously done any kind of teaching, welfare or voluntary work, so it appeared that adult illiteracy had acquired a special status as a social problem warranting immediate and personal involvement. But exactly what the appeal of literacy tuition was for such a broad cross-section of the public was not clear. It involved a practically random pairing of complete strangers, frequently from very different social backgrounds, brought together to conduct an intimate and technically difficult transfer of skills often on the basis of little more than shared optimism. The appropriate terms in which to describe the character of this transaction were not obvious, even for those engaged in it, and in the search for comparisons it was hard to tell the apt from the exaggerated. Was it the case that no comparable national welfare initiative had been seen since the war-time evacuation and relocation of city children? Was this temporary and admittedly localised liaison between haves and have-nots a symptom of a more fundamental armistice between the class trenches? Were students attracted to schemes simply by the prospect of free, personal instruction in a practical and potentially marketable skill? Was the prospect of being taught by volunteers in a relatively informal setting an incentive or a deterrent? Were tutors idealists seeking to establish a purely altruistic relationship in their lives? Were those tutors who were professional school teachers frustrated in the classroom and trying to prove to themselves in one-to-one situations that they possessed worthwhile skills?

As a small-scale study, the Nottingham project could hope to contribute in only a modest manner to the understanding of such broad issues. It set out simply to explore the expectations students and tutors brought to tuition, hopefully in ways that might be useful to scheme organisers concerned to reduce the 'drop-out' rate from both sides. It also embodied a reaction against the highly technical character of much academic research on literacy and illiteracy: at the time of the project's inception, very little attention had been paid to what illiteracy meant to people themselves. Experts, operating with Olympian detachment on the basis of cherished preconceptions, handed down methods and materials that were often entirely inappropriate to the interests and needs of their users, whose views were not canvassed. Before the details of the Nottingham scheme are described, it is worth examining the extent to which illiteracy has been misconceived and distorted in the specialist literature.

Illiteracy myths

To sociologists and social psychologists, 'stigma' is disrepute that has been organised and institutionalised within a culture to focus on all the members of a specific social category. In unfavourable circumstances any category or condition may attract suspicion and contempt, but the most familiar examples include physical disabilities, mental handicaps, homosexuality and ethnic minorities. Stigma is expressed and operates largely through the diffusion of stereotypical beliefs, as a result of which people without any direct contact or grounds for animosity can come to possess negative views about a group. Once stereotypes have been institutionalised (for example, in common sayings, cartoons and jokes) they have a life and effects independent of their original authors. By magnifying and distorting perceptions of the social distance that exists between social groups, they can become self-fulfilling prophecies that reduce the extent and intimacy of actual contact.

The small body of social research that has attempted to study adult illiteracy has not, on the whole, been very successful in correcting these kinds of beliefs or helpful to the people they victimise. At best, it has constructed well-meaning but ultimately fanciful pictures of the dependency and vulnerability of those who are illiterate, and at worst, it has directly compounded the misleading stereotypes. Exaggerating, from sympathy, the magnitude of the handicap faced by adult illiterates does them no favour. Perpetuating the idea, for example, that illiteracy is equivalent to total intellectual disablement diminishes the status of non-readers in the eyes of the majority, creates crises of self-confidence for illiterates, and generally increases their dependency and sense of inadequacy.

The academic research role requires individuals to be both highly literate and self-conscious about their language use, and this may explain why some investigators have been unable to maintain a sense of proportion when literacy becomes the object of their inquiry. Consider, for instance, the profound and disabling sense of the author's superiority that pervades the following extract from an article on the education of illiterate adults, published in 1945 by the well-known British psychologist, Sir Cyril Burt:

> the large majority [of the sample] . . . might be described as healthy extraverts – youths with well-marked concrete and practical interests, averse from anything of a sedentary, bookish or literary nature. . . . During the adolescent stage . . . [this attitude] . . . appears to develop into a protective mechanism, half unconsciously built up, not merely by the individual, but by the group to which he belongs. Those engaged in social activities

> among the so-called working-classes will be familiar with this characteristic. (1945, 22–3)

A similar tone of fieldwork among primitives characterises other contributions as if, in a collective effort to arouse sympathy, researchers had invented an imaginary tribe, hopelessly deprived and impossibly different from the literate. Members of this tribe are not credited with the capacity for either self-sufficiency or rational judgement: 'A larger proportion of illiterates than literates are among the followers of charismatic religious leaders' (Freeman and Kassebaum, 1956, 374). The article does not find it necessary to offer any empirical evidence in support of this claim, yet it is reiterated by other authors who see in this alleged loss of rationality an insidious political threat:

> It is felt by the [sic] sociologists that the illiterate is an easy victim of the propaganda which issues from radio, television, the movies, or mass meetings. They are easily influenced by *foreign* philosophies and are often prey to swindlers and false leaders. We can guage the possibility of riots in our cities by the percentage of illiterate and semi-literate males, black and white, clustered in our cities. (Sheldon, 1970, 294, emphasis added)

Having generalised a very specific incapacity, the mythologiser's next step is to make it the basis of a complete but separate cultural system:

> It is hardly accurate to consider the illiterate as just another segment of society, but rather an extreme necessity to protect what is left of self-respect and ego weld these people together into a distinctly separate society with its own system of values, its own hierarchy, and its own power structure . . . (Bowren and Zintz, 1977, 31)

Again, no clear evidence for the existence of a sub-culture of illiteracy is presented. Occasionally, the descriptions become wholly fanciful, reminiscent of a Victorian traveller's account, brought back from the heart of darkness, of an exotic culture:

> they accentuate the material aspects of the culture available to them. Ornamentation, flash, and extremity of dress are easily

> perceived phenomena and conspicuous consumption stands out more unabashedly than in most of the more sophisticated larger society. (Freeman and Kassebaum, 1956, 375)

While it would be wrong to suggest that these selected quotations are typical of the way illiterates have been portrayed by researchers, they indicate that the snobberies associated with reading and writing are subtle and deeply pervade the thinking of trained and ostensibly scrupulous 'experts'. It is necessary to bear in mind, too, that recent thinking in the academic arena of social problems has favoured what is mistakenly assumed to be an anthropological perspective. Ideas like 'the culture of poverty' and 'the cycle of transmitted deprivation' arm investigators right from the start with enhanced expectations of the 'differentness' of the poor and deprived which direct them into intellectual culs-de-sac looking for non-existent social types and processes.

The Nottingham Adult Literacy Scheme (NALS)

Set against the total range of Local Authority and other provision in the county, adult literacy in Nottinghamshire was a small-scale, diffuse and marginal educational activity. The reasons for this were national rather than local. Adult literacy has never been part of the mainstream of statutory provision, and therefore had only a low claim on education budgets. Added to this, the majority of people engaged in literacy tuition were either non-contractual volunteers, or part-time, short contract employees without job tenure. Whenever the wind of financial stringency blows, small but immediate savings can be made by scaling down literacy and similar educational operations. There are other, organisational reasons why adult basic education as a whole tends to be vulnerable. It uncomfortably straddles the well-defined ministerial spheres of education and employment. Tuition must necessarily be tailored delicately to student demand, requiring unusual arrangements that do not easily lend themselves to bureaucratic standardisation, and this, in turn, creates difficulties in integrating teachers and students within orthodox institutions. In directly vocational training, there is often a clientele with financial muscle or political influence to negotiate over provision with administrators or politicians: in the case of adult literacy, the clients are self-evidently handicapped in communicating their training needs, and, in any case, form a scattered and unorganised population. The productivity of literacy schemes and their relative success are much more difficult for educational administrators to assess and defend than is schooling with its regular timetables and diet of examinations. Finally, because it entails an amalgam of education, community and social work activities, potentially involving liaison across a range of agencies and self-help groups who work with the deprived and the unemployed, adult literacy has, and has been seen to have, unsettling political implications at a variety of institutional levels. The cumulative effect of all these factors has been permanently to depress the claims of literacy work on attention and resources, and to render it especially liable to sudden reversals of administrative policy.

Following decades of neglect, the Government decision in 1975 to set up an Adult Literacy Resource Agency (ALRA) through which to channel what proved to be a total of £3 million over the period 1975–8, represented by far the most significant of post-war policy initiatives in this sphere of education. (For further details, see Chapter 6.) Immediately before this ALRA funding took effect, only about 300 adults (excluding institutional inmates) were receiving literacy tuition annually in Nottinghamshire. In the city itself, tuition was available (a) in classes held under Nottinghamshire Education Authority auspices and taught by paid staff affiliated to Further Education Colleges; (b) in one-to-one tuition within the Nottingham Council for Voluntary Service (NCVS) home tuition scheme using volunteer tutors. ALRA funding made possible a quantum leap in the scale of provision in the area (Table 4.1). A Literacy Co-ordinator was appointed, reporting directly to a Deputy Director of Education at County Hall, with responsibility for supervising an NCVS scheme enlarged to deal with referrals from the BBC, and also for developing LEA provision throughout the County in conjunction with twelve local co-ordinators attached to Adult Education Centres. A secretary and three full-time staff were also appointed and premises in a disused school provided as a literacy centre. The County Co-ordinator who was appointed had experience in organising a literacy scheme using volunteers in the East End of London. Two of the full-time appointments had been volunteers in the NCVS scheme as well as having had primary school teaching experience. Although the salaries of the full-time staff came from different sources and they officially had distinct

Table 4.1: *Size and funding of the Adult Literacy Scheme in Nottingham and Nottinghamshire, 1975–8*

	1975–6	*1976–7*[1]	*1977–8*[2]
NOTTINGHAMSHIRE LEA:			
Grant Allocation (£'s)	10,235	11,135	12,175
Volunteers[3]	892	577	586
Students[4]	1,015	1,056	1,168
NCVS:			
Grant Allocation (£'s)	338[5]	5,042	5,571
Volunteers[6]	300	186	137
Students[4]	304	175	146

Notes: 1 Students under tuition and active volunteers in the week ending 26 February 1977.
2 Students under tuition and active volunteers in the week ending 25 February 1978.
3 Includes volunteers awaiting matching.
4 Excludes students on waiting lists.
5 Substantially aided by LEA.
6 Excludes volunteers awaiting matching.

Sources: DES, 1976, 47 and 51; DES, 1978b, 50 and 53.

responsibilities, in practice all worked jointly on both NCVS and LEA activities. By the end of 1977, there were approximately 1,600 literacy students under tuition and 875 trained volunteers in the County as a whole.

In March 1978, shortly before the research commenced, ALRA funding ceased. The home tuition scheme was preserved intact and all full-time posts were maintained with some reallocation of responsibilities. Several temporary, part-time staff were recruited to work on specific projects, usually in conjunction with teaching staff from local institutions. Over the period of the research, the activities based on the literacy centre (which in the interim had been relocated in a college annexe) proliferated. Numeracy tuition, courses for the unemployed and an English as a second language programme for Asian women all began.

In September 1979, in response to central government expenditure cuts, the Nottinghamshire Education Committee instituted a series of policy changes which forced a reorganisation of literacy work in the County and significantly reduced overall provision. For the first time, fees were introduced for literacy (and all other non-vocational adult classes) without exemptions. Classes were only permitted to take place in a severely restricted list of designated premises and a minimum attendance of fifteen students was imposed.

Although these changes were prompted by budgetary constraints, they are also recognisable as part of a process by which literacy education for adults was absorbed into the organisation of the College of Further Education to whose annexe the Literacy Centre had been transferred. The office of the Head of the Adult Education Department in the College was moved into the annexe and his permission was increasingly required for planning decisions and developments. Attendance registers made their first appearance. When, subsequently, the County Co-ordinator left, she was not replaced and the post was effectively abolished. Her predecessor, who had been on long-term secondment to ALRA as a field consultant, was eventually reinstated with the title of Lecturer in Literacy and Numeracy within the Department of Adult Education, thereby severing the long-standing direct link that had existed with County Hall. By September 1980, literacy tuition, although still making extensive use of volunteers, had been almost completely assimilated within the administration of the Further Education College.

The administrative nucleus of full-time staff organised tuition, recruited part-time staff and volunteers, carried out tutor training, selected and produced teaching matter, edited publicity materials and newsletters and liaised with other agencies. During the main period of the research (May 1978 to September 1979) there was a maximum of twenty different literacy groups operating simultaneously in Greater Nottingham. Owing to fluctuations in demand and the rapid turnover of students (and to a lesser extent teaching staff and volunteers), the number and composition of groups varied with the shifting times, venues and personnel. Three of the four main types of provision were included in the scope of the research:

(1) Twelve basic literacy groups located at eight centres (mainly libraries and large schools) with one-to-one tuition by volunteers under the supervision of a paid but part-time group leader. Normally, three of these groups took place at the Literacy Centre itself;
(2) Three classes run by part-time, paid staff dealing specifically with spelling and/or post-basic literacy. (Students and tutors in these groups were not included in the research);

(3) Up to five classes run by paid, part-time group leaders and differing from those in category (1) in that there was no strict one-to-one pairing. The tutors in these groups were mainly teachers known to, and recruited by, the group leaders. The majority of these classes pre-dated the establishment of the Literacy Centre and despite being located in its premises, they operated more or less independently of it.
(4) One-to-one home tuition with volunteer tutors.

This pattern of arrangements placed a great emphasis on the role of group leader. A conscientious leader automatically exerted a great influence on a group, for instance, by encouraging students suffering from a loss of morale and by pursuing the reasons for non-attendance, by advising tutors and implicitly setting standards of performance, by keeping in close touch with organising staff on the progress of matchings. Leaders were selected from the more experienced and highly motivated volunteers; many, but by no means all, had some previous teaching experience. Group leaders were not normally paired with specific students but covered for absent tutors and set up the group activities and language games which took up the second half of the weekly sessions in many groups.

Recruitment and matching procedures

The substantial increase in the size of the Nottingham scheme during 1976 consisted largely of referrals from the BBC publicity drive (Hargreaves, 1980, 29–35: see Chapter 6). Following this initial, uncontrolled influx of student names and addresses, which kept the limited resources of the scheme at full stretch, local recruiting publicity tended to be of two kinds. Firstly, general advertising of the Literacy Centre address, telephone number and activities via posters, leaflets, adult education brochures, local radio programmes and phone-ins, open days and city centre displays; secondly, more selective attempts directed primarily at recruiting volunteer tutors, employing press advertisements, posters and literacy logo displays in libraries and other public places.

The volume of student demand for tuition was the key variable influencing all major organisational arrangements. Once the existence of the Centre became widely known, there was a steady, 'background' stream of inquiries with occasional peaks following a successful piece of publicity. Within broad limits, the pace of recruitment and training of volunteer tutors could be adjusted to the number of students currently on waiting lists.

After the BBC referrals ceased, the ratio of referrals to personal inquiries fell. In the period 1977–8, the ratio was approximately one referral to every three inquiries, but subsequently referrals gradually increased as contact with other agencies developed. The Probation Service, Jobcentres, Social Service Departments and penal institutions provided the majority of referrals in the post-1979 period.

It was standard procedure with telephone inquiries and referrals to try to persuade the prospective student (through his or her sponsor if necessary) to visit the Centre for an initial interview. If and when this interview took place, a member of the literacy staff completed a form recording the personal details of the student and his or her preferences for type, venue and timing of tuition. In addition to asking students directly about the nature of their literacy problems, the interviewer usually attempted a preliminary assessment of their current attainments in reading and writing by means of several extremely simple exercises at the end of the form.

Speed of subsequent assignment to a group or home tutor depended mainly on the student's availability and mobility so that geographical factors tended to weigh more heavily than current literacy level. With the exception of a few people in category (2) above, neither students nor tutors were 'streamed' by ability. Students were free to insist on home tuition if they had a strong preference for it, though lengthy delays before the matching began were possible in some localities owing to the uneven distribution of volunteer tutors. The policy of the Nottingham scheme came increasingly to favour an eventual graduation from home tuition to groups for all students but those most deeply concerned with privacy and confidentiality.

During their initial interviews, both students and tutors were asked for any preferences they might have about partners for tuition. Some students had a marked preference for a same sex tutor or a tutor in a particular age-band (usually older). Within the limits imposed by availability, these preferences were respected. Where a variety of matching possibilities existed, staff employed common-sense criteria of appropriateness on the limited information on the interview forms. Both students and tutors were told that they had an option to change their partners if they so wished, though this option was rarely exercised.

Tutor training

The training of tutors took place several times a year whenever the number of volunteers justified the arrangement of a course. An ideal complement was considered to be twelve to sixteen people. Courses lasted for twelve hours spread out over six consecutive weekday evenings. Introductory training of this kind, known as 'level one' training, was carried out by all the full-time staff in turn.

Each course consisted of a general introduction to literacy work with adults, including such topics as functional literacy, student anxiety, counselling, 'theoretical' treatments of reading and spelling, reviews of direct teaching methods, aids and materials. Case studies and sample materials were discussed in the group and exercises were completed as homework. A large amount of reference literature was issued to each prospective tutor, but heavy stress was laid on the availability of staff for advice and guidance if the first matching raised special difficulties.

Trainees were provided with a copy of *Teaching Adults to Read* (MacFarlane, 1976a) which was published under ALRA auspices. This fifty-page booklet covered in outline some of the topics likely to preoccupy a tutor starting for the first time with a student. Among others, sections were devoted to learning activities (word-matching, building dictionaries, comprehension questions), phonics, selecting and simplifying texts, lesson planning and informal ability assessment. While it was pitched at an appropriate level for novice tutors, the lack of space available for detailed coverage and examples made it a useful introductory guide rather than a constantly-referred-to bible.

'Level one' tutor training in Nottingham was relatively close to the orthodoxy disseminated by ALRA through training literature like MacFarlane's booklet and resource packs, newsletters and advisors. It was based on three main principles:

(1) Adult orientation
   (a) Tutors were encouraged to relate their teaching strategy to student needs negotiated and jointly defined between tutor and student.

(b) A very marked preference existed amongst paid staff for materials and activities designed specifically for adults.
(c) Repeated invocations to use students' knowledge and interests as inputs to literacy activities.

(2) Egalitarianism
(a) A stress on the limits of the tutor's own literacy.
(b) Suggestions that tutors could and should learn from students.
(c) Encouragement given to the idea of self-help groups of students.

(3) Functional literacy
(a) Task-related teaching was given greater emphasis than reading schemes or phonic principles (although the latter two were not ignored).
(b) Teaching materials were based on messages rather than complete texts.
(c) The selection of skills taught was determined primarily by the students' current abilities and needs rather than a fixed 'syllabus'.

The training course attended by the author was extremely eclectic in its coverage of teaching methods and systems. The trainer was careful to point out that the range of student abilities and needs was so great, and responses to particular techniques so varied, that each tutor would be obliged to experiment with his or her student. The volunteers attending this particular course fell naturally into two categories, people with some previous experience of teaching (though not necessarily teaching reading and writing) and those with no teaching experience. Members of the first group tended to be more active in discussion, to put forward personal evaluations of this or that technique, and to make use of a more technical vocabulary in talking about likely problems. The trainer spent some time during discussions pointing out the differences in approach between teaching adults to read and school work, and also how important it was always to operate from the base line of a student's interests and existing knowledge. There was a sense in which the tutor training course attempted to embrace two opposite objectives – to prevent teachers transferring, in a wholesale way, existing attitudes and methods developed for beginning reading with children – to give non-teachers sufficient knowledge of available techniques to allow them to go into the rather daunting first contact with confidence. Informal remarks made by non-teacher members of the training course witnessed by the author suggested that the second objective was not fully achieved with at least some individuals. These people expressed anxiety about starting to tutor without a clear idea of how to diagnose underlying reading problems and doubted their mastery of the various techniques they had been told about. There was some fear, too, that the initial session would grind to a halt in a fog of mutual incomprehension and embarrassment. An absence of contact with students during the course probably magnified these self-doubts.

Provided volunteers attended the training sessions regularly, they were matched with students as soon as an appropriate candidate appeared. There was no selection of volunteers at the end of the course (although there was usually some fallout over the six weeks). Tutors who could not be promptly matched with a student frequently lost interest and drifted out of contact with the scheme; this could be exploited in the rare cases in which a volunteer survived training but was judged to be unsuitable by the organisers.

Further ('second-level') training was not compulsory. It took the form of evening talks on specialised aspects of tuition from full-time staff and outside experts together with occasional, whole-day study sessions held at weekends. Attendance at second-level training involved only a minority of the most committed tutors and although additional, informal contacts did periodically take place in response to tuition problems, many home tutors followed their own instincts and kept up only a tenuous contact with the Literacy Centre.

The Nottingham literacy catchment area

The catchment area of the Nottingham literacy scheme did not coincide conveniently with any major geographical or administrative boundaries. As far as adult literacy activities were concerned, the scheme was not demarcated by the city boundary but extended well beyond, especially to the north and north-west where several of the satellite centres providing suburban venues for group tuition were located. Home tuition was even more amorphous; while it was organised from the Literacy Centre, situated about a mile from the heart of the City, it operated around Greater Nottingham wherever demand and volunteer tutors existed.

This lack of clear boundaries frustrates any precise, quantitative description of the type of urban context in which the scheme operated. The 'County Deprived Area Study', conducted by the County's Department of Planning and Transportation in 1974, had identified severe problems of multiple deprivation in nine inner wards of the city. Six of these wards had achieved scores on the twenty-item index of deprivation more than five standard deviations above the mean for the entire County, indicating very high concentrations of low income, low levels of job-skill, unemployment, poor housing, single parent families, children in care, criminal convictions, etc., in combination. The inner residential zones of Nottingham were, however, extensively and continuously redeveloped throughout the 1970s. The scheme for the St Ann's area alone entailed the demolition of 10,000 dwellings, the erection of 3,500 council homes and the rehousing of an overspill population officially estimated to be 20,000. The scheme for the Meadows area involved the construction or refurbishment of an additional 3,000 homes. To these major programmes of urban renewal must be added a series of more piecemeal physical changes to the environment of the City, as well as some significant shifts in planning policy (the City Council sold off nearly 10 per cent of its stock of 54,000 dwellings between 1976 and 1978).

The extent to which physical renovation and large-scale relocation have mitigated the undoubtedly grave and concentrated inner-city problems of the early 1970s remains hard to assess. In a follow-up to their 1968 study of deprivation in the St Ann's area, Ken Coates and Richard Silburn (1980) traced 141 rehoused families from their original sample. The percentage of the rehoused families possessing selected consumer durables was, as Table 4.2 shows, with one exception, lower than the rates for either the East Midlands or the United Kingdom as a whole.

Table 4.2: *Households possessing selected consumer durables, 1975–6*

	Percentages		
	Rehoused St Ann's Sample (1976)	*East Midlands (1975)*	*UK (1975–6)*
Car	20.6	57.1	56.1
Washing Machine	66.1	81.4	72.1
Refrigerator	76.7	85.2	86.7
T.V.	96.4	95.4	95.2

Source: Coates and Silburn, 1980, 114.

Most of the other social indicators that are available conflate 'pure' characteristics of the population with levels of resource provision and local administrative policies. (Statistics on wage and employment levels can be found in Chapter 5.) While Table 4.3 shows that the Nottingham rate of acceptance of homeless families was, for the period of the research, well above the corresponding all-England figure, it cannot be treated as a direct measure of social need. Similar caution must be exercised with the perinatal mortality rate (combined stillbirths and deaths under one week old per 1,000 total live and stillbirths), which in 1978 was 18.8 for the City compared with a figure for England and Wales of 5.5.[1] In the same year, the City had more than twice the rate of under-eighteen-year-olds in care than either the County (8.6 per 1,000) or England and Wales (7.7 per 1,000).[2]

Table 4.3: *Homeless households accepted, 1978*

	No.	*Rate per 1,000[1] Households*
Nottingham	326	3.1
Inner London	8,570	4.2
Non-Metropolitan Districts	24,560	1.4
All England	53,000	1.7

Note: 1 Population base 1971 Census except Nottingham figure which is a mid-1978 projection.

Source: *Social Trends*, 1980, Table 9.21, Nottingham Housing Department.

Little in the way of education statistics is available on a City-only basis. Pupil-teacher ratios for both primary and secondary schools in the County were close to the all-England figures (Table 4.4), as was the percentage of free school dinners.

Table 4.4: *Pupil-teacher ratios,[1] maintained schools, January 1978*

	Primary Schools and Immigrant Centres	*All Secondary Schools*	*All Schools*
Nottinghamshire	24.1	16.8	20.1
England	23.3	16.7	19.8

Note: 1 Full-time pupils and qualified teachers only. Full-time and full-time equivalents of part-time teachers.

Source: DES, *Statistics of Education: Schools*, Vol. 1, 1978b, Table 27 [30].

During the period of the research (and subsequently), Nottinghamshire had a serious crime rate well above the England and Wales level and on a par with that of the Metropolitan Police District (Table 4.5). These figures undoubtedly reflect the severe prosecution policies that were operative, but the City area nevertheless made a substantial contribution to the crime level. In 1978, the Constabulary's Central Division dealt with 14,575 complaints regarding crime and proceeded against 4,347 adults and juveniles in respect of 6,860 cases. The value placed on the goods stolen within the area was over £1 million.[3]

Table 4.5: *Indictable offences[1] recorded by the police per 100,000 population, 1977 and 1978*

	1977	*1978*
Nottinghamshire	7,619	7,076
Metropolitan Police District[2]	7,269	7,282
England and Wales	5,014	4,878

Notes: 1 Excludes 'other criminal damage value £20 and under'.
2 Includes City of London force.

Source: Home Office, *Criminal Statistics*, 1978, Table 2.3.

Illiteracy careers

When the Nottingham research began, the idea of an 'illiteracy career' seemed to offer a naturalistic starting point from which to examine interactions between the personal and the social levels of the topics. It seemed reasonably self-evident that the character of the literacy skills demanded of an individual, and the ease with which they could be acquired, vary systematically (but independently) over the life-cycle. Childhood prior to school, schooling, entry into work, occupational training, are all, to a greater or lesser extent, phases in which literacy has a high salience not just for the individual but also for his or her parents, teachers and employers. In these early stages, the scrutiny of a child's or young person's competence is a quasi-public concern and major shortcomings are relatively likely to be detected. The pressures to accept assistance, supported as they are by institutional interests, are strong, but so, on the whole, is its availability. In the second major phase of the life-cycle, typically involving home creation and family building, literacy demands remain high owing to transactions with print-based organisations like banks, building societies and clinics, with the possible presence of school-age children imposing additional requirements. It is in this phase, however, that adult literacy problems are 'privatised' and personalised, gradually to become contained and perhaps concealed within the family or other intimate circle. It starts to be hard for outsiders to refer diplomatically to the existence of a possible difficulty, even in order to proffer help, because the whole matter tends to acquire a status similar to an embarrassing medical condition. Access to assistance is generally poor compared to the first phase. In the third, and for our purposes final, life-cycle phase, work and family situations have generally stabilised and demands for new or enhanced literacy skills are few. Unless some domestic crisis or other disruption intervenes, most mature adults will by this point have reached an accommodation with illiteracy. The 'You can't teach an old dog new tricks' attitude is common and assistance is psychologically remote, though in reality not significantly worse than in phase two.

The concept of 'career' has an additional relevance to illiteracy in the sense in which it has been employed by sociologists in the tradition of Everett Hughes (1937) and Erving Goffman (1968). In this usage, the stress is on the moral dimensions of a career, the trajectory of an individual's self-conception through a sequence of social contexts or situations in which the force of acceptance or rejection by others plays on and gradually transforms an identity. The processes are especially clear-cut when the individual is a member of a stigmatised social category. Goffman's work, in particular, has attempted to analyse the vicissitudes and identify management problems encountered by those who have to endure the negative social esteem they have in others' eyes. There is a rough social-psychological parallel between the situation of severely illiterate pupils in school and, to take one of Goffman's own examples (1968, 45–6), the plight of orphans,

> who become socialized into their disadvantageous situation even while they are learning and incorporating the standards against which they fall short. For example, an orphan learns that children naturally and normally have parents, even while he is learning what it means not to have any.

It is school, of course, that is the key setting in which the individual discovers the expectations governing literacy and illiteracy. It is because schooling is a lengthy and competitive process based largely on institutionalised evaluation that illiteracy can inflict such permanent damage on an individual's self-esteem. For the majority of young schoolchildren, reading and writing are academic exercises imposed by the teacher: literacy only slowly becomes a means to obtain goals that the child has developed spontaneously. Academically unsuccessful pupils can thus become aware of their low social standing before fluency in reading and writing can be directly useful to them, or a lack of it genuinely inconvenient.

In addition to its early onset, another pernicious aspect of the stigma of illiteracy is the fact that it is not, like severe physical deformity, for example, instantly apparent in all social situations. This might be thought to mitigate rather than to increase its impact, but the fact is that potentially rather than immediately 'discreditable' conditions, to use Goffman's terminology (1968, 14), generate a set of peculiarly demanding management problems for their possessors. In social encounters with acquaintances and strangers, the temptation to fake and 'pass' as normal is much greater than with a form of difference that is visually obvious. The risk of exposure while passing and the even more acute consequential embarrassment adds the strain of playing a fragile role to the practical problems of communication.

A further, theoretical issue, much discussed in the sociological literature on deviance, concerns the significance of the contact with 'official' agencies and the impact of their diagnosis on the individual's condition. In a variety of social 'deviations' among which mental illness is the classic example, formal labelling (as in diagnostic interviews) is the prelude to a new stage in the moral career. The existence of diagnostic categories generated by professionals tends to alter an individual's relationship with family and friends. Subtle changes in their treatment and expectations of the individual force adjustments in his or her self-concept, with the long-term result being an intensification/amplification of the original 'symptoms'.[4]

There are several obvious differences, however, between the impact of the medical clinic and that of the literacy scheme. Initial contact with a literacy scheme is frequently the product of prior changes in the prospective student's self-concept rather than its main determinant. There is no equivalent in adult literacy work to psychiatric treatment in specialist and segregated institutions.

Unlike the psychiatrist, literacy tutors do not have available to them conceptual categories which reinterpret and challenge the client's common-sense understanding of his or her problem, with the possible single exception of 'dyslexia' (which was not a diagnosis in common use within the Nottingham scheme). Finally, attendance at a literacy scheme never has the direct or indirect element of compulsion that surrounds many psychiatric consultations.

Initial contacts

The initial visit, enquiry or referral of a patient or client to a clinic or rehabilitative agency is a key event for the organisation, and conventionally, is assumed to be equally significant in the career of the individual. A common approach to understanding the complex of circumstances and influences that have resulted in the contact is to propose a 'push-pull' model. The very large number of factors that can always be implicated either on the basis of previous empirical research or common sense, can be placed in three main groupings: (1) 'objective push' factors related to the individual's circumstances and biography – age, stage in the life-cycle, occupation, etc.; (2) 'subjective push' factors – motivation, aspirations, perceived gravity of symptoms or deficit, sensitivity to the opinions of others, etc.; (3) 'agency pull' factors – the nature and extent of publicity and 'outreach' effort deployed by a particular agency or scheme. One of the attractions of such a model is that the factors identified can be easily translated into questionnaire items or interview prompts in research projects designed to establish the precise frequency with which particular combinations of factors occur in samples of presenting patients or clients. It appears possible by such a strategy to identify the 'average' client and also to quantify the effectiveness of the various channels of publicity used. The most serious defect of this approach is its exaggeration of the extent to which seeking assistance is a discrete decision with definite and identifiable precursors. There is a related tendency to focus attention on the events and episodes immediately prior to contact, and finally, a concern to catalogue the positive, facilitating factors while ignoring those that have been operating as delayers or deterrents to contact.

In fact, there was little evidence from the student sample of any typical or strategic events leading adults into tuition. On the contrary, fourteen out of eighteen interviewees had made one or more previous attempts since leaving school to obtain assistance with their reading and writing. These previous efforts were frustrated mainly by the students' inability to recognise in advance what kind of tuition they needed or what kind of person could help them:

> 'I've tried through years since I've left school to get on to something. I even went to night school for English, but of course it wasn't the English I wanted to learn so that [it] sort of died off. . . . I never used to bother because I was on night shifts. It seemed to be a bit impractical to go every fortnight.'

Subsequently, Ted was taught by his sister-in-law who was a teacher, but her diagnosis of the appropriate level at which to begin was faulty:

> 'my brother's wife gave me a few lessons . . . but that got a bit impractical. . . . She was willing enough but I don't think they were going the right way about it because they were just getting me to read and I wasn't up to that standard of reading because I didn't know all my vowels, did I, and my consonants and one thing or another, so reading was a waste of time. Starting above my head really . . .'

There is a belief, apparently even among professional teachers, that all adults really do know how to read, in a Platonic sense of 'know', and that it only needs exposure to print and practice to develop the skill to fluency:

> *Peter*: 'there was some chap advertised, he was an ex-headmaster of some school, which I forget, anyway he advertised, you know, reading lessons, and I went to see him and anyway he give me a reading test and he said that my reading ability was up to about eleven years old, and he said if you keep reading, he says, it'll come to you anyway . . .'
> *Interviewer*: 'Did you go regularly to this headmaster?'
> *Peter*: 'Well he had this advert in the paper if you didn't improve within ten lessons, he taught for £1 per lesson, and if you didn't improve within ten lessons, he guaranteed your money back. And after the third lesson he said, "Well, quite honestly", he says, "I think you are wasting my time and I think you are wasting

yours", he says, "If you just go and get a book and start reading, it'll come to you". But what I could read, I couldn't write. I mean it just didn't flow . . .'

It is predictable that a history of unsuccessful tuition will leave its mark in the form of reduced student morale and an increased scepticism about the value of the entire literacy enterprise. For some students, this is in addition to considerable pre-existing anxiety about other people knowing of their illiteracy. Bob was a case in point. His wife had tried to help him but they both felt acutely uncomfortable about their respective roles. He also visited an elderly couple he had known since childhood and together they used to read the sports page of the newspaper. The visits ceased when the husband suffered a stroke, and a period of inactivity followed until Bob heard on the local radio of a literacy exhibition in a city shopping centre:

> 'I waited about four year and just when I heard it on the radio I thought well I'll go now. But it took me about two, two and a half hours – I kept walking by and then actually the crunch. . . . I went down there and I saw [the organiser] and he says, "Morning". I said, "How do you do". He says, "Well, do you want anything?" I said, "No, I'm just looking", and I walked right by and he kept looking and looking. He says, "Can I help you at all?" I says, "All right then, youth, yes I'd like to know more about this here adult literacy scheme".'

Disclosure, even to people from whom sympathy can be reasonably anticipated, represents a reversal of what has often been many years of systematic and almost painfully elaborate concealment. However confidential the arrangements, the process of initiating formal tuition outside the formal circle of previous acquaintances can appear highly threatening from the student's perspective. The stresses involved are comparable to transformations like 'coming out' into a homosexual sub-culture after long suppression of a deviant sexual identity (Dank, 1971). While a group of tutors and students working together is not as encompassing as a sub-culture, it can provide similar emotional support and reassurance following the transition.

Although it was argued above that it is wrong to seek, as a matter of course, a critical event or decision as determining the path to tuition, a third of the students themselves identified a specific factor. An element common to all these cases was a major alteration in personal circumstances or a shift within the personal life-cycle. Sally, for example, was a young mother whose children had started to learn to read at school and, anxious to help them at home, she felt her deficiencies keenly for the first time since leaving school. Don wished to change jobs but had recently failed the Fire Service entry exam for the second time. Dick's aging mother was no longer able to help him because of failing eyesight. At fifty-two, Peter had reached the end of his physical resources as far as bricklaying was concerned and looked forward to some other form of self-employment. Two younger students needed training for the jobs they sought and were preparing to meet the entry requirements.

The catalogue of such events is not, in itself, especially illuminating. It does, however, underline the point that 'survival' with severe illiteracy is entirely feasible for many people, at least in typical circumstances. If the level of demand is increased, informal help removed, or a general disruption such as the 'Three Day Week' occurs, shortcomings are more clearly exposed and tuition comes to represent the only rational solution. Although the idea of returning to a teaching situation may not be intrinsically attractive for people with unhappy school careers behind them, it does have the advantage of initially preserving the self-conceptions they may have of merely being 'poor spellers' or 'not up to scratch' as readers.

Tuition and orientations to illiteracy

The overriding impression made by tuition was one of tremendous variability in concrete activities, teaching materials and teaching techniques. The interview transcripts contain very diverse accounts of how tuition was planned and executed. Each tutor-student pair seemed to have arrived at a unique synthesis of teaching and learning styles, so that even where identical procedures or materials were employed, they were harnessed to different purposes and implied different achievements and failures. In the light of what might be termed the overall 'pedagogic situation' in adult literacy, this lack of uniformity is hardly surprising. Consider the contrast with beginning reading in and out of school. It was argued above that a need for literacy does not arise completely spontaneously out of children's experience of the world. Few ask to be taught to read and write: their parents and teachers impose literacy as a non-negotiable requirement. This is not to deny that literacy does have an interest and entertainment value for at least some four- to eight-year-olds, but its utility for children in this age-group is not comparable to its importance for adults. There is simply far less children can do with the information they acquire from, or generate with, writing and print. Although the reality can and should be otherwise, school instruction remains premissed on uniformly passive and largely indifferent learners, assumptions which are broadly congruent with the use of sequential teaching systems and reading schemes.

On the other hand, notwithstanding the possible existence of strong personal and social pressures on them, adults who approach literacy schemes have chosen freely to learn. Most adults say, if asked, that they hope tuition will assist them to acquire or process specific kinds of information. They need to be literate in order to pursue various enterprises about which they have developed interests and made emotional investments. In comparison to children, they already possess a massive knowledge of the everyday world including, except in the most exceptional circumstances, the rudiments of reading and writing. Adult tuition can thus be tailored to an individually variable corpus of interests and knowledge in a way that work in the classroom is generally not.

The pedagogy of adult literacy, transmitted through training courses and widely used manuals (eg. BBC, 1975; MacFarlane, 1976a; ALRA, 1977) legitimates and reinforces this heterogeneity by resisting the idea of a preferred overall teaching system or strategy. Tutors are encouraged to start with a thorough review of the student's existing abilities in order to plan tuition, and it is suggested that wherever possible the student should participate in this planning. The watchwords are adaptation, experimentation and innovation.

Such diversity makes life difficult but interesting for the researcher, and there were, in addition, other obstacles to uncovering the processes at work in tuition. The accounts and perceptions of tutors and students (questioned separately) regarding what was taking place during tuition sessions were frequently inconsistent. For their part, the students found it very difficult to describe their activities in detail mainly because few possessed the technical vocabulary with which to identify the skills they were working on. This turned out to be more than merely a terminological deficit. It was clear that several students did not understand the point of what had been attempted by the tutor in recent sessions, so that their drills and exercises remained obscure to them. This could indicate a general failure by some tutors to recognise the heuristic importance of such understanding.

A further research problem existed with the students' accounts of tuition. There was a widespread and quite natural reluctance by students to say anything that could be construed as criticism of their tutors, especially to a third party with ambiguous loyalties. There was a marked tendency to say or imply that every aspect of tuition was perfectly tailored to their needs. The pace of tuition, for example, almost always appeared to be 'just about right'. Without it being solicited in any way during the interview, tutors were showered with gratitude and praise. On the other hand, tutors were able to talk uninhibitedly about the limitations of their students and the difficulties of the current matching. They were critical of students but also self-critical.

The deference with which students referred to their tutors appeared in most cases to be entirely genuine and presumably reflected the orthodox 'pupil' role they had adopted. This deferential stance posed a problem for tutors who favoured a participative tutorial style because their students did not expect to contribute to the decision-making in other than minor respects, such as to opt for one book title or general topic rather than another. One tutor remarked that his student seemed almost to resent having his opinion sought regularly. There was thus circumstantial evidence, in at least some pairings, of a fundamental asymmetry of approach to basic aspects of the teaching process.

Early in the data-collection phase of the research, it became clear that in order to make even tentative steps towards understanding tuition as a process, it would be necessary to construct some kind of scheme that could give an overview of the mass of detail generated by the interviews. Each tutorial pair's arrangements reflected the student's existing abilities at the start of tuition, the number of meetings and the speed of progress, as well as a host of other 'local' and individual factors interacting with each other in a dauntingly complex fashion. A key step in the interpretation of the transcripts was therefore the formulation of the concept of an 'orientation to illiteracy'. An orientation, in this context, refers to an organised system of beliefs and attitudes regarding the means and ends of tuition in literacy, including as key elements definitions of progress, success and failure, together with ideas regarding the demands each party in tuition can legitimately make on the other. Orientations are taken to have their origin typically prior to tuition: in the case of tutors, it lies in their period of training; with students, it tends to reflect their accumulated experience of illiteracy and the overall trajectory of their literacy careers. Because they come into existence before a tutor-student pair meet, orientations are relatively resistant to short-term change within tuition, and indeed, operate as frameworks by which tuition can be interpreted and evaluated.

Bearing in mind that the 'orientations' are a set of explanatory idealisations against which specific cases and relationships can be compared, three main student and two main tutor orientations were suggested by the Nottingham research (Chart 4.1).

Student	**Tutor**
Instrumental	Technical
Mastery	Pastoral
Personal	

Student orientation	**Tutor orientation**	
	Technical	**Pastoral**
Instrumental	Congruent	Problematic
Mastery	Compatible	Compatible
Personal	Problematic	Congruent

Chart 4.1: *Orientations to illiteracy and tutorial combinations of orientation*

'Instrumentally' orientated students viewed literacy in affectively neutral terms as a means to specific, personally cherished, goals. Their self-conceptions had not been deeply scarred by the stigma of illiteracy and they did not find their deficiency especially shameful or take elaborate steps to keep it secret. Despite the occasional previous attempt to get help, these were not people who felt they possessed a major social handicap. They found it relatively easy to conduct their affairs with the limited skills they had, perhaps through the assistance of an amanuensis at home or at work. It was frequently some disruption or major change in their personal circumstances that increased the level of literacy demanded of them and gave tuition a new or renewed relevance. Their goals on entering tuition were specific and had a largely practical, 'functional' character. They had more or less clear ideas about what they wanted to do with the literacy skills they hoped to acquire, and they were prone to discontinue tuition as soon as they felt they had reached a requisite standard (regardless of the hints or clearly stated views of their tutors to the contrary). Instrumental students were very often seeking an educational or vocational credential in order to gain entry to, or promotion in, an occupation. On the other hand, they rarely had recreational uses of literacy in mind or saw it as a way of increasing their social standing or acceptability. Their attitudes to tutors and literacy work were highly calculative: they were aware of the direct and opportunity costs of time spent on preparation and attendance, and they sought tangible evidence of their increasing skill to justify these costs. They were not anxious for intimacy with tutors and volunteered little information about themselves. Reserve and apparent deference were employed to keep their involvement in the tutorial relationship cool.

Students with a 'mastery' orientation also saw literacy as a means to an end, though the objectives were more diffuse. They tended to feel vulnerable and socially exposed, possibly as a result of embarrassing incidents in which their deficiencies had been suddenly revealed. They wished, above all, to shed this vulnerability and to attain an unself-conscious control over reading and writing, particularly in public use. The decision to start tuition was difficult and hedged with doubts and reservations. They may have been under pressure, or even subtly blackmailed, by a spouse, relative or close friend. The hope that an improvement in literacy would enhance the quality of a valued social relationship appeared to feature in their motivation. They remained, at least partly, ashamed of their inability to read and write fluently and their desire was to pass as fully literate within their own social milieu (although they were sometimes ignorant of what this entailed by way of skills and effort). They sought a tutor who 'understood' them in addition to teaching them efficiently, and in home tuition with certain tutors, sociability seems eventually to have displaced literacy work as the basis of the relationship.

It is probably the case that a high proportion of individuals with a 'personal' orientation do not, in fact, come forward for tuition. In this minority, the stigma of their condition has been felt especially keenly. A sense of shame and failure has been deeply internalised and generalised so that it occupies a central place in their self-conceptions. Illiteracy may be the central problem in their lives or, more likely, it has interacted with other difficulties and assumed unrealistic and perhaps neurotic proportions. They may expend an enormous amount of ingenuity and emotional energy disguising their illiteracy from those whose opinions matter. When people with personal orientations do come forward for help, perhaps after extended periods of soul-searching, they remain acutely sensitive about their shortcomings and tend to opt for the confidentiality of home tuition. These individuals bring a great intensity of feeling to tuition and they present special problems for inexperienced tutors. Even so, their desire to succeed is strong because they have fashioned literacy into a vehicle for the substantial reconstruction of their identities.

Turning now to the tutors, those with a 'technical' orientation were committed, first and foremost, to the task of teaching people to read and write. Literacy was perceived as a practical, desirable end in itself. Many technically oriented tutors were, or had been, teachers, some with ESL or beginning reading experience, but many of the remainder suffered initial anxiety about their capacity to teach effectively. The main technical preoccupations were with the selection and preparation of tasks and materials for tutorials, student performance with these materials and overall student progress. The tutorial relationship itself was of interest mainly in so far as it was believed to be promoting or hampering the goals of tuition. Some tutors appeared (consciously or not) to regulate the degree of their intimacy with the student as a reward or penalty for performance. Literacy tuition was the only form of voluntary or welfare activity that most technically orientated tutors had undertaken or considered.

'Pastorally' orientated tutors, in contrast, tended to have records of past and sometimes current involvement in other voluntary work. Literacy tuition was conceived as merely one form of assistance among many by which the disadvantaged could be helped. They defined their task as befriending the student and developing a relationship in which the language work was an important element, but not always the *raison d'être*. Illiteracy was likely to be interpreted as a symptom of a more deep-seated social or psychological malaise which the tutor was generally willing to incorporate within his or her brief. Pastoral students did not seem to be dismayed if, over time, tutorials ceased to have any direct concern with literacy and became increasingly devoted to a discussion of personal problems, or even stopped entirely to be replaced by casual visiting and pure sociability.

As should be apparent from the description above, matching was necessarily a fairly primitive procedure which could not ensure the conjunction of particular student and tutor orientations. The range of possibilities are set out in Chart 4.1. The instrumental-technical and the personal-pastoral combinations can be regarded as 'congruent' as there is a strong likelihood of mutually consistent expectations. In instrumental-pastoral and personal-technical combinations, on the other hand, each party has substantially different objectives and preferences, so that a high casualty rate can be anticipated as pairs fail to make the necessary adjustments and accommodations. Mastery-technical and mastery-pastoral combinations are logically and empirically intermediate. Expectations are not entirely complementary but there is likely to be sufficient overlap to permit adjustment in the majority of pairings.

Progress and dropping out

The Nottingham research made no attempt to measure 'objectively' gains in reading comprehension or writing fluency. Aside from the many practical and methodological difficulties of carrying out such measurements in a manner not disruptive to the pairings, a consensus has established itself opposing the assessment of adult success in terms of standardised test scores. Charnley and Jones, for example, who examine the issue of success at length, are firmly of the opinion that 'the evaluation of success in the acquisition of literacy must begin with the objectives perceived and formulated by the students, and not with externally imposed standards and purposes' (1979, 20). While the substantially increased confidence students can derive from tuition is undoubtedly a crucial extra-linguistic component of success, the implications of the previous section go further. In the case of students with personal or mastery orientations, a major preoccupation is the removal of the threat of the sudden revelation of their deficiency. Above all, such people desire to slip into the anonymity of the mass who are unself-conscious about reading timetables or filling out application forms. These students may need only a token advance in literacy skills to begin to view themselves in a more favourable light. Instrumentally orientated students, on the other hand, tend to start tuition with extremely modest expectations about their target level of achievement, partly because they believe, rightly or wrongly, that their information needs are modest. Since these needs do vary greatly between individuals, and because tuition does involve opportunity costs, the student's judgement on whether he or she is making progress must be taken seriously. The most direct confirmation is simply their willingness to continue their attendance.

The other side of the 'progress' coin was 'dropping out'. Although this phrase was used widely by the staff in the scheme and appeared frequently in the records, it is misleading, carrying with it an unfortunate implication that tuition was incomplete. The turnover of students was very high. Of the eighteen students interviewed, only ten were definitely active when their tutors were contacted six months later. While such a high turnover, by no means unusual in literacy schemes (Jeffrey and Maginn, 1978), does not give grounds for complacency, it must not be taken as an indicator of failure. An open-ended commitment to tuition is not something all students are able or need to make. While a comprehensive and sophisticated literacy will require lengthy and regular contact, it is vital that provision is not premissed on this objective only. It remains, however, difficult for some tutors to accept the realities of student turnover, as the following dialogue indicates:

> *Interviewer*: 'Do you think he has reached as far as he wants to go?'
> *Tutor*: 'I think he's getting very near because he's missing one or two lessons and I think he can tell you he's quite happy with what he can do compared to, sort of, you know, he thinks . . . he's doing very well. I mean, you don't like to say, well, there's a lot more you can do . . .'

The tutor's room for diplomatic manoeuvre in such a situation is seriously limited. This particular tutor did all he felt he could:

> 'I try to show him other things that he hasn't touched on at all to try and make him realise that there are more things that you can learn. But whether it will work, I don't know . . .'

It did not work. The student almost immediately stopped attending for good.

One element in student turnover is made up of clients prepared to accommodate to life with comparatively low levels of competence. Members in this category rarely announce their departure in advance or explain the reasons for their decision not to continue. A quite separate element is constituted by those unsuited to, or dissatisfied with, tuition as they have experienced it. Since literacy schemes are not in a position to calculate the relative size of each of these categories, a sound and conservative general policy would be to ensure a range of types of provision in addition to tuition.

Summary

There is no reason to suppose that the five orientations described above exhaust either the theoretical or the empirical possibilities. Literacy schemes with different referral networks and arrangements can be expected to throw up further orientations, or at least, distinctive distributions of tutorial combinations. The question of the generalisability of the categories is clearly one that can only be settled by attempts to apply them within different schemes.

The Nottingham research provided no grounds for giving any credence to the stereotypes of illiteracy described at the beginning of the chapter. It seems to be the case that substantial illiteracy is nearly always a grave social disadvantage, setting a low ceiling on educational achievement, and thereby barring entry, as the following chapter will demonstrate, to a wide range of employment. The evidence also indicates that individual responses to it are extremely variable, with feelings ranging from the slightest hint of personal inconvenience through to the occasional case of deep embarrassment: exceptionally, where it comes to blight personal relationships, it can inflict lasting psychological damage. But it is rarely, like ethnicity, the single crucial determinant of the individual's relationships and destiny. There is no social force impelling adult illiterates to form self-protective and exclusive groupings. To a greater extent than many other physical, psychological and social handicaps, it is possible to make an accommodation to illiteracy and to circumvent the situations and activities in which reading and writing loom large. Indeed, there is a major irony in the way some adults exercise such ingenuity and skill, either reducing literacy's demands or finding substitutes for it, so that when they finally seek tuition, the tutor is driven to despair looking for materials with a practical relevance for them.

5
Illiteracy and work

Introduction

There is little doubt that the occupational implications of possessing or lacking literacy skills are generally profound, but in the face of the enormous variety of kinds of work and work setting, past investigations have largely been restricted to anecdotal accounts of individual triumphs and failures. In the light of this stress on the personal perspective, the Nottingham research approached the topic of employment on two fronts: while the interviews with literacy students covered work histories and experiences in detail, a separate programme of inquiries was arranged with representatives from the personnel function of selected employers who were involved in the local market for unskilled and semi-skilled labour. The objective was to understand how their concrete selection policies and procedures affected the employment prospects of the kind of people who were seeking help from the NALS.

The chapter begins with some factual information about the Nottingham and East Midlands labour market for manual work as a backdrop for the discussion that follows of the employment experiences of some of the Nottingham sample. The final section attempts to identify the economic and social processes that lead employers to recruit 'literate' workforces even where the work itself does not necessitate it.

The Nottingham labour market

At the time of the research, Nottingham had a labour force of about 250,000. Despite a handful of very large employers (including Boots, Plessey, John Player, TI Raleigh, the National Coal Board and the Local Authority), few of the 9,000–10,000 enterprises in the area involved more than 500 people, and the great majority, especially in the textile and hosiery industry, were very much smaller. The latter has been affected by a long-term decline which severely reduced the opportunities for part-time and full-time work for women for which Nottingham is traditionally known. Energy crises have helped to arrest rather than reverse a similar long-term decline in coal mining on which the Sutton/Mansfield area to the north of Nottingham remains dependent, while the extended coal-mining dispute of 1984–5 has introduced deep schisms into many previously united communities.

The quantitative data that are available do not suggest that the local labour market is, in any basic respect, distinctive. As far as wage rates are concerned, Table 5.1 implies a consistent shortfall in comparison with national averages in the semi- and unskilled sectors. However, some allowance must be made for the fact that these Nottingham rates are derived from a survey of starting salaries offered to job-seekers and would not incorporate various kinds of increment and supplement available to employees of long standing.

Table 5.1: *Average gross hourly earnings (excluding overtime), national*[1] *and Greater Nottingham*[2]*, 1979*[3]

			Pence
Occupational Category		*National Rate*	*Greater Notts. Rate*
Machine Tool Operators	– Men	209.7	142
	– Women	160.7	
Cleaners	– Men	156.1	126
	– Women	129.4	
Storekeepers	– Men	172.0	126
	– Women	139.6	
Sales/Shop Assistants	– Men	173.0	108
	– Women	114.4	
Bar Staff		109.8	107
Kitchen Hands/Porters	– Men	136.1	105
Kitchen Hands	– Women	126.2	

Notes: 1 *New Earnings Survey* rates are for full-time men aged 21 and over and full-time women aged 18 and over whose pay in the survey period was not affected by absence.

2 Greater Nottingham rates are taken from a survey of starting salaries offered by employers to job-seekers and conducted by the Nottingham District Employment Service Division of the Manpower Services Commission. It was based on vacancy data from six Jobcentres/Employment Offices. The number of vacancies in each category is not available.

3 *New Earnings Survey* figures are for April 1979, Nottingham figures for June 1979.

Source: *New Earnings Survey*, 1979, Part D, Tables 86, 87.

Table 5.2: *Average gross weekly earnings, manual and non-manual workers*[1], *1979* (£'s)

Manual	*Nottinghamshire*	*East Midlands*	*Great Britain*
FT Men 21 and over	98.9	92.3	93.0
FT Women 18 and over	52.4	53.9	55.2
Non-Manual			
FT Men 21 and over	106.2	105.8	113.0
FT Women 18 and over	(67.3)[2]	63.1	66.0

Notes: 1 Whose pay during the survey period was unaffected by absence or unemployment. Full-time workers only.
2 Standard error exceeds 2.0%.

Source: *New Earnings Survey*, 1979, Part E, Tables 108, 109, 111, 112.

Table 5.2, which reports average gross weekly earnings (for the County rather than the Greater Nottingham area) suggests, somewhat inconsistently, that local male manual workers are paid substantially better and male non-manual workers substantially worse than the national averages. In the corresponding groups of female employees, the reverse situation obtains, but to a much less marked degree. As a consequence, the averages for all full-time men and for all full-time women, not reported in Table 5.2, are close to national averages. A partial explanation for the high earnings of some male manual workers in the area may lie in the percentage of total earnings made up by overtime pay and payment by results bonuses (28.3 per cent) which is above the national average (24.4 per cent).

Table 5.3, which deals with the percentage of the workforce

Table 5.3: *Unemployment rates*[1], *selected areas, 1978–9*

	10 Aug. 1978	*7 Dec. 1978*	*9 Aug. 1979*	*10 Dec. 1979*
Nottingham	6.1	4.9	5.3	4.9
Nottinghamshire	6.0	4.9	5.4	5.0
East Midlands –				
Males	6.3	5.6	5.6	5.5
Females	4.5	3.4	3.9	3.3
Total	5.6	4.7	4.9	4.6
United Kingdom	6.7	5.7	6.0	5.6

Note: 1 Denominators for 1978 percentages were based on estimates of total employees (employed and unemployed) for mid-1976; for 1979 percentages, denominators are based on estimates for mid-1979 number of total employees.

Source: *Dept. of Employment Gazette, Regional and Area Statistics on Unemployment*, Sept. 1978, Jan. 1979, Sept. 1979, Jan. 1980.

registered as unemployed at selected dates in 1978 and 1979, shows that Nottingham had a slightly but consistently lower rate than either the East Midlands region or the United Kingdom as a whole. These figures may, however, present an overly optimistic picture of the situation at the unskilled end of the labour market which was affected by substantial redundancies during the course of the research, as well as by the contraction of the hosiery trade referred to above. Little reliance can be placed on the extremely low female unemployment rates for the region which probably reflect the unwillingness of married women to register if they are ineligible for benefit.

Work histories

It is sometimes assumed on common-sense grounds that anyone who is illiterate will be lucky to find any type of legitimate employment, but the work histories collected from the student sample revealed a complete absence within a two-year time-span of long spells (defined as over four weeks) of involuntary unemployment for reasons other than sickness, but two individuals were unemployed at the time of their interviews, while one young mother was not seeking work. This absence of long-term unemployment needs to be placed in perspective. Firstly, it is, of course, based on a small sample of cases gathered from one city. Secondly, the sample did not cover the vocational courses on literacy that catered specifically for the currently unemployed in the Nottingham region and therefore it would tend to under-represent their numbers. Despite these limitations, interviewees' remarks are sufficiently consistent to suggest that illiteracy operates as a much more selective handicap than has previously been appreciated. Its main impacts on the Nottingham sample could be summarised as follows:

(1) It appeared to constitute an unsuperable entry barrier only to jobs which had a supervisory component or whose job descriptions contained a discrete clerical element, though not to jobs which entailed reading and writing on a casual basis.
(2) Sub-literate school leavers without qualifications spent longer than their qualified and literate peers in finding an employer willing to take them, an effect that is probably especially marked in areas of high existing unemployment.

(3) When mature adults with literacy problems do find work, it is often insecure and they are likely to be among the first groups to be laid off during recessions or seasonal troughs.

(4) Applicants who possess another attribute that employers regard as unfavourable, in addition to illiteracy, will not be considered by some potential employers regardless of any positive characteristics they may be able to present.

These consequences are mostly predictable and self-explanatory, but the final category can be amplified by an illustration. Jean, an independent and spirited seventeen-year-old, whose childhood had been spent in institutions, was in local authority care at the time of the interview following several minor skirmishes with the law, none of which were connected with or affected her work. Jean maintained that her background was held against her in job interviews despite her proven capacity to do the work:

> 'That's another thing, when I go to a job. I mean, I went to one before I went to Parkinson [a knitwear firm] and do you know all they said to me was – I explained you know – I said I have to have this lady come home with me because of me moving and that. Well, once they heard that they sat down and they says well we don't know if we can take you on and I was giving them all the details, you know, and he was saying to me, "Why were you in care? Why did you go here?" And when I was telling them about running away he says, "Why didn't you want to live with your Mum?", and things like this. He says, "I can see you're the type of person to go for a fag every ten minutes". I said, "I don't think so because I go for one every hour . . .'

Jean finally got a job with another small garment firm making underwear. Whether she was considered a model employee there is impossible to say, but she encountered no problems in reaching the output targets and collecting her production bonus.

The past and present employment of the students interviewed was concentrated, without exception, in 'semi-skilled' or 'unskilled' jobs. None of those who were currently 'economically active' had ever held positions which entailed formal supervisory responsibility for other employees (except over trainees). This was expected since the vast bulk of work roles entailing supervisory or managerial authority (with the exception of some forms of self-employment) require credentials based on reading and writing. However, labels like 'semi-skilled' or 'unskilled' are not, despite their currency, reliable guides to either the real complexity of jobs or the actual skills of the people that perform them. The interview data threw up several individuals who possessed a collection of manual skills, apparently as a result of their 'horizontal' rather than 'vertical' job mobility.[1] Peter, for instance, was a labour-only subcontractor in the building trade who had never served an apprenticeship or even received formal training, but had clearly acquired a variety of high-level manual skills. His first job on leaving school had been as a dental mechanic:

> 'Anyway, I did it for two years. I could do the job quite well but then again handicrafts and things like that at school were always my top line really because going back to. . . . I mean I don't know what to call it now but in those days you used to call it handicrafts and the teacher was a teacher named Grimshaw. In actual fact, I was so good at it that half of the time I used to teach one half of the class and he used to teach the other. Anything to do with my hands, I could do. You know, bookbinding, anything like that.'

Peter turned to bricklaying when he was sixteen, following in his father's footsteps even though the latter tried hard to discourage him:

> 'I progressed a bit as a bricklayer and quite honestly if I'd been better at this game [reading and writing] I think I could have done quite well really. I own my own house sort of thing which I've built myself. . . . I've done it twice.'
> *Interviewer*: 'Twice? You've got two houses?'
> *Peter*: 'Two houses. Well, a bungalow and then a house sort of thing. Got myself a plot of land and built the bungalow in my spare time. Mind you, I done the house the same way so I've progressed a little bit and I've actually built one or two houses to sell, but as I say, if I'd been better at reading and writing I think I could have done a lot better.'

Although he is physically fit and does not look his age (forty-seven), Peter realises that it will be increasingly difficult for him to earn a decent wage as a bricklayer on piece rates. He appreciates that most men of his skill and experience are site foremen or jobbing builders and he has a 'secret' hope that literacy tuition will open up one of these avenues to him.

Bob, though half Peter's age, was similar in many ways. As well as having several unaccredited skills at his disposal, he illustrates another theme that turned up persistently in the work histories. Because form filling is a major element in the job finding process, many skilled illiterates fail at the first selection hurdle. Bob could not get a job in any of the large organisations he approached. Working in a brickyard after leaving school, he happened to pick up a good knowledge of welding. After a serious accident (which wasted his left arm, shortened a leg and left him classified officially as disabled) he needed lighter work. He visited a steel firm in the area:

> 'I went there and I was given a piece of metal, these heavy bars what's on your windows and I welded it right across in ten minutes. They just take an hour to do one bit. And he said, "You're worth £100 to me without any overtime", and he says, "We got to ask you this now mate", he said, "Where's your papers?", and I said, "I'm sorry me duck but I can't write very well". I said, "I can read a bit but I can't write very well and I got no papers", and now its union rules that you got to have papers. So that was it.'

Despite his difficulties with literacy, Bob had become shop steward while he worked at the brickyard:

> 'This is what makes you laugh, I couldn't read or write yet I was shop steward, union man. . . . Transport and General Workers. And they knew down at the Head Office and they said as long as you are doing your job we're not bothered. And I got their money there every month and that was it . . .'

Bob had experience as a centre lathe operator and a fork-lift truck fitter, both skills he had picked up in the brickyard. When he was made redundant he went to an interview with a large metalworking firm (referred to as 'Brown's' in the next section):

> 'Although I was a welder/fitter/mechanic – I could do it blindfolded – but just to pass that writing exam, fill that form in, was just a dead loss. See what Brown's did when I went there for a

job, er, she more or less said well if you can't fill this form in you are useless and that really cut me and I thought. . . . I nearly turned round. That nearly got me right to boiling point and I just walked out. I said, "Stuff your job", exact words. Personnel officer, she was.'

Experiences like these probably lie behind the noticeable concentration of the sample in small organisations, but more is probably involved than simply the rejection of illiterate applicants by large, bureaucratic firms. There appears to be a complex affinity between illiteracy and small, informal work settings within the secondary labour market.[2] In such settings, there is often little concern with official regulations, credentials or job demarcations. Flexible employees who can demonstrate that they have several skills at their command are welcomed even if they lack formal training and certificates. From the employee's point of view, learning on the job suits the individual who might not gain much from conventional chalk and blackboard training. Bob again, talking about the brickyard:

> 'I did sweeping up for one year then I did fork-lift driving for I shouldn't have done because I wasn't insured but the gaffer said I'll give you 3d. extra. It sounds daft but he said I'll give you 3d. a week extra till you get better.'

The small entrepreneur can get skilled work out of an unqualified employee without paying the market rate, and the employee is better off than he would be doing the least skilled jobs in large plants. Several of the people in the sample, who, like Bob, had substantial skills to sell, were nevertheless driven into the informal ('black') economy to earn a decent living.

> *Interviewer*: 'Do you ever think of doing contract welding or anything like that where you would be working for yourself?'
> *Bob*: 'Well you've got to have if you go to a place like [the brickyard]. I did one place, I did it on the side and for about three month there was about £150 every Sunday for five hours work. And I'd like that job and I could do it every week now but the tax man would do me.'

Bob had also been involved in similar 'unofficial' deals involving scrap metal. Doing 'foreigners' (that is, work on your own account in the firm's time) and 'bits on the side' is, of course, a staple of the industrial sub-culture and it would be wrong to suggest that only workers without formal training are engaged in it.

To bring Bob's history up to date, he was working at the time of the interview in a small printing firm, operating large multi-colour presses. This entailed very long shifts, often twelve hours from 2 pm until 2 am, but his pay packet was usually, by his standards, big. Bob has an irrepressible personality and an unshakeable determination that will not let illiteracy or physical disability stand in his way. This comes out in his description of his first encounter with his future boss in the print shop, following his interview.

> 'I just went, "Right, see you then me duck", I said, "Let me known then, I said, "I'll wait till about Wednesday then, youth". I kept calling him youth (my missus said, "I don't know what he'll think of you calling him it, it should be Mr Jenkins"). Well now, when he comes round he said, "Morning me duck", I say, "Morning youth", but I just keep forgetting and he never tells me off. I mean from when I started here on the floor inside three months I'm on a quarter of a million pound machine. I'm the only one that's been there three month and moved onto a big machine. And I'm going in for this new big one, we got a one million pound machine coming in that big, the 800, and I'm after that one . . .'

While Bob's career indicates some of the recurrent difficulties illiterates face in the employment sphere, his strength of character cannot be taken as standard. His evident pride and satisfaction in the responsibility for expensive machinery which he had been given was congruent with an external and objective confirmation of success. Bob, unlike any other literacy student in the sample, had managed to make the transition from unskilled to (effectively) skilled work independently of any improvements in his literacy skills (although he was, in fact, reading for pleasure and beginning to write his own correspondence). This type of upward occupational mobility was atypical of the rest of the students in the sample. Consider the case of Wilf, now in his late thirties, who was more typical both in terms of personality and career. Wilf left school to get a job in a soft drinks firm, loading crates onto a conveyor. He then had seven years in the building trade as a labourer for his grandfather, who was a jobbing builder. A two-year spell of 'unemployment' followed during which Wilf claims he applied unsuccessfully for 385 jobs. During this period, he actually did casual work in a fun fair:

> 'I was just travelling around with the fair 'cos you pay no tax or nothing on . . . poor money but it was better than signing on each day. . . . I was on the merry-go-round, dodgems. . . . Oh, its hard work, very hard work, not as easy as you think. You have to put up, build up one day, open up and then take it down the same night, then travel through the night and then build it up ready to open up the next day. Really hard work.'

Recently, Wilf got a temporary job as a cleaner and porter for a Local Authority recreation centre. This was a double breakthrough. After extensive literacy tuition, Wilf had successfully completed his first job application form. Three months after starting the new job, he was put onto a permanently employed basis. Shy and hesitant in manner, he felt that for the first time in his life he had a regular, 'proper' job which guaranteed him sufficient continuity to settle down and furnish a home rather than living in digs. Despite these gains, Wilf's life remains hard. With low basic wages, he relies heavily on long hours of seasonally available overtime. His tutor reported that he was sometimes too exhausted to concentrate on his reading and writing exercises; he had given up his favourite recreation, fishing, for the same reason. His work prospects are poor. As he gets older, he will find the physical demands of his work, like Peter, increasingly onerous. There is little likelihood that the attainment of even a relatively high level of literacy will open up employment possibilities beyond the kind of manual work with which he is familiar. This is the case with many older literacy students doing manual work and it poses a serious dilemma for tutors and schemes. One of the almost inevitable consequences of extended tuition and contact with an interested tutor is the generation and formalisation of expectations regarding progress at work. Raising the aspirations and confidence of young literacy students is desirable since so many feel their 'failure' at school so keenly and undervalue their prospects. It is another matter to sow the seeds of dissatisfaction in a mature adult who has no realistic prospects of promotion and who, however uncongenial their job might seem to be to a middle-class tutor, has probably reached some kind of successful adjustment to it.

A rather different pattern was detectable among the work histories of the younger literacy students. These had left school at fifteen or sixteen, normally without any qualifications, and had then found themselves blocked in tolerable but often promotionless work roles. Literacy was a means either to a specific vocational credential, or to general self-improvement, often prompted by boy or girl friends. Thus Don, in his late twenties, had repeatedly failed the entry examination for the Fire Service through poor spelling and grammar. While he was quite happy in his current job in a supermarket provision section, the great attraction of a job as a fireman was that the shiftwork gave greater opportunities to 'moonlight'.

Norman, twenty-two years old, had been a trainee butcher on leaving school but cut himself so often that he decided storeroom work in a supermarket would be safer. Unfortunately, he appears to have been accident-prone there too, and a series of self-inflicted injuries culminated in an incident where a pile of cases fell onto him, broke several ribs and necessitated a long spell of recuperation. Norman found a job in a small garage workshop and, enjoying the daily variety of jobs, stayed for five years. His literacy studies, crammed in between long hours of overtime, were not directed toward any particular career goal, but he was being encouraged strongly to 'get on' by his fiancée, and the idea of being a car salesman was beginning to appeal to him.

The common feature of these younger students' concern to improve their literacy was their matter of fact approach to it. Although they tended to regret getting so little from formal schooling, they were not ashamed of their shortcomings and were far less secretive about their illiteracy than older students. To most of them, tuition was merely a relatively minor but necessary preparation to a change in work roles, although this change might in itself loom large in their hopes and plans.

Employers and illiteracy

When it became evident during the early part of the research that few students had succeeded in getting jobs with the larger local employers, a decision was made to explore the recruitment arrangements set up by these large firms. Interviews were conducted with personnel managers and training staff from four major and one

Table 5.4: *Profiles of organisations studied*

Organisation	*Type of Activity*	*Major Job Categories*	*Total Number of Lower Grade Employees*
Austin's	Retail Sales	Shop Assistants Warehouse Staff	450
St Peter's	Service	Cleaners/Orderlies Porters Gardeners	2,000
Brown's	Metalworking Assembly	Machinists Assemblers General Labourers	4,000
White's	Electro- Mechanical Assembly	Assemblers Wirers Machinists Adjustors	4,000
Green's	Packaging	Packagers General Labourers Storekeepers	6,500

small Nottingham organisations, which between them accounted for about 17,000 semi-skilled and unskilled workers (see Table 5.4). During the interviews, the content of a wide variety of manual jobs was discussed (including cleaning, machine-tool operation, gardening, portering, general labouring, metal parts assembly, warehouse work and packing machine operation), together with recruitment, selection, training, promotion and job advertising policies. As more information on the job descriptions accumulated, it became clear that reading and writing constituted minuscule aspects of 'lower grade' work, that is, those semi-skilled and unskilled job categories located towards the bottom of each plant-wide hierarchy.[3] This did not square with the considerable importance the recruitment policies of large employers appeared to attach to the selection of a literate workforce. If literacy was used as a criterion of worker suitability even where the work did not depend on it, it presumably served latent functions that merited further examination.

The industrial significance of literacy and illiteracy can be understood best in relation to the three successive phases into which the recruitment process to large organisations naturally falls: (1) the job search stage; (2) the selection stage; (3) the job performance stage.

Job search

As far as the initial stage is concerned, literacy competences can determine or at least strongly influence the search activities undertaken by an individual seeking a job. The pattern of the search in turn determines the information that can be accumulated about the state of the local market. For example, in the absence of any assistance, a very weak reader may find great difficulty in deciphering the column of classified job vacancies in the local newspaper, the display cards in a Jobcentre, or the internal vacancy sheet on the noticeboard of their current employer. Even if help is available there may be reluctance to call on it. At home, asking for assistance may raise expectations or generate alarm. At work, the fear may be that news of the search will filter back to supervisory staff, endangering job security. While it is quite possible to supplement personal searches with informal inquiries among friends, these can produce information that is inaccurate or obsolete, particularly if the friends have not themselves recently been active job-seekers.

Writing skills are also relevant to the search for a job. In professional and executive occupations, there are some opportunities to secure work directly by a demonstration of advanced literary skills. Graduate employment, especially in fields like advertising, public relations and publishing, may significantly depend on a letter of inquiry displaying stylistic verve, originality and wit, and this is sometimes systematically exploited by applicants who write the same, suitably original, application to every major employer in the area of work they desire. While such a strategy is clearly less common and less relevant to the acquisition of manual employment, one advantage of a neatly written and grammatical letter of inquiry or application is that it is likely to be processed by a relatively senior member of the personnel function, rather than by either receptionists or line personnel like foremen. An additional advantage derives from the fact that a letter can go into the files and be retrieved when vacancies occur, whereas telephone inquiries and personal visits are not necessarily recorded in any permanent form.

Although the telephone is increasingly used to make initial inquiries, and while it is potentially available to anyone who can use a directory, even here practical problems exist. Access to a telephone during working hours is difficult for many manual workers already located in large plants. There are frequently queues for the use of public telephones during work breaks; responsible members of the personnel departments in employing organisations may not be available to answer queries in the lunch hour.

Up to date information on vacancies and general advice on employment are available from Jobcentres and Employment Offices, but whether justified or not, the reliance many manual workers place on formal job-finding agencies is low. None of the respondents in the current research mentioned these agencies as featuring importantly in their job hunting. Other research reveals a similar lack of confidence in Employment Offices and their staff (Hill *et al.*, 1973; Daniel, 1974; Blackburn and Mann, 1979). In the latters' sample, only 8 per cent (N=949) of Peterborough manual workers had found their current jobs from an Employment Exchange. In Hill *et al.*'s study of the unemployed in three English cities, well over 30 per cent felt that not all the facts in their case had been considered by the Employment Exchange staff, and over 35 per cent believed more could have been done for them. As the authors point out, such reactions may simply be generalised frustration, and in recent years, considerable effort has gone into meeting the problems inherent in providing a usable employment service for the disadvantaged. Towards the end of the research, a pilot scheme was set up in a central Nottingham Jobcentre in which the initial inquiry form was streamlined and simplified, and staff were specifically trained to assist discreetly anyone admitting difficulty with form-filling. Despite such desirable innovations, it is unlikely that the suspicion that Employment Offices are outposts of employers' personnel departments can be easily dispelled, ingrained as it is in the working-class sub-culture.

To summarise, the evidence from labour market research indicates that few job-seekers starting out on a search for unskilled work have much information to hand beyond the names of a few of the largest local employers. If they are halting readers and poor writers, it is probable that their search will be narrower in scope, briefer in duration and less systematic than that of a competent reader. The results of their search are correspondingly less likely to be satisfactory, not only from their own point of view, but also from their prospective employer's.

Selection

In each of the four large organisations in which detailed inquiries and observations took place, lower grade vacancies occurring through normal labour turnover were filled largely from casual inquirers or Employment Office referrals. All the organisations operated recruitment offices with staff to deal specifically with personal visits, telephone calls and interviews. Since three of the four organisations were 'household names' in the locality, the volume of casual inquiries was great (in 1979, Green's had 22,000), and advertisements in the local press were only occasionally needed. For lower grade jobs, all the firms operated a 'first-past-the-post' hiring method; except for some part-time, 'twilight' shift work, shortlists and waiting lists were not used. (On the other hand, all the larger organisations advertised higher grade and supervisory vacancies internally and used shortlists for appointing to these jobs.)

Selection procedures were generally simple and uniform. If there were vacancies, inquirers were asked to fill in a job application form given to them by a receptionist. When they had completed the form, they were interviewed, often immediately, by selectors. If the applicants were deemed satisfactory, they were sent for a medical examination. In some of the firms, applicants for some job categories were subsequently re-interviewed by line personnel (supervisors or department managers) who retained the power of veto over hiring. References were normally taken up after employment had started. School leavers, disabled employees, part-time staff, etc., were dealt with by slightly different arrangements.

At this point, a rough distinction can be introduced between two justifications employers use for desiring literate recruits. The first derives from any elements of the work cycle or set of job tasks that require the worker to read or write – this can be termed 'job literacy'. The second and more general justification is in terms of the employers' perceived need to document aspects of the relations that exist between themselves, employees, trade unions and the state – which can be called 'employment literacy'.

All the large employers studied used either or both of these justifications to operate a 'literacy screen', the purpose of which was to discriminate between levels of literacy among job applicants. A screen can literally come in a variety of forms. At its most sophisticated, it can consist of a pencil and paper test designed from scratch specifically for that particular work situation. Alternatively, a pre-existing general-purpose test of functional literacy may be 'borrowed', or at the least sophisticated pole, recruiters may simply rely on a part of the selection process that already conveniently entails reading and writing operations by the applicant.

The literacy screening for lower grade jobs in the five surveyed organisations could be described as unsophisticated and haphazard. Professionally designed tests of functional literacy were not employed and the screens that were used were not calibrated in any way against the literacy components of the work tasks allocated on entry to new recruits. They generally consisted of a casual jumble of 'on-the-spot' reading and writing operations which bore little relation to work activities.

The job application form was the principal, and at Austin's, St Peter's and White's, the only test of literacy in use. At Green's, it was backed up by an insistence that forms were filled in immediately in the reception area, and receptionists were briefed to ensure that it was the applicant who completed the form in person. Brown's were also careful about this, and were reluctant to send out forms through the post.

All the forms themselves were similar in design and sought the same basic information under very similar rubrics with only minor differences in layout. Despite the great reliance placed on the applicant's ability to fill in the forms, their relevance to establishing levels of either functional literacy in general, or the job literacy requirements of specific job categories, was minimal. There was no evidence that the forms had been designed with any literacy assessment function in mind. Selectors at Brown's and St Peter's described in detail how they used the forms during an interview. In each case, they went verbally through the information provided by the applicant, section by section, but despite their considerable experience these selectors appeared to make little or no distinction between various interview objectives for which the application form was the common means. These objectives included checking the consistency of the information on the form with the applicants' verbal accounts without sight of the form, establishing whether non-completion of sections indicated non-comprehension of rubrics, assessing the plausibility of applicants' reasons for job changing, and eliciting the reasons for gaps in employment histories.

Selectors at Brown's and St Peter's, in particular, were concerned with a composite picture and its overall consistency with, or discrepancy from, implicit stereotypes, rather than a fine evaluation of specific strengths and weaknesses. These selectors were supremely confident in their diagnostic capacity. Phrases used included '. . .

he doesn't add up . . .' and 'I always know if something's wrong somewhere . . .'. There can be little doubt that these selectors held negative stereotypes which equated, or strongly linked, low literacy with low intelligence.

Green's was unique in that selection staff had a variety of specialised materials that could be used in an interview to screen applicants who appeared from their forms to be poor readers or writers. Firstly, there were two typed lists of alphanumeric product codes whose function will be described below; applicants were asked to identify instances of the same code in both lists. Secondly, there were printed prohibition notices on small cards (e.g., 'DANGER, FLAMMABLE') that could be presented to applicants for recognition. These were the only examples in the five organisations of an attempt to reproduce in the interview a functional literacy task directly relevant to job performance. Elsewhere, judgements regarding literacy were sometimes made on the basis of much more irrelevant and incongruous 'tests'. For example, Green's incorporated into their screen the applicant's ability to make sense of a four-page printed form dealing with trade union membership which they had agreed with the union concerned to place before all recruits. This form was extremely complex in format: one of the pages contained a table with twenty cells, eight notes and references to twenty-eight different sums of money. The reverse page consisted of a difficult passage of continuous prose based on the Trade Union Act, 1913. It was not clear exactly how the selectors determined adequate understanding, but the exercise would have given a professional accountant pause for thought.

Equally fortuitous materials were in use at Brown's. Although the selector interviewed was certain that she personally could identify cases of illiteracy from the application form alone, the medical department had been briefed to check that the applicant could read aloud passages from a Curry and Paxton eye test card designed to rate visual acuity. (The card consisted of paragraphs of prose from a novel, beginning and ending in the middle of a sentence and printed in a variety of type sizes).

Thus, all five organisations operated selection procedures which they believed made it likely that illiterate applicants for at least certain jobs would be identified and rejected, though the official standing of these procedures varied. Only in the case of St Peter's was there written authority for screening (in the form of the interview procedure manual which included ascertaining standards of literacy as an objective of interviewing). In Brown's, a member of the Personnel Department responsible for selection said that it was Headquarter's policy that all employees had to be able to read and write, but the requirement was not documented (and, in actuality, the job literacy levels were the lowest of the firms visited).

Only in Austin's (the smallest firm) and White's was it claimed that severe illiteracy constituted no bar to employment in selected job categories. In the case of Austin's, non-readers were placed in warehouse work largely because the director who had the final discretion in hiring them himself worked on site and knew the personnel and work arrangements intimately. Provided there was adequate supervision by a competent reader, the minimal 'job literacy' element could be circumvented. The Training Manager at White's did not think that the recruiters in the organisation had ever rejected people with skills adequate to do the job owing to illiteracy. This manager was the only one interviewed to suggest directly that discrimination against illiterates capable of carrying out the work was not defensible. His location in a training rather than a personnel function may have coloured his views, and although White's was considered to be a generally progressive employer, informed observers doubted that known illiterates were regularly hired.

The justifications offered for the literacy screens, whether official or unofficial, were usually in terms of the nature of the manufacturing process (or the product) and its relation to the embracing provisions of health and safety legislation. Two managers interviewed together said that the Health and Safety at Work Act had obliged them to formalise previously haphazard literacy screening arrangements. When pressed, both conceded that legislation did not specify literacy per se, but they claimed that in the event of an accident they would only be able to demonstrate that they had completely fulfilled the employer's obligations if they could point to written information and printed warnings plus literacy screening of applicants.

Job performance

It has long been accepted that automation removes the skilled elements from industrial work, but the understanding of the processes involved was greatly advanced by the publication of two influential works, Ivar Berg's *Education and Jobs* (1970) and Harry Braverman's *Labour and Monopoly Capital* (1974). In the latter, Braverman (1974, 438) quotes a director of Monsanto Chemicals to the effect that, 'Most factory jobs require only sixth grade competency' (i.e. eleven-year-old level). Blackburn and Mann's study of the market for unskilled labour in an English town (1979, 12) reports along the same lines that:

> Using technical notions of 'skill' we find that almost all workers use less skill at work than they do, for example, in driving a car . . . . We have estimated that in Peterborough about 85 per cent of the workers possess the necessary ability to undertake 95 per cent of the jobs . . .

Significantly, despite this low level of skill, competence in literacy loomed large in the selection process in Peterborough firms. Blackburn and Mann note that:

> Literacy in English was without question the most important formal requirement. Without the ability to read and write English, an applicant could work at only labouring and cleaning jobs at four of the nine firms. . . . Furthermore no responsible jobs in any firm could be held by anyone who could not read and write English. (1979, 103)

In terms of both technical and literacy skills, the Peterborough situation was repeated in Nottingham. There was a negligible 'job literacy' element in the content of most of the numerically large job categories (such as machine minder, assembler, cleaner). Where reading was necessary in these jobs, it largely entailed simple instructions that used a highly restricted vocabulary and syntax. Examples included order chits for machine tool operators, 'instructions for use' on cleaning materials, stock lists in warehouses. The ability to assimilate passages of prose was not normally needed or exercised, and readers with only a highly limited social sightword vocabulary would have been able to handle the literacy content of all the jobs successfully, provided they were familiar with the materials and plant layout (a constraint that would operate equally upon competent readers). A few storekeepers and van-drivers had a genuine clerical component in their job tasks, but the total number of employees involved was small in relation to the major job categories mentioned above. In non-supervisory manual roles, writing was restricted to initialling, ticking or logging-in figures or coded categories. The need to write passages longer than a sentence connected with the job was almost exclusively limited to supervisory roles above the level of chargehand/supervisor/inspector.

The almost total elimination of a literacy component from low-skilled manual work is clearly not accidental. Job design appears to have been deliberately premissed on a worker without reading and writing competences. For example, some machinery controls had elaborate fail-safe devices to back up written labels and operating instructions. One training manager said, 'the presses kick you out if you mishandle them. They don't allow you to operate them incorrectly'. Green's, the largest of the five organisations, operates in an industry which has introduced a code of practice governing the labelling and packaging of its potentially hazardous products. A straightforward, industry-wide system of alphanumeric codes applies to all packaging, and substitutes character recognition for reading. In White's, words for wire colours in wiring diagrams have been replaced by codes made up of the unique combinations of the initial letters of colour words in order to prevent confusion springing from the rival colour vocabularies that are in use among the multi-racial workforce. St Peter's employed two separate colour codes in place of technical descriptions, one to ensure that lower grade staff do not confuse different types of cleaning materials, another to signify exceptional requirements of special categories of client.

In the four large organisations, manufacturing processes were organised in such a manner that the first level of supervision required only marginally more sophisticated literacy skills than the shop-floor grades. Communication between supervisors and operatives was almost entirely verbal, memos and notes not being widely used. Even the communication between higher management and supervisors remained predominantly verbal; changes in technique or methods were often demonstrated by a deputy department head to a meeting of supervisors, with documentation playing very much an auxiliary role. Close supervision of shop-floor activities appears to be generally complementary to the elimination of a literacy content from lower grade work.

The situation with respect to employment literacy provided a marked contrast. The four large organisations all held brief induction courses which presumed a literate workforce by distributing very large quantities of duplicated sheets and booklets on payment systems, sick leave, holiday and recreational arrangements, trade union membership, disciplinary procedures, etc. Some of these documents dealt with complex legal and financial matters of considerable importance to employees, but the quality of the writing and the design were highly variable. Few made any systematic attempt to avoid or explain technical jargon. The poorest, indistinctly reproduced sets of unbound sheets with corrections in biro, bore the hallmarks of hurried and careless production. It is significant that organisations which were very careful to transmit information about production in a verbal form should consider such documentation to be an effective way of communicating with employees about their general rights and duties.

The main factors that underlay the more or less systematic elimination of a need to read or write on the shop floors of the firms studied appeared to be high labour turnover and the character of the manufacturing technologies. Labour turnover was itself the product of a complex network of variables including the extremely monotonous, short-cycle job tasks, bonuses determined by work group output norms (which some newcomers were slow to reach), and high proportions of married female employees not wholly dependent on the wages, and thus only prepared for a very qualified involvement with the organisation. In the face of the resulting labour mobility, the larger firms were unwilling to invest in training for their lower grade workforce and preferred instead to accept the lower productivity that results from brief on-the-job training. Literacy was only at a premium where employee flexibility was required or the production process was so specialised that substantial training had to be given. This interconnects with the nature of the technology employed. White's operated primarily in an electromechanical assembly technology based on numerous small components which can either be purchased or manufactured on site, while Brown's utilised a traditional light engineering assembly technology. In both cases, a very fine division of labour was possible and this offered a multiplicity of options for job design. The skills (or lack of them) of the lower grade labour force can be treated as a fixed input even in the face of product changes. It is easier for technical staff to redesign the product and the configuration of its components than to make greater demands on the dexterity, knowledge or training of the machinists or assembly workers.

At points where reading and writing are unavoidable, specialist job categories involving small numbers of employees can be created. White's was engaged in reviewing its stock control and storekeeping functions in the face of an imminent technological change which would miniaturise components and make identification of them much more difficult. The storekeeper's role was expected to absorb the increased clerical burden, and there was a probability that it would eventually come to incorporate the operation of a computer terminal, but no more general restructuring was anticipated.

The claim that recent legislation surrounding employment imposes a literacy requirement on organisations which they are obliged to 'pass on' to workers does not stand up to scrutiny. Most legislation relevant to communication with employees simply states that a particular kind of information must be displayed in the working environment or be available to the workforce, but it does not insist that assimilation is monitored. Since much of the information concerned related to employee rather than management interests, a ritual observance is possible (hence the piles of leaflets issued during induction courses).

Why, then, do organisations expend effort to recruit only literate employees when the work they will do does not entail and will not benefit from their literacy skills? Is literacy a desirable attribute in unskilled employees because it is a convenient indicator for employers of 'trainability' on the one hand, and a 'schooled' (that is, compliant) workforce on the other? And if the latter beliefs are prevalent, is there any objective basis for them, or are they merely rationalisations legitimating prejudice and 'pure' discrimination?

Explaining literacy screening policies

In recent years, labour economists have devoted considerable attention to discriminatory hiring, mostly in relation to women and black people. 'Human capital' theorists, working in a neo-classical framework that is concerned with the marginal productivity of individuals, have tended to start from an assumption that 'pure' discrimination will automatically lead, in fully competitive market situations, to lower profits for racist and sexist employers (Becker, 1971; Arrow, 1972). One basic reason for this is that discriminatory employers are effectively reducing the supply of potential employees and raising their labour costs. If a particular form of discrimination persists, it is, however, assumed to entail some mechanism that confers real economic advantages on the discriminators. Along these lines, for example, it has been argued that lower investment in education and basic skills by individuals results in lower productivity from them which, in turn, is penalised by employers with lower wage and higher unemployment rates. However, for the lower grade jobs considered above, there is no reason whatsoever to believe that greater educational attainments would raise individual levels of output. Furthermore, since lower grade work is so simple and on-the-job training minimal, there is no great need for employers to select for 'trainability'.

A suggestive modification of this human capital approach is the idea that employers always prefer long-staying workers as the basis for building a cooperative labour force. Since there are no selection tests that can reliably detect these desirable characteristics in recruits, employers require convenient indicators of them. On common-sense grounds the most relevant indicators that are immediately available are the individual's previous work and school records. (Schooling is relevant because it takes place in an institutional setting involving production and discipline: educational qualifications are significant not for the skills and knowledge they denote but as measures of application and persistence.) Within the limitations of an interview situation, these indicators are tapped via the requirement that the recruit be able to complete an application form that is mainly concerned with school and work records. Literacy thus becomes the ultimate proxy for employability.

The formal models that have been constructed for the general process of discrimination (Phelps, 1972; Spence, 1974) deal with a variety of situations in which the proxies for desired employee characteristics become stable prerequisites of jobs, irrespective of the validity or strength of the correlation between them and productivity. Once the initial beliefs of employers are translated into differential job offers (and possibly differential wage rates), they become self-fulfilling and self-confirming. New entrants are encouraged to invest in educational 'signals' by the success of their predecessors, while employers who only hire literates will never be in a position to review their prejudices. (The solution that human capital theorists offer to this state of affairs is to recommend basic remedial education for the disadvantaged.)

A complementary explanation for the ubiquity of literacy screening can be proffered, based on the structural differentiation of large bureaucratic organisations. In each of the four large organisations studied, recruitment was the responsibility of a designated personnel function consisting of at least three levels of seniority. The recruiters who held selection interviews were normally the lowest in seniority within the function. Furthermore, although they had an overall knowledge of job content and work organisation throughout a site, because of the plants' size they tended not to know all the individuals working in each section or department personally, or appreciate all the technical aspects of the various technologies. (As noted above, this sometimes led to the standard practice of giving a veto on appointments to a member of line management from the department concerned.) It is probably generally true that the personnel function in large organisations is remote from production areas and ignorant of the details of shop-floor operations. This seriously erodes the claims of recruiters to have a distinctive selection expertise, particularly for those recruiting to lower grade job categories where there is usually no vetting of qualifications or actual testing of skills. A literacy screen can in these circumstances be useful as an apparently objective and impersonal criterion on which to reject people who simply 'don't feel right' to the selector. The costs to the firm of consistently rejecting illiterate applicants can never, of course, be calculated, but in view of the evidence from the work histories of substantial mechanical and technical skills possessed by literacy students, there are grounds for doubting the wisdom of such a policy. As far as the selectors are concerned, the costs to them of rejecting an able illiterate are negligible compared to the costs of picking a 'wrong 'un' in the form of recriminations from line personnel and superiors. If, in addition to their vulnerable organisational location, selectors as individuals tend to associate illiteracy with slow-wittedness, discrimination is almost inevitable. Although unambiguous evidence on possession of stereotypes is hard to gain, it is probably not coincidental that three recruiters, when interviewed about illiteracy problems in their organisations, each produced similar, rather vague, stories about employees who caused problems because they could not read warning notices.

A summary statement can now be made about the local labour market situation and the mechanisms that lead to discrimination against illiterates. (Because most of the mechanisms are intimately bound up with modern training and personnel procedures, it is at least probable that they operate widely in large-scale enterprises.)

The majority of lower grade jobs (assemblers, machinists) contained no significant literacy element but a minority had a small character recognition and reading component (storekeepers, shop assistants). Yet, roughly only one half of 1 per cent of the 17,000 jobs covered were effectively available to adults unable to complete the application forms. Large employers rejected illiterates for the following reasons:

(a) Such organisations use literacy as a proxy for cooperativeness and 'trainability' among recruits. Once such a belief is institutionalised in selection procedures, it becomes a self-fulfilling prophecy and the organisation is never confronted with contradictory instances.
(b) Large organisations tend, through bureaucratic inertia, to rely for information on forms and records designed by highly literate staff who are either unconcerned with the problems of illiterates, or alternatively, lack the knowledge to design properly calibrated tests of functional literacy. Consequently, selection procedures build in an unnecessarily high literacy requirement which guarantees the rejection of a proportion of applicants with adequate, or more than adequate, manual skills.
(c) While contemporary manufacturing technologies mainly require very low levels of job literacy, the employment relationship is increasingly mediated by state regulation and intervention. Where legislation places an obligation on organisations to provide information for employees, this may be interpreted as imposing a literacy requirement on the workforce.
(d) Selection personnel in junior positions may not have sufficiently detailed knowledge of work arrangements in large plants to waive literacy requirements that are justifiable prerequisites for only a minority of jobs and job categories. They may also be slow to relinquish stereotypes that associate illiteracy with general stupidity and lack of skill.
(e) The job search activities of illiterates are unlikely to produce comprehensive, accurate and up to date information on vacancies and sources of advice and training. Although they are more likely to be initially aware of large local employers, anticipating that a literacy screen will be one of the hurdles to employment with them, they may steer themselves towards smaller and more informal work settings.

6
Dealing with illiteracy

Introduction

A necessary preliminary to understanding any malaise that has already been accepted as a social problem is to reconstruct the process of acceptance. In the case of illiteracy, such a reconstruction adds much greater resolution to the map of reading and writing's place within the communication systems of modern societies. The first section below presents a potted summary of the Adult Literacy Campaign in Britain in the 1970s, and it is followed by an attempt to describe the operation of the economy which sustains the demand for and supply of literacy skills. This, in turn, provides a basis from which to evaluate the frameworks of ideas and institutions which currently guide and deliver intervention and 'treatment' for illiteracy. The final section takes up the conception of literacy developed in Chapter 2 and offers an outline of the kind of agency within which it could be effectively persued.

The British Adult Literacy Campaign

In three years in the mid-1970s, adult illiteracy became a major social problem in Britain. This is not to say that the numbers of people with severe reading and writing problems increased dramatically in the period: the change that took place, roughly between 1972 and 1975, was initiated by a transformation in educational policy and public awareness. Research reported that in 1972 only 5,170 adults were receiving tuition in literacy skills, including teaching organised not only by LEAs but also the work done in hospitals, prisons and the armed services (Haviland, 1973). Then, quite suddenly, illiteracy was elevated from a non-issue appreciated only by a handful of field-workers in pioneering tuition schemes to a (temporally) high priority on the agenda of national politics.

Although the adult literacy campaign in Britain is an interesting case study in the 'natural' history of social problems, this is not the place for a detailed account and, in any case, not all of the facts are in the public domain. What can be stated briefly is that there was an apparently coincidental convergence of interest in literacy from several different official and semi-official quarters. One element was certainly the publication in 1972 of research by Start and Wells on behalf of the Department of Education and Science (DES) which suggested that about 3–4 per cent of the annual cohort of fifteen-year-old school leavers had reading ages of less than nine years (quoted in DES, 1975, 12). The report of the Russell Committee on Adult Education approached the same territory from a policy and planning standpoint by endorsing the notion of a comprehensive service which would cater:

> for all the people, including those hitherto untouched by adult education. Many of them are handicapped or disadvantaged in various ways, discouraged from participating in existing provision. . . . They merit special consideration. (DES, 1973, 61)

The third element was the early interest of BBC Education Officers, possibly stimulated by the Start and Wells findings, who initiated discussions with production staff about the possibility of a televised series for non-readers (Hargreaves, 1980, 1–2). The BBC's plans, now incorporating radio, were made public at a conference held in November 1973 entitled 'Status Illiterate – Prospects Zero'. This was organised by the British Association of Settlements, whose member groups in London and Liverpool had considerable first-hand knowledge of dealing with problems of illiteracy. The event, chaired by Lady Plowden, was a considerable success and attracted extensive media coverage. The figure of 2 million functionally illiterate British adults was repeatedly quoted and seemed to capture public attention. The conference lead to the formation of a committee, also chaired by Lady Plowden and eventually called the National Committee for Adult Literacy, to ensure organisational liaison. A bandwagon had begun to roll.

In 1974, BBC management approved plans with a budget of £800,000 for a three-year programme of broadcasting for the illiterate and semi-literate. Key elements in the plan were the use of volunteers, a telephone referral service for intending students and tutors, and independent research into the effectiveness of the project as a whole. Since these were non-broadcast activities, the BBC and the National Institute for Adult Education jointly approached the Department of Education and Science for financial assistance, and received a grant of £45,000. An approach to the Ford Foundation for similar support was also successful and finally produced (in 1975) a grant of £175,000 towards the non-broadcast activities (Hargreaves, 1980, 7–11).

The skilled lobbying of the voluntary agencies and the BBC initiative produced another governmental response in the form of £1 million earmarked to 'pump-prime' the literacy efforts of LEAs and voluntary bodies during the initial phase of broadcasting (April 1975–March 1976), primarily by the appointment of full- or part-time literacy staff to voluntary agencies and education authorities. An Adult Literacy Resource Agency (ALRA) was set up to distribute this money and support regional work with expertise and training materials, and its existence and funding were extended in February 1976 for the years 1976–7 and 1977–8. A Scottish Adult Literacy Agency was also established from April 1976 with funds of £200,000 for two years from the Scottish Education Department.

That a strong demand for literacy tuition existed was demonstrated immediately the BBC's central telephone referral service began on 1 October 1975. In the words of the broadcasting project leader:

> We had arranged that the Jimmy Young programme on Radio 2 should do an extended item [about the referral service], with Jimmy Young interviewing a non-reader, playing the record [of the title music of the television series], talking to Chris Longley about the need for volunteer tutors, and publicising the phone number. The ten staff stood by to man the lines for the first time, with the help of volunteers. By the time Jimmy Young had spoken the last figure of 01-992-5522 they were overwhelmed by an instant flood of calls on all twenty lines. The flood continued unabated for five hours and into the next day. The calls were from adults in every sort of circumstance. For many it was the first time they had ever spoken to anyone about the problem. Many were disguising the problem even from their husband, wife and children. When it was explained that it would take a few weeks before they were fixed up with help many said a few weeks would make no difference – they had been waiting for thirty years. (Hargreaves, 1980, 30–1)

Despite clear-cut evidence of client demand, responses by LEAs to contact with ALRA were variable. Some allocated sums as large as £80,000 to literacy work, while others with apparently comparable responsibilities committed as little as £3,000, giving rise to the suspicion that allocations were sometimes more a matter of 'internal juggling with the further education estimate' than a specific policy decision by the elected members of education committees (quoted in Open University, 1979, 29–30). In a patchy way, however, ALRA funding did stimulate a sharp, short-term expansion in basic education provision with some spin-off into numeracy and English as a foreign language. By February 1978, a total of 125,000 adults had received tuition, 80,000 volunteer tutors had come forward, about 4,500 full- and part-time, paid personnel were involved in literacy work and roughtly 70,000 'places' existed for tutees (Open University, 1979, 29). In February 1978, the completion of the pump-priming operation was marked by the phasing out of ALRA and its replacement by the Adult Literacy Unit (ALU, later renamed the Adult Literacy and Basic Skills Unit, ALBSU) whose annual budget of £300,000 was intended to support advisory work and special collaborative and experimental projects, with bread and butter literacy work now being financed directly by LEAs. This transition coincided with the introduction of general local government cuts in education expenditures and the widespread adoption of the principle that non-vocational adult education should be self-financing through course fees. Different authorities treated basic education differently, but in many areas, the introduction of charges reduced numbers and, as a result, provision levelled off and in some areas began to decline (see Table 6.1).

This outline has covered only some of the major institutional events that took place during the short but crucial period in the 1970s when adult literacy established itself as a deserving recipient of political time and public money.[1] It is not possible to continue the account in comparable detail because of the great heterogeneity of the initial local responses to central funding, and the subsequent turnover of projects, schemes and organisational arrangements, to which justice could only be done by means of a detailed national survey. It is, however, worth mentioning in passing one new element to enter the scene in the 1980s, that is, the increasing involvement of government departments other than Education in literacy and basic skills training. It has principally been the various arms of the Manpower Services Commission that have been

Table 6.1: *Adult literacy provision, England and Wales, 1979*[1]

	Students		*Staff*						(Thousands)
			Volunteers				Paid		
	Receiving Tuition	Waiting List	Teaching	Waiting List	Other	Total	Teaching	Admin.	Total
LEAs	63.0	2.0	29.7	4.8	0.6	35.2	3.6	1.0	4.6
Penal Est's	4.1	—	0.1	—	—	0.1	—	—	—
V'try Orgs.	2.4	0.2	1.6	0.3	0.1	2.0	—	—	0.1
Totals	69.5	2.2	31.4	5.2	0.7	37.4	3.6	1.0	4.7

Note: 1 As at February 1979.

Source: *Social Trends*, 11, 1981, Table 4.23.

especially active, with the Prison and Probation Services involved to lesser degrees. Apart from the scale of funding and the number of personnel involved in miscellaneous training roles, this development is notable in two respects. In accordance with the changed political and employment climate of the times, it has renewed the influence of 'functional' and vocational conceptions of literacy. While many of the 'grass-roots' literacy schemes originating in the 1970s took as their objective the development of the student's general powers of self-expression in an encompassing but ultimately ill-defined way, the new programmes tend to be concerned with much more specific and circumscribed goals related directly to the current demands of the labour market and employers, and to 'official' perceptions of the needs of employees. Secondly, the involvement of centralised bureaucracies in literacy training reinforces the formalising and standardising processes noted in Chapter 4 in respect of the incorporation of the Nottingham literacy scheme into the local further education framework. While there are losses and gains entailed in such developments, one almost universal consequence is diminished opportunities for volunteers.

Although these recent institutional involvements in adult literacy work are significant, they are subject to rapid repeal and reverse as political administrations are replaced or the economy moves into a new phase. If we are going to understand the deeper roots of illiteracy and recognise the different manifestations in which it presents itself as a social problem in 'advanced' societies (which we can take, for these purposes, to be those with an effective, nationwide network of elementary schooling), it will be necessary to explore the way it connects with the economic and status systems of a modern industrialised state.

The political economy of illiteracy

The characteristic conception of literacy in the contemporary world links two fundamental ideas, that literacy is a universal, basic human right that all governments are obliged to make strenuous efforts to deliver to all their capable citizens, and that it is a personal and collective economic benefit. The discussion of the history of literacy in Chapter 3 attempted, among other things, to demonstrate that neither notion has particularly deep roots. For most of recorded European history, at any rate, there has been a pronounced social stratification of literacy with entire sections of the population excluded, a state of affairs long regarded as part of the natural order, and as a result, politically uncontentious. Similarly, the theory that literacy generates economic returns and that these are the main reasons for encouraging instruction in it, a view which will be examined more fully below, is a relatively recent development certainly post-dating industrialisation.

If the proclamation of literacy as a universal human right has any serious philosophical ancestry, it is the classical, Aristotelian, conception of the 'good citizen'. Aristotle regarded it as a citizen's duty to educate himself in the conventions and procedures of the prevailing constitution, and to be familiar with the current tenor of public opinion and its likely shifts, so that he had a rough idea of what was and was not a practical policy (Parry, 1978). Because contemporary political philosophies diverge considerably from Aristotle and each other on the significance they attach to political participation, there is no consensus on what additional intellectual skills and knowledge are desirable. Those who adopt a minimalist line on participation, that is, who see it simply as a series of opportunities to express pre-established personal and collective interests, argue that the individual requires little more than a menu outlining which representatives and parties currently support his or her interests. Such a menu does not have to be in writing, and if levels of illiteracy are high, electioneering can be by public meeting or debate, with party identification established entirely by means of coloured banners or graphical logos, as is not uncommon in the Third World. Even if illiteracy is not a serious problem and press coverage is extensive, political leaders may have an affinity for oral and broadcast channels through which to make important appeals to the population.

Most of the viewpoints which give considerable importance to 'real' participation have a correspondingly high regard for the role of literacy. Those who see a close analogy between economic markets and the way the electoral process operates tend to be concerned about potential threats to the exercise of rational choice by the voter, on the one hand from the latter's possible ignorance, and on the other from the appeal political broadcasts and mass rallies make to the emotions. Since what the candidates and parties say (or write) on their own behalf may be unreliable, the informed voter should, according to this view, be able to draw on background political information covering, for example, the record of recent regimes and non-partisan assessments of the feasibility of manifesto policies. The conventional liberal-democratic wisdom for large-scale centralised, political systems is that compulsory education, plus a politically independent fourth estate, can normally guarantee mass access to this information.

Despite the genuflexions to an informed public and a free press that are required by this concept of democratic participation, there are more universal forces within the political sphere sustaining literacy. Modern regimes of all ideological complexions are obliged to conduct the bulk of their routine business with intermediary organisations and citizens by means of postal correspondence (which combines the advantages of reasonable speed and economy with the conservation of a permanent record). The preparation and maintenance of written records by career officials is close to the essence of the classic, Weberian definition of bureaucratic administration.[2] In the earliest bureaucratic systems, the corps of officials had a monopoly over the written word, but as the scale of governmental operations increased, effective political control over nations and empires necessitated the co-option of ever more literate agents. The general literacy of the population with which officials deal, normally completed by means of schools, is the logical end-point of this process of co-option. Thus, there is an especially intimate connection between bureaucracy and literacy: mass literacy is the creation of bureaucratic institutions and, at the same time, one of the principal agencies of its irresistible diffusion.

Radical practitioners and theorists of literacy invariably assert that it is a fundamental individual right, but the implications of this are not always clear. Those influenced by the work of the Brazilian educator, Paulo Freire, which is briefly considered later in this chapter, claim that tuition in reading and writing is inherently emancipatory, liberating illiterates from a state of powerlessness and giving them access to their cultural heritage and a political awareness. It is important not to react to such claims with automatic approval or instant dissent because they entail highly complex arguments. The political consequences of becoming literate in a particular society depend on a constellation of factors including, to list merely some of the most obvious, the initial social situation of the student, the character of the teacher, the teaching materials and the philosophy underlying tuition, and the prevailing political environment. At the same time, however, as these more or less straightforward aspects, there is an ideological component to be taken into account. Whether the experience of tuition is liberating or not involves judgements about the interests and consciousness of individuals and the potential of various kinds of political action and organisation. If it is to be more than an empty piece of jargonising, liberation through literacy must reflect sound linguistic and realistic political analysis.

A contrasting argument that has sometimes been employed by conservatives is that literacy (and in situations of ethnic conflict, often literacy in a specified tongue) is the price of admission to the franchise, an obligation rather than an entitlement. The history of literacy and the electorate is particularly interesting in the case of the United States. Backed by popular 'Know-Nothing' sentiment against immigrants, and particularly Irish Catholics who tended to be active supporters of the Democratic cause, Connecticut passed legislation requiring electors to take a literacy test in 1855, and Massachusetts followed two years later with a test that included a writing component (Heath, 1981, 36). The Connecticut law specified that every prospective voter had to be able to read any article of the Constitution or any section of the state statutes. Through a drafting oversight, no language was specified, obliging the registrars to gain a nodding acquaintance with a range of foreign tongues until an amendment could be passed stipulating English (Bromage, 1930, 951–2).

No other states introduced similar provisions until after the Civil War and the passage of the Fifteenth Amendment to the Constitution enfranchising the black population. As an attempt to circumvent this measure, eight Southern states introduced electoral literacy tests, starting with Mississippi in 1890, while eight other states including California, Washington and New York followed suit with miscellaneous objectives. The clear intent of the Southern states to exclude blacks is indicated by their elaborate regulations which entailed expedients to admit illiterate whites, provisions eventually declared to be unconstitutional by the Supreme Court (Bromage, 1930, 955). In the case of New York state, legislation of 1923 placed the responsibility for administering the literacy test and issuing certificates in the hands of the school rather than the electoral authorities. 'Scientific' tests were designed by educational psychologists which incorporated a standard that approximated to the reading ability of fifth grade school pupils. Comprehension questions tested for patriotism and included such topics as America, Americanisation, American history and government, citizenship and naturalisation, civic duties and institutions.

By and large, however, the contemporary debate in both highly industrialised and developing societies has long since shifted from the rights and obligations of literacy to its economic value. In the late 1950s and early 1960s, work in education, the media and development began increasingly to implicate literacy as a catalytic factor in the broadest societal processes of urbanisation and industrialisation.[3] Some of these studies, such as that by H. Golden (1957), attempted to correlate the empirical data on literacy rates and indices of economic development in particular countries, using quantitative techniques too unsophisticated to establish genuine historical linkages. Other contributions, like that of Talcott Parsons, were, as we saw in Chapter 1, too abstract to make contact with the empirical data that was available. Nevertheless, attention was aroused by findings that suggested that literates were more willing to adapt to technological and social change than illiterates (Schuman, Inkeles and Smith, 1967), and that education and literacy correlated well with support for democratic values and political parties (Lipset, 1959). As a whole, this literature was exploratory and tentative, and it was frequently culture-specific, but its non-academic audiences tended to sweep aside the footnotes and qualifications. It was read as a general encouragement for Third World investment in schooling and literacy training as a necessary ingredient in the creation of labour forces capable of utilising advanced agricultural and manufacturing technologies.

In the mid-1960s, some of these themes were taken up by the influential 'human capital' paradigm in economics which we met in the discussion of literacy and work in Chapter 5. Originally associated with the work of Theodore Schultz (1963) and Gary Becker (1975), 'human capital' is in simple terms the present value of past investments in training and skills. One of the framework's attractions was that it enabled economists to relate and consolidate two areas of interest: firstly, the demand for non-compulsory education and off-the-job training (which could be understood as workers investing in themselves by foregoing earnings during the course of training); secondly, the size of the cumulative, lifetime wage differentials between jobs that required specific qualifications and those requiring less stringent or no credentials (which could be understood as employers investing in the potentially more productive worker). As we saw in Chapter 5, this has a bearing on the explanation of how literacy has become the ultimate employment criterion even for manual work. To recap briefly, the human capital explanation rests on two key assumptions: that competition will in the long run eliminate any kind of discrimination by employers between job applicants that does not result directly in superior productivity and/or lower costs (Becker, 1971; Arrow, 1972); that while employers do not believe that degrees and other educational certificates automatically raise productivity, the latter are taken to 'signal' a disciplined and persistent personality who minimises costs by staying with a firm and remaining cooperative (Arrow, 1973a; Spence, 1974).

The 'pecuniary calculus' that human capital economists developed to evaluate the costs and benefit of increasing labour force skills had applications to literacy in both developed and underdeveloped contexts. Research by Blaug, specifically addressed to educational planners in poor countries, identified several ways in which adult literacy programmes, as against the enlargement of school enrolment, were cost-effective means of increasing productivity, stimulating the demand for technical training, and strengthening the appeal of economic incentives. Blaug calculated (1966, 395) that the economic benefits of school education would have to be four or five times greater than the benefits of adult literacy to produce identical benefit-cost ratios (mainly because schooling requires capital investment well in advance of any returns, and also because adult students can continue producing). He did not, however, accept the then prevalent view that literacy was a sufficient condition for the transformation of subsistence economies into modern cash-exchange economies, and he remained cautious about its role in established industrial settings. He cited evidence that possession of less than six years of primary schooling appeared to confer little advantage in terms of higher wages, but on the other hand, repeated the orthodoxy that 'the aim of a functional literacy campaign is to bring the illiterate to a level where they can make profitable use of vocational and technical training, whether in industry or agriculture' (1966, 410). This latter statement is an example of the sin of economism, the reduction of a complex and multi-faceted activity to only those of its elements that have a market value that can conveniently be measured. The disastrous international consequences of treating literacy as an appendage to the process of transferring advanced productive technologies were dealt with in Chapter 2.

A further demonstration of literacy's economic importance, this time in a Western industrial context, is offered by Bormuth (1978) who marshals a very large set of indicators to produce a societal cost-benefit analysis of literacy. In summary, his approach entails the calculation of the aggregate contribution of literacy to the US gross national product – via such factors as the monetary value of the time expended on reading and writing at work, and the value of the printed material in circulation – set against the total costs of instruction. Bormuth argues that the evidence points to increasing amounts of information being exchanged in the printed channel, that the personal and social investment in literacy is rising, and that the (monetary) benefits of literacy exceed the costs by a factor of five. Perhaps significantly, he does not attempt to demonstrate that the marginal return from further investment in literacy will be greater than that from investment in any other medium of communication.

Both the human capital and Bormuth's cost-benefit analyses embody a fundamental misconception about the nature of literacy, one whose clarification can help to resolve several theoretical and practical difficulties. This misconception is partially articulated in passing by Bormuth himself who concludes his accountancy with the remark that:

> being the only literate in a society is about as desirable as owning the only telephone in town – the greater the number of literates in a society, the more valuable is the literacy of those who achieve it. (1978, 157)

Restating this in rather more precise terms, public and private investment in literacy has been justified on the grounds that it is capable, when mastered beyond the functional threshold, of earning monetary rewards for its possessors. Furthermore, the higher the proportion of a population acquiring functional literacy, the greater its per caput value.

There are two major flaws in these assertions. The first is that, difficult though it may be to price, literacy is undoubtedly more valuable, both individually and collectively, in certain political and cultural environments, for example, those with a relatively uncensored press, public libraries, affordable books, progressive legislation on access to official information, efficient and secure postal services, a tradition of imaginative literature, adequate controls on the content of advertisements. In such an environment, almost any attainments in literacy will have a great variety of potential applications and uses, and it is likely to be valued by its possessors irrespective of the marketability of their skills.

We have already seen that in order to use the monetary indicators so crucial to cost-benefit analysis, literacy has been shrunk to its utilitarian and instrumental core. One of the factors that has been left entirely out of account is the important dimension of social status. Chart 6.1 attempts to reintroduce status into the picture. It offers an admittedly crude graph of the relations between various levels of literacy competence and the status associated with them. At the foot of the curve are the performances below fluency that are liable to earn negative status or 'stigma', severe in the case of total or near-total incompetence, milder in the case of minor grammatical errors or misspelling. In the central region is a plateau which represents 'average' or 'correct' performance which tends to pass unremarked and neither earns nor loses status. The stigma of not being able to read or write is, in structural terms, the counterpart of the very high public esteem available to those who are able to exercise their accomplishments creatively (novelists, journalists, published authors generally), an esteem that is not always associated with commensurate financial rewards! There are also many private and domestic opportunities to display above-average fluency conspicuously and to earn prestige by doing so (for instance, by completing crosswords, or conducting a witty correspondence).

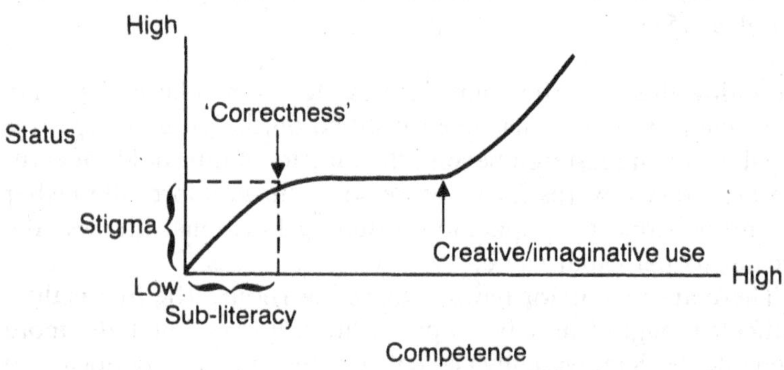

Chart 6.1: *Levels of literacy and social status*

In any arena of social status, esteem is at least partly derived from exclusivity, and applied to the case of literacy this means that a widespread mastery of a particular competence will devalue it. Literacy, and education in general, belong to what has been called the 'positional economy'. Popularised by Fred Hirsch (1977, 27), this concept refers to goods, services and social relationships that are either intrinsically scarce, or whose attractiveness declines as the number of owners or participants increases. The positional economy is perfectly exemplified by the inflation that affects literacy and other credentials in the industrial labour market. In the unskilled sector, 'lower grade' employees must increasingly demonstrate a literacy competence where once a respectable employment record sufficed. At the top end of the labour market, examination certificates and diplomas remain good investments to the extent that they raise an individual's income relative to what it (hypothetically) would have been if that person had remained unqualified but had been compelled to compete with qualified rivals. In situations where everyone is similarly qualified, certificates cease to improve incomes. To use Hirsch's own analogy, once some people stand on tiptoe in order to gain a better view, others will be forced to do the same, everyone ending up in their original relative positions.

The consequences of the process of inflation in required standards of literacy reach out well beyond the sphere of work and do not only affect the severely illiterate. Consider, for instance, those people whose attainments place them just on the left edge of the central plateau of Chart 6.1, that is, who have achieved an 'average' competence. Such people will expect to be accepted as fully literate in almost any public situation and anticipate no threats to their self-respect. Although they make slips and are parties to misunderstandings, there is normally no reason for them to doubt their capabilities. Suppose, however, that schools and literacy programmes were suddenly to improve their performance and increase the overall percentage of people falling within the band of average competence. The inevitable result would, over time, be a rise in the minimum standard of performance deemed to be competent and 'acceptable'. As long as literacy is associated with considerations of social standing, any collective improvement must always be to the disadvantage of the least able. This is not to say, of course, that individuals will not benefit from raising their skills or that initiatives like adult literacy campaigns are somehow undesirable. On the contrary, the implication is that sympathetic but effective assistance will always be needed for those experiencing difficulties. Furthermore, it indicates that some aspects of the illiteracy problem are not amenable to comprehensive solutions, and it undermines the ideal of a functional literacy for all: there is no fixed level of attainment, even within a specific society, that guarantees the least literate parity of treatment with their more literate peers.

The scale of illiteracy: misreading the problem

The last section paved the way for recasting the problem of illiteracy so that it can be related to the basic economic and social realities of Western market societies. With certain honourable exceptions, however, the mass media presentation of illiteracy (and many other social problems) encourages a popular understanding in narrower, almost entirely quantitative, terms. The historical and cultural circumstances out of which a prevailing distribution of communication skills has been created, the effectiveness of current forms of intervention, the proper place of a problem in the hierarchy of policy priorities, are all presumed to be 'technical' issues of interest only to specialist audiences, and they take a back seat as coverage is built around the most basic statistical trends and the bald question of whether the situation is getting better or worse. In this way, illiteracy comes to be 'naturally' encapsulated in estimates of the percentage of adults that have severe difficulties with reading, spelling and writing.

Less commonly, concern about literacy may be expressed in another form. It is alleged from some quarters that a long-term decline is in progress in reading as an adult activity valued in its own right. The sustained 'deep-reading' of book-length texts has become a casualty of new lifestyles and leisure preferences and this, it is claimed, both reflects and accelerates the loss of higher-order literacy skills. As reading for its own sake declines, the capacity to appreciate and respond imaginatively to the heritage of 'serious' literature is diminished to the point where it is retained only by a tiny minority, endangering literature's role as a source of pleasure and intellectual and moral enlightenment. Let us examine, in turn, each of these two ways of representing the scale and character of illiteracy as a social malaise, and pinpoint their limitations.

It is safe to say that we do not know from any form of direct measurement what percentage of the adult population could reasonably be considered to be sub-literate. (Direct measurement would entail monitoring the materials individuals actually encounter and generate in daily life and how well they and their recipients handle them.) The technical difficulties of the various forms of indirect measurement have already been examined in Chapter 2, and we can concentrate here on the substantive questions.

What data that are available fall into two broad categories. The first category is made up of research that in terms of conventional educational thinking is regarded as 'hard' because its results are derived from repeatedly applying standardised reading tests to national samples of school pupils. The statistical analysis in *The Trend of Reading Standards*, to take perhaps the best-known British illustration, culminates in some cautious generalisations about a gradual post-war elimination of total illiteracy combined with a reduction in the percentage of 'semi-illiterates', though the latter trend appears to have been partly reversed in the 1960s (Start and Wells, 1972, 52). It is worth noting that in order to ensure comparability, the criterion of illiteracy was a 1938 reading age of under seven years, and that of semi-literacy, a reading age between seven and nine years. The tests employed were the Watts-Vernon and the National Foundation for Educational Research's NS6, silent reading comprehension tests of the sentence completion type. The use of measures which deal only with highly restricted aspects of reading and not at all with writing, in combination with arbitrary, and by most contemporary criteria of functionality, very low, 'reading age' thresholds of illiteracy, was severely criticised in Chapter 2 and again those arguments should need no recapitulation.

As its title indicates, *The Trend of Reading Standards* set out to measure the long-term changes in one staple kind of school reading task, and since the research did not attempt to address the crucial 'demand' side of the literacy question – the relative difficulty of everyday reading and writing tasks and their possible alteration between 1938 and 1970 – its bearing (and the bearing of most other school-test-based reading research) on adult functional literacy is extremely tenuous.[4]

The second category of information derived from research studies is conventionally regarded, rightly or wrongly, as 'soft' because it depends on respondents' self-assessments rather than 'objective' tests. A recent example is the special analysis of the literacy (and numeracy) of a national sample of twenty-three-year-olds based on data collected in a longitudinal study of a cohort of people born during one week of March 1958 (ALBSU, 1983). As part of a broader inquiry into physical, educational and social development known as a whole as the National Child Development Study, interviewers asked the subjects about whether they had experienced difficulties since leaving school with reading, writing and spelling. Problems with reading were reported by 4 per cent of the sample with a further 6 per cent admitting spelling or writing problems. Out of the total of 10 per cent with some kind of illiteracy problem (12 per cent of men, 7 per cent of women), just under a third claimed that they experienced difficulties in daily life, especially with forms, letters and the job application process. Even among the group who experienced daily difficulties, only 15 per cent had attended some kind of remedial class or course (ALBSU, 1983, 4–5).

What one person considers a problem, another is likely to regard as too trivial or perhaps too demeaning to admit, but with the resources available the exact nature and scale of the problems respondents encountered could not be accurately established. Moreover, twenty-three-year-olds cannot be taken as typical of the entire population (though the report quotes numeracy evidence which suggests that this cohort is possibly more able than the average). Despite these considerable limitations, these 'soft' data bear more significantly on illiteracy than the reading test statistics just reported. In the light of the perspective on literacy and illiteracy developed in Chapter 2, it is clear that we need to consider the information requirements of the person concerned, the relative ease of access to the appropriate written channel, the aims and character of the available materials, and not solely the individual's text-processing capacity in the abstract. Whether or not individuals feel they have a problem is, in a sense, a blanket measure of all these complex and interdependent variables. Admittedly, it is a 'personalised' measure that does not lend itself to sophisticated statistical manipulation, but this is by no means a fatal defect. Such data are able to shed light on the decision to seek assistance and are therefore relevant to the intelligence requirements of the agencies and groups attempting to estimate need and allocate resources. There is, in any case, little prospect of more reliable or more sophisticated figures becoming available on a national basis because of the expense involved.

It is easy to seize on the figure of 10 per cent and make capital out of it. A lobby exists that would use it as a club to bludgeon teachers and schools for failing in their basic mission, and there are others who would take it as evidence of a permanent pool of ineducability and possibly deteriorating levels of intelligence. The danger of a preoccupation with crude social rates of this kind is that they imply that the essence of the problem is an incompetent minority of individuals unable to deal with the transparently clear communication of the majority, and it is this emphasis that fuels wild diagnoses of intellectual decline and extravagant critiques of the educational system. The current situation may much more profitably be seen as the consequence of the long historical process, featured in Chapter 3, in which more and more areas of social life are gradually penetrated and affected by written materials. As the bureaucratisation of work and the specialisation of leisure and domestic activities increase, so formal written transactions and procedures become escapable only at considerable cost.

While it is a relatively easy task to establish that there is more written information in circulation than ever before (some very basic figures are given in Chapter 7), it is more difficult to confirm the equally important and parallel trend, an increase in the complexity of these written communications. The translation of scientific and technological developments into consumer products and services, and the growth in the number and size of the organisations with which the ordinary person has transactions, bring 'problematic' printed materials into most homes and workplaces. These documents are problematic either because they contain specialised information at the boundaries of the recipient's technical knowledge (operating instructions for equipment, interlocking rules of eligibility for pension schemes, formally expressed conditions of guarantee), or because their internal organisation, clarity of expression and overall intelligibility pose severe difficulties for their intended consumers (or commonly, of course, because of a combination of the two attributes).

The proliferation and greater complexity of printed information is a global process and few are unaffected. Even those who have received higher education or possess demonstrable skill in communication are unlikely to be able to apply these resources outside their own specialisms. The professional scientist or engineer, at home with calculus, computer languages and circuit diagrams, is not always the person to interpret a company balance sheet, to decipher the diplomatic statements released during international negotiations, or to unravel the paperwork generated by a local government planning inquiry. At the same time, the lawyer and accountant may be equally at sea outside the fairly narrow boundaries of their knowledge.

Even within a specific sphere of technical information, those wielding expertise may be poorly equipped to pass on their professional judgements and understanding of the matter at hand to lay people. (This kind of communication is presumably both in their own and also in their clients' interests: professionals, however, have an understandable if not justifiable reluctance to share the theoretical or informational base on which their judgements draw.) This inability reflects attitudes to communications with the laity engendered during professional training. The lawyer's standard approach, for example, to improving the precision and resolving the ambiguities in a draft document is likely to be a resort (or greater resort) to linguistic formulas that are legally tried and tested, that is, to legalese. Whether legalese is capable of establishing fixed and juridically indisputable meanings is open to question,[5] but assuming this is so, any modifications in its direction will make a document less accessible to the lay people whose interests it is intended to serve, with the result that the control of the transaction shifts a little from the client. A legal illustration is used only for convenience; the same dilemmas arise in most dealings between occupational specialists and their clients. The growth of advertising and public relations agencies inside and outside large organisations is testimony to the strategic role the management of information now plays in business and commerce. Even where there is no desire to flatter or deceive, manufacturers of equipment designed for the mass market (such as hi-fi systems, microcomputers and large consumer durables such as cars and kitchen equipment), sensitive to complaints from customers about their engineers' incomprehensible manuals, increasingly subcontract the writing of documentation to outside companies skilled in the authorship of instructional texts.

Illiteracy rates have little to reveal about these matters. Arguing over the true percentage is a distraction governed by the belief, unfortunately not always a groundless belief, that governments and publics are only responsive to social problems that threaten by force of numbers to swamp the status quo. As we have repeatedly emphasised, illiteracy rates even when protected from statistical massages to get them to the right magnitude, are extremely unreliable. UNESCO regularly and solemnly produces weighty tables of rates for Third World states that have been unable for several decades to mount an efficient population census: such countries are locked into the production of specious returns by the need to show their neighbours and aid-givers that they are making satisfactory progress towards the impossible goal of the total elimination of illiteracy.

Although it is still keenly played as part of the struggle for resources, the illiteracy numbers' game is especially irrelevant to the leading industrial nations, all of whom can claim similar, single figure rates. In the environment of well-established systems of compulsory schooling, the threat may appear in the form of the 'higher illiteracy', fears that mass education diminishes, or fails to preserve, a heritage of 'classic' or 'creative' learning. According to George Steiner, one of its most eloquent defenders, classic literacy entails an intimate familiarity with an essential tradition of European literature running back to the Homeric and Vergilian epics. In Protestant societies, it covers not only a mainstream of poetry and drama but also the committal to memory of parts of the Authorised Version and the Book of Common Prayer. Classic literacy is described in terms of a facility with the structure and language of the texts and a capacity to pick up their internal allusions and echoes, but its ultimate expression is a sensibility, a recognition of the authority of the intellectual and moral standards which the books enshrine, and a respect and love for books themselves. Steiner accepts that classic literacy has always been the possession of an elite and that it requires for its perpetuation 'a bourgeois order founded on certain hierarchies of literacy/purchasing power, leisure, caste, servants, relations between sexes and generations, segregated zones of silence and inactivity' (1978b, 189). Since it cannot supply the foundations for classic literacy, mass education is 'organised amnesia', conducive to shallow and semi-attentive reading adequate to the caption, the hoarding and pulp fiction, but inimical to the 'full' reading which 'will more and more become the craft and pursuit of a minority trained to do the job and who themselves probably hope to write a book' (1978b, 201).

Steiner's writings on literacy are undisguised special pleading on behalf of a social minority dedicated to the preservation of a very particular and exclusive sub-culture. He is complacent about the values celebrated in this sub-culture being destined always to remain the concern of a minority, and he discounts the possibility that the visual media (or any other technological or social development) will bring the written classics to new audiences capable subsequently of returning to the original texts.

The critics of Steiner's position, like Edmund Leach (1977, 1978), seized somewhat predictably on the fact that it treats those familiar with a relatively narrow corpus of humanistic writing as fully literate even though they may be ignorant of even the barest fundamentals of science and technology, and are totally dependent on the 'life-support' services provided by less literate technicians to sustain their cultured existence. The thrust of Leach's argument was precisely to devalue 'classic' literacy and to question its privileged position in the curriculum (particularly in relation to artisanal skills and the 'practical tools of everyday living' that since the invention of the telephone and television depend decreasingly on a facility with the written word).

Much of the dispute between Steiner and Leach has little to do with literacy as such. It is very largely rhetorical, the stylistic clash of a conservative absolutist and a radical relativist. Leach is clearly correct in suggesting that modern systems of education judge intellectual merit too narrowly in terms of literary sensibilities. Steiner is right to say that only a minority are interested in and capable of the engagement of these sensibilities with a classical literary tradition. But the key point that both seem to overlook is that the ability to carry out a sensitive, 'deep' reading of a text is in fact a highly practical skill, entirely relevant to everyday circumstances and fully applicable to utilitarian documents. An awareness of the logic of a text, its innuendo and nuance, its unstated premisses and its persuasive definitions is potentially just as significant to the unemployed teenager with a supplementary benefit form, or the householder about to sign a contract for double-glazing, as it is to the literary critic settling down to one of his or her favoured authors. What holds true of reading is also applicable to writing. Despite Leach's disparagement of it in the *Observer* (19.3.1977) and elsewhere, the ability to compose a clearly expressed and grammatical piece of prose is not a skill that telecommunications and word-processors devalue. We have seen the evidence in Chapter 5 that it is an extremely valuable asset, socially and economically. To point out that many aspects of written style and the etiquette of correspondence are tied up with the antiquated social snobberies of educated elites is to state the obvious. To suggest to sixteen-year-old school leavers or adult literacy students that they are dispensable is to mislead them gravely.

Responding to social disadvantage

The objective in any sociological analysis is to explain the collective and institutional aspects of social events, and in line with this, the previous sections have emphasised the educational, labour market and social prestige mechanisms affecting the demand and supply of reading and writing skills. This is not, however, the main perspective from which illiteracy is viewed by those professionally engaged in combating it. While a variety of convictions and stances currently co-exist, the abiding concern especially among tutors and literacy organisers is to persuade individuals and groups who have experienced hardship as a result of illiteracy to take advantage of the services they provide. For such practitioners, and indeed for those at the 'sharp end' of many other welfare initiatives, a social problem naturally manifests itself in the most concrete of human terms, a stream of individual clients. This is the raw material that embodies the 'problem' and which presents itself for treatment. In comparison with this reality, theoretical explanations in terms of causal factors the practitioners cannot manipulate can appear to be remote and impractical.

Reconciling an apparently abstract sociological stance with the practical concerns of literacy workers necessitates a two-stage operation. In the first stage, we must locate what is actually done on behalf of adults with deficiencies in basic skills within the range of possible modes of social intervention for this type of social problem. This is the objective of the present section. Then (in the next section), the implications of the sociological analysis can be teased out and translated into broad policy options.

Socially organised reactions to social need, disadvantage or deprivation can take any or all of at least five analytically separate forms. (Since we are preoccupied with illiteracy, we can restrict our attention to forms of intervention applicable to illiteracy.) The significance of these forms or modes of social response is that they not only circumscribe the content of policies designed to alleviate or eliminate a particular problem, but also determine the character of the agencies set up to implement such policies. More specifically, each mode demarcates a limited range of possibilities with respect to the way a problem can be authoritatively defined, the organisational structure and goals of the responding institution(s), the social origins and training of personnel, client admission/recruitment procedures, treatment regimes, criteria of success, etc. The classification of a form of social welfare by its mode of intervention provides, at a minimum, a convenient shorthand for the overall style and objectives of a piece of social welfare engineering, but one of the other major purposes of this present classification is to indicate how much can be achieved by looking at illiteracy through a 'wide-angle' lens and by considering the less obvious alternatives and complements to training. The five modes which will concern us are set out in schematic fashion in Chart 6.2.

Condition	Response	Means	Goal	Application to illiteracy
1 Sickness	Treatment	Clinical intervention	Remittance	
1 Handicap	Rehabilitation	Compensatory aids	Alleviation	Dyslexia
2 Ignorance	Training	Instruction	Mastery	Orthodox literacy tuition
3 Incapacity	Therapy	Counselling	Adjustment assimilation autonomy	'Conscientisation'
4 Deprivation	Welfare	Reallocation of material resources	Benefit	Positive discrimination
5 Deviance	Control	Isolation containment Physical coercion	Correction conformity	Negative discrimination

Chart 6.2: *A classification of social responses to disadvantage*

Before examining these modes in more detail, it should be stressed that it would be unrealistic to anticipate a consistent one-to-one correspondence between one of the modes and the structure and policies of concrete institutions; nearly all 'welfare' agencies operate in different modes at different times, or attempt to combine separate modes in different spheres of their activities. The characteristic problems universally encountered by prisons can, for instance, be understood in terms of the way their regimes attempt simultaneously to combine features from modes 2, 3 and 5. Furthermore, it would also be wise to bear in mind that all welfare interventions are politically delicate, and with agencies sensitive about their public relations, the definitions and terminology they themselves employ can rarely be completely reliable indicators of the activities actually taking place on the ground. Finally, too much importance should not be attached to the terms selected as labels for each mode: familiar words have been preferred to neologisms despite the fact that they are far from neutral or impartial, but in most cases the connotation is much narrower than common usage.

Mode 1 covers the orthodox medical model of 'treatment', that is, any intervention designed to re-establish physical and mental equilibria by repairing perceived physiological or neurological lesions (or other defects) in the individual. The aim of clinical treatment is, of course, the remittance of sickness or disease and the return of normal functions to the sufferer. 'Rehabilitation' is very similar and differs only in that it embraces irreversible physical and mental handicaps where the aim of medical or para-medical agencies has to be the limitation of (or compensation for) impairment rather than full remittance.

While illiteracy is not generally understood to be an illness, there are some clinicians and psychologists who believe that a proportion of the people who experience difficulties are suffering from a medically recognisable condition: dyslexia. 'Dyslexia' originated as a term for symptomatic problems with reading within a syndrome of impairment that followed discrete brain damage in hitherto competent adults. Later, a quite distinct condition, 'specific developmental dyslexia' was postulated which involved similar reading and writing problems in children who were not known to be brain injured or retarded and were often of high intelligence.

The existence and character of dyslexia remains a topic of controversy among experts, and some literacy schemes discourage their personnel from employing it as a diagnosis of adults' difficulties. It is sufficient to note here that no distinctively clinical 'treatment' is available for people diagnosed as dyslexic. Although some educational psychologists prescribe practice drills and programmes of exercises for dyslexic children, their content differs only in emphasis from orthodox techniques of reading instruction.

Mode 2, 'training', embraces those operations which attempt, using varied strategies of instruction, media and types of instructor, to create or renew personal capacities, skills and knowledge for an individual or group's benefit. In the current sense, it is restricted to specialised programmes of instruction which attempt to make a recognisable cognitive input of some kind. This distinguishes 'training' from, among other things, forms of rehabilitation like physiotherapy or mobility instruction for the blind, which seek to increase physical capacities.

At one extreme of mode 2 lie forms of what is sometimes euphemistically termed 'corrective training', typified by traditional custodial regimes, where the resort to means like punishment and stern discipline render them indistinguishable from interventions in mode 5. At another extreme, the skills being inculcated may be taken to require distinctive attitudes for their successful application or, alternatively, the course of instruction may be so rigorous or so lengthy that a substantial alteration in the personality of the trainee is inevitable, at which point the response merges with mode 3. (Schooling itself can be excluded since in the setting of industrial societies it has developed into an entire phase of the individual's life-cycle with extremely diffuse objectives that include elements of both modes 3 and 5.)

Training is the mode that has acquired a virtual monopoly over welfare responses to illiteracy: it is the principal means employed by the great majority of literacy programmes and literacy agencies, and its central problem, shared with all types of training institutions, is the recruitment of suitable trainees. In the case of Britain, the linkage between the condition of illiteracy and the training response has become virtually reflex particularly in the thinking of those volunteer tutors whose experience encompasses little else. In a process that is not unfamiliar in other social problems in which a single form of response dominates, the condition being confronted comes to be perceived 'back-to-front' through the refracting lens of the response. As literacy schemes and centres become increasingly established and integrated into the mainstream of adult education, their freedom to manoeuvre is reduced and there are decreasing opportunities to break out of a role that begins and ends with the provision of instruction. More importantly, the 'operational' conception of illiteracy gradually narrows to exclude those kinds of cases or types of difficulty not thought likely to benefit from tuition. The open door policy that some literacy centres believe themselves to operate is necessarily always a romantic ideal. The established referral network with other welfare agencies will intercept and deflect at an early stage some marginal clients (such as, for instance, those who have been designated as ESN, educationally sub-normal, for whom the specialised help needed is not likely to be on hand). However, the principal filtering mechanism for 'difficult' types of case felt (often with some justification) to be out of a scheme's range is its use of selective channels of publicity in combination with a particular pattern of arrangements for tuition. The times and venues of tuition, waiting lists, access to home tuition, all these are selective mechanisms which can be manipulated more or less deliberately to attract a client population of students with 'manageable' characteristics. Finally, the initial interview provides some scope for the nature and severity of the client's 'presenting' problem to be interpreted or re-interpreted by literacy staff, with the result that it is rare for clients and their sponsors to have to be told directly that they cannot be helped.

The selection and 'creaming off' of preferred types of client can be expected to take place in all social problem agencies, but where a range of response modes are offered in parallel, clients excluded by one mode stand a chance of fitting in elsewhere. Where a single mode of response dominates a social problem, the consequences of exclusion are much more serious, and this places a premium on developing alternatives to the training response. These will be examined in the next section.

Returning to the classification of responses, as implied above, mode 3 approaches the individual client on a broad front and aims to induce comprehensive changes in attitudes, ideology and self-definition. The condition the potential client is experiencing is conceived to lie within him or herself and to be treatable by a process that transforms key aspects of that self via an assortment of therapies and resocialisation techniques whose common objective is the creation or enhancement of personal autonomy. These techniques range from 'classical' psychotherapies through many varieties of counselling to the conversion activities of 'born-again' religious sects.

It was suggested in Chapter 4 that in the minority of students with a 'personal' orientation, illiteracy could give rise to disabling anxieties and general feelings of inferiority. Whatever the student's orientation, severe illiteracy may just be one element in a collection of interacting personal problems which, as they come out into the open, can swamp the skills and resources of the average tutor. Literacy schemes face a dilemma over the lead they give to their tutors over intervening in these problems. They can say little or nothing in the course of tutor training on the grounds that tutors will ignore all advice anyway and get involved or not as their instincts dictate. Alternatively, they can issue explicit warnings about the hazards of amateur counselling and stress the importance of formally referring all delicate problems beyond reading and writing for specialist advice.

A therapeutic response based on counselling as a specialised supplement to training for those whose illiteracy is exacerbated by psychological problems is not the only way mode 3 bears on literacy work. The writings of the Brazilian educator, Paulo Freire, can be seen as an attempt to synthesise the key aspects of modes 2 and 3. Although the key term used in connection with his approach is the almost untranslatable 'conscientacao' rather than 'therapeutic', it does have among its objectives the kind of transformation of identity characteristic of mode 3. Freire argues that the illiterate peasants of the Third World have been pacified and spiritually impoverished by a 'culture of silence' which serves the interests of the politically powerful. Literacy tuition is an opportunity not simply to transfer a basic skill but to introduce the learner to a new and literating culture. His form of tuition seeks to open up a dialogue between educator and learner, exploring their common linguistic heritage in a way calculated to promote the development of a critical consciousness and political awareness.

Freire raises some fundamental issues concerning the value of acquiring literacy and its social and political functions, but the cultural gulf between the societies within which 'conscientacao' was developed and the settings of the literacy campaigns of the industrialised First World render any direct importation of materials or organisation impossible. His influence has been, broadly speaking, on the creation of a pedagogical climate which places great importance on treating the adult learner as an adult, entailing a recognition of the learner's existing experience but opening the way to a self-critical stance towards it. One of the fundamental obstacles to any more direct application is that the appeal of mode 2 training derives partly from the way it can be bolted on to bureaucratically organised education systems, while a Freire-style mode 3 response requires something much closer to a political movement, the necessary support for which is only likely to be forthcoming in highly charged and socially polarised situations.[6]

Mode 4 is the most miscellaneous of the categories of response and it covers 'welfare' operations of two major kinds. In the first, benefits in the form of cash payments, materials or services are allocated directly to the deprived individuals to reduce the personal costs of the depriving condition (a hypothetical illustration might be subsidised telephone rental for 'registered' illiterates). The second kind represents a form of indirect, collective subsidy via an attempt to modify the physical or social environment in the deprived group's favour. Examples of this would include publicity campaigns to inform the general public of a group's needs and problems, and any legislation that enforces special consideration, standards or priorities for a group's benefit (such as non-discrimination against illiterates within certain categories of employment).

Although a reasonable case could undoubtedly be made out, it is, of course, unlikely that the provision of direct cash payments for illiteracy will be incorporated into any welfare system in the foreseeable future. A more realistic strategy might involve the introduction of self-financing subsidies. As an example, consider the economics of a scheme to improve the readability of materials in mass circulation (such as official forms, leaflets, instruction manuals, timetables). The task of affecting the improvement would necessarily extend the production time of the publications involved, and possibly necessitate more expensive production methods (multiple type founts, more pages, the incorporation of graphic devices, colour printing). In some instances, experts external to the producing organisation would have to be employed, so the improvement in comprehensibility can be expected to incur significant costs. The publishers involved might well need to be persuaded that the extra expenditure could be recouped under other headings, and indeed, an improvement in the intelligibility of official or commercial documentation should bring benefits in the form of a greater understanding of the product, service or arrangements described by the documentation, which in turn should result in a reduced number of queries from the public to be dealt with by counter staff, fewer office-staff hours spent on the telephone and a less voluminous correspondence to produce, post and file. The delivery of this form of assistance is discussed further in the next section.

The fifth and final mode to be considered here adopts, as we have seen, the 'corrective' stance more commonly accepted as appropriate to crime and serious political or organisational deviation. It consists of an armoury of negative sanctions designed to marginalise and stigmatise those defined as deviant, with the objectives both of deterring others and of removing individuals from familiar (and thus supportive) settings in order to inculcate new values and behaviour. In relation to illiteracy, mode 5 rarely if ever takes a fully institutionalised form: it operates informally at a face-to-face level via slighting remarks and other kinds of interpersonal rejection. The disparagement of personal incompetences of various kinds is a diffuse phenomenon with complex psychological roots and a broad role in the determination of individual prestige within peer groups. However, while the transmission of stigma has a local and low-level character, the creation of semi-institutionalised hierarchies of prestige, as described earlier in this chapter, becomes possible if popular sentiments are indirectly supported by selection and competition based on literacy attainments in classrooms, the job market and work organisations.

Remedying illiteracy

It was suggested above that although training responses have dominated the adult literacy scene in the so-called advanced societies, important alternatives and complements as yet largely untapped exist within what has been termed the 'welfare mode'. A need to consider alternatives springs directly from some of the institutional processes discussed in the penultimate section, particularly the inevitable selectivity of instructional agencies, a selectivity exacerbated by the reluctance of adults, with certain of the orientations outlined previously, to come forward for this type of assistance. The sociological conception of literacy presented in Chapters 1 and 2 provides a further reason for seeking new strategies. To recapitulate briefly, it was suggested that practically usable literacy, whether we wish to call it 'functional' or not, always has to incorporate substantive information and extra-linguistic skills. It was further suggested that illiteracy should not be seen solely as an attribute of the consumers of written information, for it reflects, in part, the abilities and intentions of its producers and publishers. By excluding these aspects, the relatively narrow operational definition of illiteracy that prevails confines attention to only one of the parties in literacy transactions. The teaching of basic reading and writing skills to adults has been artificially divorced from its objective – the task of transmitting information – giving rise to a proliferation of helping agencies operating in an independent and uncoordinated fashion. Improvements to the comprehensibility of widely disseminated written information, a kind of positive discrimination on behalf of its consumers, would benefit not only those who are clearly, even in their own eyes, sub-literate, but many who presently handle printed materials with difficulty but still resolutely resist designation as illiterate. The rest of this section explores, in necessarily broad terms, a strategy for assisting a very wide range of consumers of written information by means of a modest reorganisation of existing literacy agencies and services.

At the heart of the proposal are twin aims: firstly, a desire to coordinate and strengthen all activities that promote literacy (in its extended sense of text-handling skills plus information) in whatever guise and under whatever aegis they currently take place; secondly, to foster worthwhile literacy initiatives and developments which to date have taken place only on an experimental or localised basis. The primary means of attaining these objectives is the creation of an organisational umbrella, the Community Information Service (CIS). This would consist at a local level entirely of representatives of agencies involved either in basic skills training or the dissemination of written information to the public. The core would consist of representatives drawn on a part-time basis from the staff of existing organisations and groups such as the public library service, Citizens' Advice Bureaux (CAB), health, legal and consumer advice centres, claimants' unions, skill training workshops, Social Service departments of local authorities, the other miscellaneous welfare, minority and voluntary schemes. The objectives of bringing together representatives of such an assortment of agencies would be to develop the kind of liaison that at present seems to be exceptional. The work, for instance, of the average public library touches on the problems of illiteracy at many points, yet the display of a literacy logo by an issue desk often means no more than the provision of a shelf of books and pamphlets for use alongside tuition, instead of underlining the availability within the library of specialised skills or services backed up by comprehensive cooperation with literacy centres. The reverse problem arises at literacy centres where the training in assimilation skills is available but the information the clients wish to acquire is often lacking.

At their regular meetings CIS members would coordinate their established activities into coherent patterns and programmes. It is true that referral networks already exist in some areas but where they consist of little more than lists of the appropriate telephone numbers, they are unlikely to promote more fundamental cooperation. Out of sustained contact and planning of the kind envisaged could come the mutual confidence to promote new joint ventures. These ventures could develop in many directions including arrangements to permit the exchange of skills and expertise among CIS personnel themselves, but a couple of more detailed examples might suggest the range of possibilities.

Established professional occupations like the law and medicine handle their subject-matters by means of specialised technical vocabularies acquired during training. The use of this vocabulary in oral or written communication with clients is a frequent and familiar source of bewilderment and confusion. It is not easy to counter the dominant professional view that these difficulties are inherent and attributable to the complexity of the bodies of theoretical knowledge being applied. Nevertheless, for many, the suspicion remains that at least some technical obscurity serves the latent function of placing the client at a strategic disadvantage within the professional relationship. Even if it is not deliberately designed to intimidate the laity, this obscurity undoubtedly causes a great deal of everyday misunderstanding that advice agencies and self-help groups struggle, not always effectively, to repair. A CIS-sponsored programme of publication on behalf of such groups could bridge the gulfs that exist between professionals and the public. Such a programme would entail the preparation of fact-sheets, background notes and digests of information, designed with the appropriate expert help but written in a non-technical and non-patronising manner, presented in free or inexpensive formats, and aiming at a wide distribution among the designated readership, distribution to whom would be facilitated by the broad base of CIS itself. Many voluntary bodies already publish this type of material but its effectiveness depends on accuracy, precision and simplicity of expression, a design brief that requires the subtle blending of a variety of communication skills and publishing crafts that are more likely to be available or to build up within a group with varied backgrounds and training. A full client involvement in all publication ventures would help to ensure documentation suited to its audiences.

This type of expertise can be placed at the disposal of local authorities and other organisations involved with communicating on a mass scale with the public. One powerful argument in its favour is that, properly applied, the costs it entails can be covered by producing more effective materials out of which fewer queries but greater comprehension arise.

In the light of their separate histories and varying sources and levels of funding, the task of turning existing agencies operating with dissimilar staffs from different locations into a linked network is not a simple one. One new facility that could act as the hub for a literacy network could be a 'drop-in' centre in high-street premises along the lines of schemes pioneered in Leeds, Glasgow and elsewhere. A drop-in centre can combine the functions of an advice bureau, a specialised library and a literacy centre. It can provide letter-writing and form-filling and interpretation services for individuals in the community embroiled in correspondence with bureaucracies, and provide a setting for advice clinics run by CAB staff and outside professionals, together with reference facilities covering standard published material and the fact-sheets referred to above. The high-street location of such a centre is crucial if it is to have visibility and accessibility, although it could be situated in suitable premises already owned by CIS agencies.

Drop-in centres would be able to supply print-handling skills for individuals reluctant to embark on full-scale tuition, but staff would also be able to recruit for tuition in those cases where it appeared appropriate. Instead of the client having to make an initial commitment in advance of any concrete evidence that they can be helped, tuition could be a natural development out of more specific services and consultations which would hopefully demonstrate that something worthwhile was on offer. Within the framework of a drop-in service run by CIS, tuition would remain a vitally important activity, but it would perhaps be merely one of many available rather than the pre-eminent mode of intervention and the 'natural' destiny for any client. In addition, the client need no longer be thought of necessarily as an individual: the pooling in central premises of any reprographic, printing and microcomputer equipment available to the network of participating agencies could provide the basis for an association with many community and minority groups whose participation could further extend the centre's range of operations.

In view of the enormous variety and the possible complexity of many potential inquiries, the staff in such centres need careful training and good support, but there would clearly be opportunities for both volunteer and full-time contributions in appropriate functions. Just as many clients are not ready or are unsuited to tuition, so many tutors are more valuable in other roles and have other contributions to make that at present may be unnoticed and untapped. One deliberate by-product of this form of response is that it brings together print-users of all levels of skill and sophistication, a mixing that contributes to the destigmatisation of illiteracy.

The idea of CIS is, of course, very much a blueprint. Financial and administrative arrangements would inevitably pose many local difficulties. Cooperation and coordination between a range of agencies with their own traditions, professional preoccupations and political cultures cannot be instantly wished into existence, but requires patient negotiation and creative organisation design. But CIS is, in fact, a very modest and achievable proposal. In an era of stringency on public expenditure, it makes no significant additional claims on budgets, adds no personnel to welfare payrolls. It preserves intact existing agencies and disputes no one's expertise (except the deliberate mystifications of some public officials, some advertisers and some professionals). It seeks merely to avoid the duplication and dilution of the modest resources already invested in adult literacy work, and to promote a mutual recognition among the many people who are already working in this field without fully appreciating the fact.

7

The future of literacy and literacies of the future

Introduction

It has been argued consistently throughout this book that written communication must be understood against the backdrop of the social arrangements of which it is a part, and also in relation to the types of information to which literacy can and cannot give access within a particular environment and epoch. The more familiar approach which depicts literacy as a collection of interrelated cognitive and linguistic capacities that have an apparently self-contained and detached existence is arguably not so well able to confront the wider issues about the present role and future development of literacy in technologically advanced societies with which this final chapter is concerned. Unfortunately, recognising the complexity of the interactions between linguistic and social realms is easier than creating a synthesis that resolves and explains them. Part of the price of opening the door to insights from a variety of social, historical and critical perspectives is a lack of conceptual order and integration. Out of the disorder no overarching theoretical system has yet emerged which can be presented with any confidence to the reader, and moreover, the possibility of a unified theory of literacy, dealing with its comparative development in different societies and (necessarily) with interactions between written and non-written channels of communication, itself remains contested.

In the absence of a satisfactory theory, a relatively small body of agreed facts has been enveloped by a great deal of impressionistic interpretation and judgement, much of it directly in conflict. We are faced, for example, by a claim underwritten by the official literacy agency that there are as many as 5 million British adults who have experienced problems since leaving school with reading, writing or spelling (ALBSU, 1983, 4). The arguments about standards and the presumed cultural decline in literacy were critically reviewed in the last chapter, but even allowing for the moment that this estimate embodied what would be an understandable element of exaggeration, it would still raise some searching questions about whether our designation of ourselves as a fully literate society was justified.

There are, at the same time, quite contrary images of our societal achievements and abilities, images which have already gained considerable political and popular credibility. The notion of the arrival of an 'information society' is based directly on presumptions of a relatively wide diffusion and application of 'computer literacies' which overlay and depend upon more basic literacies and numeracies. It is on this foundation that major shifts both in the nature and availability of employment and also in lifestyles and patterns of communication are premissed. This appears, at first sight, hard to reconcile with a population apparently so slow to master a communications technology in continuous use for at least 2,000 years. There may, in fact, be no contradiction: it is quite possible that both interpretations incorporate substantial elements of the truth. If so, what we could be witnessing is the emergence of a new pattern of information transmission and distribution, but one rather different to the expectations of its more complacent advocates and engineers. Its distinguishing feature could be a technocratically-based sophistication at one social pole balanced by ignorance and helpless dependence at the other, and the overall result could well be some disturbing and unanticipated social and cultural schisms, a dystopia rather than a utopia.

The assessment of these and rival prognostications about the future of written communications, to which we will later return, is hampered by the absence of an agreed base-line from which to make judgements about the scale and character of the social transformations wrought by successive forms of literacy. The polar case of a community entirely dependent on oral communication should occupy a strategic conceptual role here, but there is a surprising lack of agreement over how to portray its fundamental features. A discussion of the nature of these disagreements will, among other things, serve to give warning of the dangers of simplistic dichotomies in the study of communication. This will have a bearing on the subsequent analysis of likely future trends in the demand and supply of literacy skills, and on the discussion of the relations between different literacies with which the book concludes.

The oral-literate transition

In discussing orality and literacy, an initial distinction can be drawn, following Walter Ong (1982, 11), between 'primary orality', the state in which cultures and communities entirely without access to writing exist, and 'secondary orality', typical of 'advanced' societies, where the transmission of speech frequently employs electronic technologies like the telephone, radio and tape-recording which are themselves ultimately dependent on the existence of writing and print. Primary orality will be dealt with first.

Playing a parallel role to the concept of a 'primitive mentality' within anthropology and sociology, the idea of a phase in which human communication had a wholly oral character has furnished a conveniently blank screen on which contemporary hopes and fears can be projected. In a survey of 'voice' and 'print' as metaphors in the history of communications theory, Leed (1980) has suggested that this pairing has been used as a vehicle to represent a primordial opposition between social solidarity and individuality. Leed notes that Johann Herder's theory of language, set out in *Über den Ursprung der Sprache* [1772], was a seminal source for that perspective in which language is treated not merely as a highly effective tool of the intellect, but rather as the basic mode of human self-expression and a distillation and encapsulation of the character of community life. Such views came to appeal to conservative critics of the French Revolution who sought a source of solidarity that antedated all consciously fashioned institutional arrangements (Leed, 1980, 45). In time, too, they were to influence a nineteenth-century 'rediscovery' of folk-culture by literate European intellectuals who travelled far afield to collect traces of song, dance, myth and fable from peoples uncontaminated by modernity. In the introduction to one of the most monumental nineteenth-century studies of folk lore, *The Golden Bough* (1951, vol.1, xii), Sir James Frazer commented:

> literature accelerates the advance of thought which leaves the slow progress of opinion by word of mouth at an immeasurable distance behind. Two or three generations of literature may do more to change thought than two or three thousand years of traditional life . . .

The remnants of oral culture that were obtained in the earliest, often clumsy, attempts at reconstruction came to be endowed with all the virtues assumed to be lacking in the industrial ethos – simplicity, authenticity, practicality. Oral performances were believed to involve an especially immediate and intimate relationship between performer and audience and were supposed to resonate with the pulse of national and cultural origins.

Similar themes are reiterated and developed in more recent work such as the tradition of classical scholarship on the epics of Ancient Greece by Milman Parry (1971), A.B. Lord (1968) and Eric Havelock (1973, 1976, 1982). It was pioneering work by Parry that shifted attention away from largely unproductive disputes over the time and place of the authorship of the Homeric epics by showing that the *Illiad* and the *Odyssey* contained metrical and linguistic characteristics that could best be explained by recognising their oral origins. In what has come to be known either as the 'oral-formulaic' or as the Parry-Lord hypothesis, the poems are treated as a set of stock themes, plot incidents and phrases that are reworked by the performer for and during each recital. Even if the latter's powers of recall had been commensurate, he would not have been able to memorise a fixed, canonical version of the story because, in the absence of writing, there cannot be one. In an oral tradition, it is the formulas that are passed on to the next generation of minstrels, part of whose skill and creativity lies in giving spontaneous renderings subtly tailored to the audience in question. Work on the oral traditions of Yugoslavia and several African cultures has largely confirmed the outlines of the Parry-Lord picture of oral composition.[1]

Nevertheless, there are respects in which it falls short as a contribution to the general picture of pre-literate societies. It has licensed a rather exaggerated belief in the solidarity and corporatism of communities characterised by primary orality, and it has encouraged an oversimplified view of the associations linking speech with expressivity and print with impersonality (e.g. McLuhan, 1962, 1964). Lord himself (1968, 129) held the view that writing is incompatible with oral modes and in time comprehensively eclipses them, while we saw in Chapter 2 that Eric Havelock's work, directly in the Parry-Lord lineage, encourages acceptance of an oral mentality incapable (in the absence of the alphabet) of analytic thought (1976, 37ff).

The dichotomy between speech and the written word and the sensibilities based on them has been reinforced by some dubious generalisations about print and its supposedly global effects. Print has been portrayed as an isolating and individuating force, weakening networks of kin and other primary attachments and partially displacing their social-psychological support for the self with remote sources of identification and an enhanced sense of personal determination. McLuhan, Eisenstein and Ong all present versions of this thesis.[2]

The dangers inherent in creating disassociated mentalities to represent each side of the voice/print divide become clear when these constructs are confronted by the complexity of detailed empirical cases. In *The Domestication of the Savage Mind*, Goody employs widely drawn illustrations to demonstrate that devices such as written lists, tables of classification and non-phonetic written formulae (such as algebraic equations) do represent substantial advances in reasoning power over the tools and resources of primary orality; in his own words:

> writing, and more especially alphabetic literacy, made it possible to scrutinise discourse in a different kind of way by giving oral communication a semi-permanent form; this scrutiny favoured the increase in scope of critical activity, and hence of rationality, scepticism and logic to resurrect memories of those questionable dichotomies. It increased the potentialities of criticism because writing laid out discourse before one's eyes in a different kind of way; at the same time it increased the potentiality for cumulative knowledge, especially knowledge of an abstract kind . . . (1977a, 37)

It is not simply, however, that intellectual operations impossible in solitary contemplation or speech instantly become possible in writing. In situations of primary orality, an intellectual apprenticeship requires extended and intimate contact between teacher and taught, but such contact tends to create as a by-product a human relationship that may leave little psychological space for dispassionate, self-critical deliberations. Even if these sceptical analyses take place, they are very likely to be contained as private understandings within the relationship since, as Goody emphasises:

> continuing critical tradition can hardly exist when sceptical thoughts are *not* written down, *not* communicated across time and space, *not* made available for men to contemplate in privacy

as well as to hear in performance. (1977a, 43, emphases in original)

While it is accepted by social anthropologists that the capacity to institutionalise scepticism concerning established beliefs and understandings appears to require the alphabet, Goody's argument must not be pushed beyond its intended limits. Writing does not promote the automatic development of analytical philosophy, empirical science, or any other specific belief system. The only truly universal guarantee offered by writing is that the products of any cognitive activity considered worthy of record by a literate group within a culture can be efficiently preserved and accurately transmitted within that group: the determination of the content and the possibility of wider diffusion is always contingent on the local context. The potential for scepticism and criticism opened up by writing may be ignored or by-passed in a host of ritual or bureaucratic applications, and indeed, these 're-directions' may be encouraged by literate elites as part of a strategy of political containment.[3]

Other allegedly general differences between oral and literate situations turn out on examination to be susceptible to alternative and localised explanations. In a brief overview of the field entitled 'The myth of orality and literacy' (1982b), Deborah Tannen casts doubt on the longstanding assertion that written communication is necessarily more 'decontextualised' than speech. She queries, in other words, whether the structure of written discourse insulates it from the situation in which it is being used in a manner impossible in conversation. In her own research[4] which entailed groups of Greek and American women recounting from memory the details of a specially made silent film, Tannen detected substantial ethnic differences in approach. The Americans were preoccupied with accuracy, detail and the formal features of film as a medium, while the Greeks used conversational strategies to relate a story with a message, freely attributing motives to the characters, and generally making judgements and working the material into narrative shape. The inference that Tannen wishes to be drawn is not that the American narratives were influenced by a 'literate' environment and the Greek narratives by a mainly face-to-face, oral lifestyle, nor the commonplace that each group of women had alternative strategies available within oral discourse and selected one which was thought to be appropriate to the circumstances in which they were doing the recounting (the Americans did their recounting in a university setting, the Greeks did not). The point for students of orality and literacy, anticipated many years ago in the early work of Basil Bernstein, is that some oral styles exist, possibly in all cultures, that detach speakers from the setting and give them a virtually impersonal 'voice' and perspective that mimic written discourse without necessarily being derived from contact with it. One reason these codes, to use Bernstein's term, are likely to be mistaken for a spin-off from literacy is that they are selectively reinforced and cultivated in homes and classrooms which have come to recognise and value them as aids to the process of formal schooling.[5]

The indications of a complex and variable interpenetration of orality and literacy gather strength when we turn to secondary orality. We have seen that a prevalent assumption of print-orientated observers is that traditions generated within and transmitted solely by oral discourse tend to be displaced quickly by mass literacy, losing their cultural centrality and visibility. Classic researches like the Opies' [1959] account of the sub-cultures built upon children's stories and rhymes supply powerful reminders of the resilience of distinctively oral modes in the heart of societies with centuries of familiarity with paper and print. Yet despite the recognition the Opies' work has received, its full significance is often missed; the social and linguistic marginality of the social groups selected for research on oral transmission tends to reinforce the impression that it is a remnant of the past, and its products a series of isolated 'survivals' from obsolete patterns of communication. The recent use of anthropological and historical techniques to investigate the communicative patterns within whole communities uncovers evidence to the contrary. In a comparison between two small mill settlements located close to each other in the southeastern United States, Shirley Brice Heath (1983) documents the way in which speech and the written word are integrated into the activities and lifestyles of white working-class and black working-class neighbourhoods (Roadville and Trackton respectively). It is impossible to summarise adequately Heath's detailed descriptions, but she insists that it would be fruitless to categorise either neighbourhood as essentially oral or essentially literate:

> there are multiple uses of written and oral language, and members have access to and use both . . . . It is impossible to characterize Trackton and Roadville with existing descriptions of

> either the oral or literate traditions: they are neither and they are both. Yet the forms, occasions, content and functions of their reading and writing differ greatly from each other, and each varies in degree and kind from patterns followed by the townspeople. (230–1)

A somewhat similar picture can be gained from Milroy's (1980) linguistic study of long-established Belfast working-class neighbourhoods. It indicates that despite having English as a first language and normal access to basic schooling, these entire localities function in a way that is remarkably independent of the written word. Although not directly concerned with literacy, Milroy found that her research was hampered by the difficulty she had persuading her informants to read passages or even word lists aloud (1980, 100); she interpreted the resistance both as a sign of inability and as an indication that reading (at least, reading aloud) played a negligible role in the group's interactions.

With some localised and notable exceptions like the work of Heath, little systematic and detailed knowledge is available about the way different social strata in advanced societies employ and select between the literate and oral skills and resources available to them. In the Trackton neighbourhood, Health was struck by the relative absence of situations in which extended, solitary reading or writing was necessary (1983, 196); both activities tended to be public and conversation featured prominently in the process of deriving applicable information from the written word and interpreting its significance. Such a finding may seem to smack of the self-evident but there is surprisingly little recognition, in the existing academic literature at least, of the way in which some practical transactions allow or encourage switching between oral and written discourse, while others restrict or prevent it. Where there are opportunities for switching, individuals may be able to 'survive' on very limited literacy skills (such as social sightword recognition and signing). A couple of Carolina mill towns cannot, of course, be taken as representative of other types of community or sub-culture, but the powerful image of the solitary and silent reader and author that lies behind much contemporary theorising about the oral-literate transition almost certainly invokes an atypical case.

These researches leave intact the assertion made previously about the absence of extensive pools of total illiteracy in Britain. There are almost certainly pockets like Trackton and parts of

Belfast even in the most economically developed and literate societies of Western Europe and North America, but we have seen that they are characterised not so much by a comprehensive incompetence with the written word as by a systematic avoidance of those activities and situations in which it is impossible to substitute conversation for reading and writing. It reflects repeatedly-made individual and collective choices that favour both speech and personal contact over both print and formality. Total illiteracy, on the other hand, does not generally entail or reflect any choice at all. This difference has an important bearing on remedial policies. Because these 'oral' values may arise from and express a rejection of school and a distancing of its standards, conventional educational palliatives are unlikely to be effective agencies of change.[6]

Literacy and the information explosion

The way in which oral and literate channels can substitute for and supplement each other are not immutable or divinely ordained, neither are they strictly comparable in different periods or cultural circumstances. The significance to the adult of a particular capacity to read and write can be affected by major alterations in the communications technologies available, or by changes to the economic or socio-legal arrangements regulating access to these channels. The future of literacy and illiteracy cannot, in other words, be abstracted from the problem of predicting general changes in the structure of communications and the structure of society. That said, however, the developments and trends in progress or in prospect that are loosely drawn together by the idea of an 'information revolution' appear to carry direct implications for basic skills, and therefore warrant close investigation. Which developments will be most relevant to literacy depends very much on whether the scenario chosen to depict the immediate future is painted by a pro-technology optimist or a sceptical critic, and the implications of some of the more plausible possibilities from both camps will have to be investigated cautiously. The initial step will be to assess whether measures of the volume of written and printed information bear out the suggestion of fundamental changes, although since 'information' is such a catch-all, the rate of its accumulation can only serve as a rough pointer.

The metaphor of an information 'explosion' based, in part, on the world-wide accumulation and proliferation of all kinds of printed material, but also on the post-war development of sophisticated telecommunication and computer systems, has through relentless repetition become a true cliché, robbed of its power to arrest or enlighten. The image of an explosion is not, in fact, particularly apt for a process that has been characterised more by steady growth on many fronts than by sudden localised spurts. The available statistics, though limited in scope, do give a general impression of expansion in written material. If we take, first, books, the estimated total number of titles published annually world wide rose from 269,000 in 1955 to 607,000 in 1977, a rise which considerably outdistanced world population growth (from 131 to 187 titles per million people). Not unexpectedly, the wealthy and technologically advanced nations saw larger increases than the Third World; in North America the expansion was six-fold, in Europe two-fold.[7]

In the case of serial publications, the picture is understandably complicated by the immense variety of types in circulation, a variety that frustrates the compilation of truly comprehensive figures. As far as newspapers are concerned, the most encompassing (but therefore rather crude) statistic, the total world production of newsprint, was marginally less in 1981 than in 1970, while per caput consumption of newsprint remained more or less on a plateau (Table 7.1). The more detailed statistics of numbers of titles and levels of circulation of principal dailies and weeklies contained in the standard sources confirm a general impression of overall stability with some slight declines. However, even in countries like Britain where the number of daily newspapers has been in long-term decline, there are exceptional areas of growth: the number of local freesheets, for example, more than doubled from 234 in 1979 to 581 in 1983.[8]

For periodicals other than newspapers, there is a definite upward trend in the number of titles. Ulrich's *International Periodicals Directory*, the most comprehensive listing available, contained around 50,000 titles in its fourteenth (1971–2) edition, but by the twenty-first (1982) edition, this had risen to about 65,000 titles.

The proliferation of scientific periodicals which announce results and advance in basic research, thereby triggering further publishing activity over an extended period, has been monitored closely. The number of scholarly scientific and technical journals published in the United States increased from 2,800 in 1960 to 4,600 in 1979, while the total number of journal articles has risen annually by

	Total newsprint production, millions of metric tonnes 1981	Newsprint consumption, Kgs per inhabitant				Production of other printing and writing paper, millions of metric tonnes 1981	Consumption of other printing and writing paper, Kgs per inhabitant			
		1970	1975	1980	1981		1970	1975	1980	1981
North America	10.8	42.4	38.0	45.6	42.7	15.1	47.4	44.6	59.9	59.4
Latin America	1.3	3.8	2.9	3.3	3.5	2.0	3.3	3.9	5.0	5.3
Developing Countries	2.8	0.9	1.0	1.3	1.4	6.4	1.2	1.6	2.0	2.3
World	25.9	5.9	5.4	6.0	5.8	41.5	7.3	7.3	9.0	9.2

Table 7.1: *Production and consumption of printing and writing paper*
Source: UNESCO Statistical Yearbook, 1983, Tables 6.3 and 6.4.

between 2 per cent and 4 per cent for more than a decade. Contrary to popular and academic wisdoms, there is survey evidence to indicate that each of the more than 400,000 journal articles published annually is actually read on average 600 times (King, 1980, 99). This picture of the rapid accumulation of knowledge is broadly consistent with a classic study of the scientific literature of the post-war period which concluded that in an expanding scientific discipline it doubles in size within an interval of roughly fifteen years.[9]

Traditional book and serial publication, important though it is, accounts for only a small fraction of the amount of paper with printing in circulation at any point in time. The more ephemeral forms of written communication are not dignified by specific statistics on volume, but the right-hand side of Table 7.1 reveals that the personal consumption of printing and writing paper other than newsprint increased steadily during the 1970s, and while levels are a great deal higher in the developed than they are in the developing world, the rate of increase is greater in the latter, suggesting that further substantial growth is likely.

At the opposite end of the writing spectrum from mainstream publishing, the number of 'personal' letters sent from one private United Kingdom address to another increased by 37 million to 679 million between 1981–2 and 1982–3.[10] The overall letter/parcel traffic in Britain increased from 8,753 million items in 1956–7 to 10,493 items in 1982–3.[11] These increases, although not remarkable in scale, have taken place during a period of steadily increasing telephone ownership and usage.

Since 1960, when transistors were first incorporated into computers, the most rapid rates of growth have taken place in information in machine-readable formats, that is, texts and numerical data which can be stored electronically in various kinds of computer memory and retrieved and reproduced either on paper or display screens. Some of the information in this medium duplicates what already exists in print or 'backs up' other memories in case of failure; some of it is constantly being revised or updated; the information in many computer systems is destined for consumption by other electronic systems and consequently exists transiently, or only in forms not directly meaningful to its human beneficiaries. For these kinds of reason, almost no inclusive statistics on machine-readable information are available. Growth has, however, undoubtedly been astronomical. It has been calculated, for instance, that expenditures in the American data-processing industry grew eighty-fold between 1955 and 1975 to reach $41 billion.[12] The number of bibliographic references available on-line to scientists and scholars increased from less than 250,000 in 1968 to 65 million by 1980.[13]

Since the early 1960s, commentators and forecasters have speculated that this great and increasing weight of printed and written information is the key element in a fundamental social and cultural transformation. In the first formulations, this transformation was closely linked with the long-term growth of service enterprises and occupations (in, for instance, health, education, business administration and scientific research and development) and a corresponding decline in the size of the workforce involved in traditional extractive or manufacturing industry. In 1973, the American forecaster, Daniel Bell, published a work popularising the conception of a 'post-industrial' social system in which the influence of theoretical knowledge and the professional elites that wield it becomes paramount.[14] Bell suggested that technical knowledge was now the 'axial principle' of the most developed economies, its pre-eminence sustained by the enormous information processing and retrieval capacities of microelectronic technologies. Bell's views on the centrality of information processing have been reiterated in many more recent publications. A 1979 OECD report surveying similar territory even borrows Bell's metaphor:

> The production, transmission and processing of the most varied information will be at the heart of economic activity and social life . . . through its links with data processing and telecommunications, the electronics complex during the next quarter of a century will be the main pole around which the productive structures of the advanced industrial societies will be reorganised. (quoted in A. Smith, 1982, 14)

The management of these developments is largely in the hands of technocrats and committed engineers whose priorities consist in securing adequate capital investment to maintain the pace of technological development, the laying down of a foundation of technical education and training, and overcoming what they regard as misguided resistance and short-sighted protectionism in the labour market. Extensive public relations exercises (like 'Information Technology Year' in Britain) have marketed the idea of an information age and sought acceptance for it, with the result that an awareness of the impact and the fruits of the new communication technologies is no longer only the preserve of specialists. On the assumption that more equals better, the enthusiasts point to the consumer cornucopia as proof of the benign character of the revolution, and the high streets of Japan, Europe and North America are indeed fully stocked with audio and video systems, calculators, cameras, watches and home computers. More crucially, great play is also made of the technology's capacity to distribute seemingly limitless amounts of any kind of machine-readable information through a variety of networks in a way that is said to retain the important selection decisions for the end-user rather than the provider of the service. In the case of some computer and cable networks, transmissions are designed to be possible in both centre-periphery and periphery-centre directions. It is argued that developments of this kind could, in time, come to challenge the commercial newspaper and publishing empires based on the centralised mass production of titles destined for single-copy purchase by the end user. The existence of a demonstrable consumer demand for new communications products and services and the possibility of two-way traffic are among the attractions that lead the optimistic camp of commentators including, for example, De Sola Pool (1983), to suggest that the information 'revolution' is inherently decentralising and egalitarian, a true 'technology of freedom'.

The more pessimistic onlookers see information technology in Europe and North America merely extending and intensifying market forces as the determinants of what information is available to whom. The current realities and future developments these critics have in mind include the continued domination of the information scene by multinational corporations such as AT&T, ITT and IBM (the latter has sold between two-thirds and three-quarters by value of all the world's large computers, and it earned more than $40 billion in revenue in 1983); control over the transmission of time-sensitive financial information such as stock market prices and currency exchange rates by private agencies hard to regulate or make accountable; in Britain, the introduction of commercial criteria to govern the production of information by the statistical services of the state itself, with consequent reductions in the quality of statistics covering politically delicate matters like levels of unemployment and take-up rates of welfare benefits, and the 'economic' (that is, prohibitive) pricing of official reports and series (Robins and Webster, 1983, 348–50); the diminution of public service as a basis of broadcasting by commercial initiatives such as the introduction of teletext services and Direct Broadcasting by Satellite; the distribution of valuable cable franchises in Britain and the USA to private interests with the most minimal safeguards for the public interest (Elliott, 1982).

The main argument of the critics, then, can be summed up in the assertion that there is every prospect that the benefits flowing from the greater throughput of communications will fall disproportionately on already privileged and propertied groups – the shareholders of large corporations which will be obliged to 'cover' new technological developments if only to protect their established interests, their employees (often small in number relative to the size of capital employed), and a few entrepreneurs. A further objection sees a threat to civil liberties from the enhanced capacity for surveillance and social control by the state (and possibly other rich institutions able to purchase large computer systems capable of supporting databases containing millions of records relating to individuals).

A British example of the kind of installation that critics have in mind is the Police National Computer located at Hendon, Middlesex, which is reported to contain 90 per cent of its maximum capacity of 40 million separate records, and for which increasingly sophisticated links with the computers belonging to county constabularies are being constructed (Robins and Webster, 1983, 352). Because of the importance to their work of round-the-clock monitoring of radio and telecommunications, together with general information retrieval and encryption/decryption, security agencies are regular customers for the largest, fastest and most expensive computing equipment. The complaint of civil liberties activists is that prejudicial information on individuals and dissident or heterodox groups can be and is passed from one large government-controlled database to another without the subjects' knowledge and without the possibility of impartial verification or correction. The experience from non-security contexts like credit-checking bureaux suggests that the mechanisms set up by the gathering institutions themselves cannot be guaranteed to eliminate inaccurate, obsolete and illegally-obtained information from the records even where commercial pressures favour accuracy. The optimists point to the data protection acts that already exists in many countries. Largely owing to EEC pressure, a Data Protection Bill has passed through the British parliament, but press comment has been sceptical ever since its originally published form showed the hallmarks of hurriedly drafted and cosmetic legislation. Doubts persist especially over the special status and broad definition for security/police related information and the access security services are explicitly given to private information systems, sloppy definitions of key concepts like 'data user', the exclusion of paper records, and the massive problems of ensuring the compliance of both departments of state and private organisations whose operations have never in the past been open to direct public inspection.

What impacts, then, will this new environment for communication have on traditional literacy skills and more particularly on the people that lack them? How will it affect the demand and supply of literacy competences and to what extent will it redefine the status curve discussed in the last chapter? These are not easy questions to answer in general terms, but to try to do justice to the often contradictory forces at work, we will begin by exploring the likely occupational fortunes of groups with different kinds of literacy asset to bring to the labour market and daily survival.

Much of the nominally semi-skilled and unskilled work considered in Chapter 5, and especially the repetitive and short-cycle machining, assembly and packaging tasks, are of a type well-suited to full or partial automation. For most of the common work-tasks in manufacturing industry, automated techniques and equipment are readily available and their introduction depends largely on organisation size, managerial judgement of the likely costs and savings, and the local industrial relations climate. The larger manufacturing firms generally in the vanguard of automation are, as we have seen, precisely those that already discriminate most thoroughly against adults with a literacy deficit, so it might be thought that this type of applicant will not be materially affected by the shrinking pool of jobs in this sector. In fact, what is likely to happen is that those presently pushed by their illiteracy towards the smaller, 'secondary' employer will encounter increased competition with people 'shed' by automating firms. Although literacy credentials seem in the past to have mattered less in the small manufacturing organisation, this type of employer will be able to pick and choose more than in the past and will often opt for large-firm experience (so that literacy is taken into account in an indirect fashion).

Another group who will be affected are the long-serving employees in the larger organisations who are semi-literate or worse but whose arrival pre-dated literacy screens (or who somehow circumvented them). It was suggested in Chapter 5 that many of these people are coping quite easily in their work because the factory shop-floor has traditionally been a world of predominantly oral communication. The introduction of numerically-controlled machine tools, process control and other equipment operated by typewriter-style keyboards or requiring VDU screens to be read could expose their limitations immediately. The warehouseman, accustomed to receiving instructions directly from a chargehand or supervisor who could be consulted at any time in the event of problems, may now be presented with a computer listing of stock with advice available remotely, perhaps only at the end of a telephone. Alf, the removal man with reading problems played by Bob Hoskins in the pioneering television series dealing with illiteracy, *On the Move*, would now be facing the literacy and numeracy hurdle of a tachograph in the cab of his van.

As the historical survey in Chapter 3 emphasised, most nineteenth-century manual workers were expected to acquire their work skills through verbal instruction on the job and would not as a matter of course be expected to read and write as part of their work (although many could). Farm work, despite the relatively early introduction of mechanisation, has traditionally been one of the occupational areas least dependent on print. This was probably originally due to the limited education available to the rural poor in the late eighteenth century, but the capital-intensive character of modern husbandry and cultivation has drastically reduced demand for the kind of unskilled labour that might encounter problems reading the instructions on a bag of fertiliser, calculating dilution ratios, or noting down milk yields correctly. Farm workers now need to handle sophisticated equipment which may require formal training including attendance at 'chalk and talk' courses of classroom instruction. The transformation in agriculture by which (often) high-level manual skills learned on the job are displaced by (often) lower-level skills obtainable only through the medium of writing, exemplifies a process operating throughout the economy: a significant number of manual occupations once open to the unqualified and the illiterate have incorporated subsidiary aspects and sub-tasks requiring literacy and numeracy, and access to them has been closed off.

While the work prospects of the severely illiterate, regardless of age, are bleak and are becoming bleaker, the daily task of life-support has simultaneously become more and more bound up with handling the written word. The difficulties this group faces in money matters are perhaps symptomatic. One of the features of traditional working-class communities was and largely remains a marked preference for buying and selling in cash and an ingrained (and not unjustified) suspicion of 'credit' transactions, broadly defined. Attitudes favouring the use of cash can probably be best understood as part of a wider cultural pattern, incorporating the oral strategies and the affinity for face-to-face dealings with known individuals, discussed in the last section. One source of evidence on the avoidance of non-cash transactions is the marked class gradient in the use of bank or giro accounts (Table 7.2), and although there is no comparable statistical evidence, it is probable that the severely sub-literate and sub-numerate are among those most reluctant to become involved in this type of financial arrangement. In the past, such sentiments were congruent with financial prudence and close control of household finances, but it is no longer easy to manage the home economy efficiently entirely in cash. For one thing, there is mounting pressure from employers to induce an ever wider range of personnel to accept payment by credit transfer. For another, those without bank accounts are unable to take advantage of conveni-

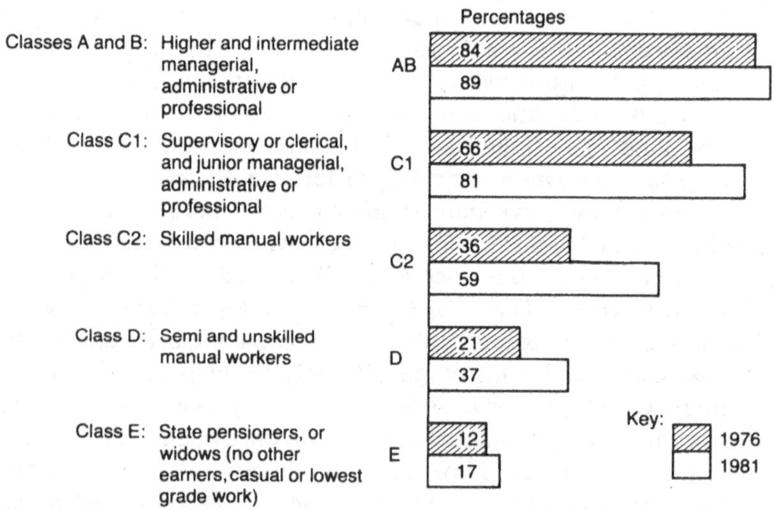

Source: Inter-Bank Research Organization, Research Brief, October 1982.

Table 7.2: *Current chequing accounts by social class, 1976 and 1981*

ences like cash dispensers and instalment arrangements for domestic payments, while they also deny themselves access to the least disreputable end of the credit market.

Far from eliminating print, most of the imminent innovations in information technology destined for use by the general public will require considerable textual accuracy and self-assurance by users, often in the sight of other users and against the clock. The telegraphic kinds of messages generated by computer systems will baffle those able to read but needing a clue-giving context plus verbal redundancy to make sense of instructions. Although high-street and living-room systems are supposedly designed with inexpert users in mind, the needs of the barely literate have not been prominent in design specifications to date.

Severe illiteracy, as we have emphasised, is an intricate blending of incapacity and self-protective hostility towards activities and transactions based on writing. Even where the software in a computer system has been carefully designed to be, in an overemployed phrase, 'user-friendly', anxiety and confusion can easily be provoked. For most people heavily dependent on oral exchanges to achieve understanding, interactions with keyboards and VDU screens of whatever kind are likely to be extremely intimidating. Consider as an example the likely consequences of plans, given coverage in both the daily and specialist press (e.g., The *Guardian*, 5.4.1984), to replace some of the Department of Employment's network of large Jobcentres (where job-seekers can receive a comprehensive range of advice and counselling services) by 'automated teller machine-type terminals in the walls of local government buildings'. The scheme proposes that new-style, machine-readable, National Insurance cards will be the means by which the unemployed will gain access to job information held on seven regional and one central computer. The consultant who conceived of the project is quoted as saying:

> On the screen will appear an index to job classification and by punching the code key appropriate to needs, the viewer can display a synopsis of all current vacancies, each with a reference number or letter. (*Computer News*, 5.4.1984)

Such 'menu-driven' arrangements are a well-established way of shielding users as completely as possible from the internal complexities of computer systems, but even with the benefit of such devices, the scheme, in its original form at least, appeared to make no provision for those handicapped by poor reading skills. Any policy decision to make interviews and job counselling less accessible and to substitute a session in public in front of a keyboard and screen for the possibility of a sympathetic human hearing will certainly deter those who, on the evidence of Chapter 5, are already reluctant to use Jobcentres. The plans, initially estimated to be worth £200 million to equipment suppliers, but subsequently scaled down, appear to have been motivated much more by the salary savings involved than by any likely increase in the effectiveness of the service that would result.

In the more distant future, voice-sensitive devices might obviate the need for any word or even character recognition on the part of the user, but such sophistication will be expensive and selectively taken up. In the interim, there will be several generations of 'automated teller machine-type terminals' providing a wide range of important services and information but which will not speak or respond to speech, and to which a substantial proportion of the population will therefore give a wide berth.

A climate of opinion already exists that accepts that little can be expected by way of new learning or adaptability from adults with low or obsolete educational attainments, but which looks with possibly unrealistic optimism towards the rising generations that are being educated with a computer in the classroom. There is little doubt that existing microcomputer systems have capacities very relevant to a wide range of learning tasks and problems. Aside from the storage, representation and manipulation of information in the form of combinations of text, graphics and sound, there is the potential for interaction and dialogue between user and machine at a pace regulated by the learner's performance. There is often, too, the possibility of machine-generated speech to accompany displays of text and, a little in the future, the capacity to respond to the speech of the user. Because the connections between visible objects, articulated sounds and written forms can all be handled on the same piece of equipment, we have a tool with great potential to help children and adults to learn to read and to reason numerically and logically.

Is there, then, any sense in which information technology can compensate for its disproportionate distribution of employment and direct economic benefits to the educationally successful by making a balancing contribution to basic education? The answer that is given to this depends on how the relations between conventional and computer literacies are interpreted and developed within the educational system. Not unexpectedly, 'computer literacy' is at least as ambiguous as its parent notion. In many schools and colleges operating with shortages of trained staff and equipment, computer literacy is a remote ideal that may mean little more in practical classroom terms than occasional demonstrations by the teacher of commercially-written software, with the bonus for selected students of limited 'hands on' keyboard experience. (It could be added, in passing, that such experience may be of limited value since there is wide agreement that very little of the educational software currently available either exploits the potential of microcomputers, or significantly enhances the learning process for conventional subjects: in too many cases, it merely transfers to the VDU what could and probably should take place on the blackboard.)

In a more systematic sense, computer literacy suggests the assimilation by pupils of sufficient operational knowledge and skills to free them from a total dependence on particular equipment or program packages, and which equips them with the basis for continuing self-instruction. The educational arguments for this intermediate sophistication particularly emphasise the importance of exposure to computer technology for those not destined for science or technological careers. There is a belief, correct or not, that one method of arriving at such mid-range competences for all pupils is to incorporate computers into the existing curriculum wherever an opportunity presents itself, with possible support from a general 'computer appreciation' course.

In another interpretation, computer literacy necessarily includes, in addition to the skills already mentioned, some understanding of underlying principles as reflected in an ability to write and modify simple programs in an established high-level computer language (such as, for example, Basic, Fortran or Pascal).[15] Such relatively advanced objectives normally presume a timetable slot in the secondary curriculum dedicated to 'computer studies', formal syllabus and examinations, specialist teachers and the like, and are regarded very much as the preserve of those that have already assimilated solid foundations of numeracy and natural language literacy.

There is little in any of these fairly familiar kinds of educational arrangement that could be expected to have much impact on either the 'underclass' of remedial pupils or adults other than those already firmly 'plugged in' to continuing educational courses or institutions. The need to ration user-access to what is, at best, rarely more than two or three machines per class or group prevents many adults and children discovering that a microcomputer could be an unconventional route into orthodox literacy skills. The word-processing packages obtainable for the more sophisticated home computers are tools usually thought of as the preserve of the professional writer or business person, but they incorporate several features that are invaluable for individuals struggling to express themselves. As a writing instrument for young children, the keyboard needs less control and dexterity than a pen and always produces perfectly formed and legible letters; errors can be removed from the screen leaving no visible traces of previous flawed efforts. Printed versions can easily be set out with a polished and professional appearance. Above all, as Seymour Papert has pointed out (1980, 30), the word processor, by providing a short-cut to the stage where learners have created some recognisable sentences, enables them to concentrate on the more rewarding considerations of content. By making the whole process of constructing a text much less laborious, the possibility of revision and refinement becomes far less daunting. The advent of word-processing systems designed specifically for educational use with simple menu and command structures is therefore very much to be welcomed, but it is vitally important with adults (and with children, too) not to, in Papert's term, 'infantilise' the learner. One of the great contributions microcomputers could make in adult basic education is to place at the learners' disposal sophisticated equipment worthy of their attention and interest, capable of drawing out their latent powers of self-expression, and nothing should be 'bowdlerised' or appear toy-like.

Word-processing equipment has already wrought a thorough transformation in the nature of office work in larger organisations, and aside from the very substantial long-term impact on the secretarial and clerical labour market, there are some quite subtle consequences for the literacy of everybody on and around the 'plateau of competence' depicted in Chart 6.1 (page 162). The main implications of the new technology for the office are usually reckoned to be an increase in secretarial productivity and a de-skilling of key aspects of the production of correspondence. Various typing skills like centering headings or the tabulated layout of tables of figures can now be performed automatically by electronic typewriters and word processors. Spelling checkers are available that will scan a text and identify all the words not contained in the program's vocabulary (which, even in home computers, may be in the region of 20,000 words). Facilities often exist to add any specialist terms or names used in a particular activity to the basic lexicon provided. In the future, similar programs will be able to examine the grammatical structures in a text and identify tense and case errors, or even highlight poorly located or connected dependent clauses. By 'mechanising' some of the elements in the production of formally correct written discourse, information technologies could make the plateau of competence more easily accessible (at least to those within reach of the necessary machinery).

There is, however, a very real possibility that this latter facilitation of correctness and linguistic orthodoxy will be swamped by a set of countervailing forces. Although the costs are by no means negligible, the cheaper variants of the new information-handling systems bring the possibility of publically broadcasting printed information within the economic reach of a much wider spectrum of individuals and small groups than ever before. It has, for example, been suggested that one reason why the volume of posted material has been maintained in the face of the spread of the telephone is that clubs and community associations are increasingly able to produce newsletters, journals and magazines entirely in-house through the voluntary efforts of their own members. By removing some of the social and economic barriers surrounding it, the new technologies have made the printed word much less exclusive, placing many people in authorial and editorial roles whose education and social background barely prepared them to be consumers let alone producers of print. The novelty of their situation lies in the fact that notwithstanding their lack of writing experience and their unfamiliarity with established writing conventions and techniques, there is no longer the need for their work to pass under the pen of a copy editor or be rationalised for a printer's benefit. The author is increasingly his or her own editor and censor. The sheer volume and accumulation of oddities of form and content may have a destandardising impact on the written form of the language. When there is as much *samizdat* as there is official propaganda, the reader can be forgiven for not being sure on occasion which is which.

At the same time, the physical appearance of printed material is no longer a reliable indicator of its social origins or the authenticity or quality of its contents. The improvements in reprographic technologies give many documents and materials produced in spare rooms or garages an appearance indistinguishable from the output of large and prestigious institutions (recreating the problems of authenticating documents encountered in the scribal era). At the other end of the continuum, established publishing houses are increasingly willing to experiment with forms of 'direct' publication which often result in books and magazines with an 'economy' appearance (composed in, for instance, unjustified typescript), and also works associated closely with, or actually in, other media. The extra-textual cues that remind the reader of a text's provenance and how to approach it are either being shed completely or becoming harder to interpret.

A likely upshot of these trends is a major disturbance to the long-established cultural hierarchies institutionalised in and through print. Who appears in print (in the sense of the social identities and self-conceptions of authors) and what appears in print (both in the sense of what is thought to be worth communicating and the way it is expressed in prose) are likely to be extremely heterogeneous, even by current standards. As more people have something they have written produced in print in one format or another, the mere fact of authorship itself will inevitably lose some of its salience and prestige (though the standing of professional 'stars' is unlikely to be affected). The very generalised and culturally diffuse respect for the written word and the skills for handling it has long been on the wane on account of the erosion of traditional supports such as deference to the educated elites that historically monopolised it, and the special awe emanating from sacred religious texts and legal codes. This diminution is likely to continue. In a social environment containing so many textual varieties and formats in circulation, the pre-eminence of the book as a repository of distilled knowledge and an exemplar of 'complete' literacy certainly cannot be taken for granted. But what is not likely to be diminished is the use of whatever it is that people read and write as a basis for fine social evaluation and discrimination.

This analysis of the social dimensions of literacy has concentrated on three main spheres: the arrangements for training children and adults, as a result of which particular combinations of reading and writing skills have a definite distribution in a society; the technical means available to record and retrieve print; and the mechanisms regulating the content of the knowledge and information in circulation. The importance of information technologies for literacy and illiteracy does not lie in any particular product or service that will irrevocably transform the future. The pace of innovation and the uncertainties of market forces and government policies can overturn any prediction that extrapolates crudely from what currently seems influential or promising. Its importance lies in the manner in which it operates directly upon each of the three spheres mentioned above, having effects on such a broad front, institutionally and culturally, that it is hard to conceive of the policies that could contain or counter its impact.

A much-repeated assertion alleges that membership of a community of speakers of a natural language is an automatic source of social solidarity and integration, but that common literacy in a language is a source of differentiation and division. Such a simple dichotomy could hardly be the whole truth, but even so, it captures well the ironies and contradictions that attend our inescapable need to communicate in words.

Appendix 1

Details of sampling and interviewing procedures

The sample of students from NALS was intended to be representative of the 380 students who, according to the index-card records at the literacy centre, were active on 1 May 1978. The original design called for a random sample stratified by (a) sex of student, (b) amount of tuition received, and (c) mode of tuition (home-based, one-to-one in classes, or true group tuition). The tutors were to be those currently matched with the selected students at the time of the interview, and at the request of the Education Authority, all contacts were to be made through tutors or class leaders. Students awaiting matching and non-anglophone students were excluded.

It became apparent that (c) was not an entirely appropriate factor for stratification since students were being increasingly encouraged to 'graduate' from home tuition to one-to-one tuition in classes. In addition, there were only small numbers receiving class tuition (mainly spelling groups), so this factor was dropped.

The selection procedures encountered some major practical difficulties. The alphabetical card-index which was employed as a sampling frame contained the names and address of every student contacting or referred to the centre since 1975, together with initial interview date, venue of tuition and current tutor. Since cards were not removed from the index, the numbers had accumulated to several times the active complement of students. In principle, the cards were marked 'D.O.' (dropped out) when tuition ceased, but many students never informed their tutors or the organisers that they had finished, and their status remained in doubt for many months, at least until they had failed to respond to several inquiries. Some students normally attended intermittently, while others excused themselves temporarily for reasons of health or work, but never actually resumed tuition. There were thus many doubtful cases about whom tutors and organisers preferred, perfectly reasonably, to err on the side of optimism. Where originally-selected names turned out (after investigation) to be dormant, substitutes were selected from a reserve list.

The distinction between low- and high-contact students also presented difficulties. The cut-off point was arbitrarily set to ten meetings, but in the delays that occurred between selecting student names and establishing their eligibility, willingness and availability for interview, many low-contact cases matured into high-contact ones. New sampling frames had to be drawn up for low-contact cases for the periods 1.9.78 to 31.12.79 and 1.1.79 to 1.5.79. The numbers and types of interviews conducted are set out in Table A1.1.

The original intention had been to collect an additional comparison group consisting of people who had severe literacy problems but had never received tuition as adults. Permission to approach students who were 'on the books' but had never been matched or who had dropped out before tuition commenced was denied by the Local Authority. The plan was therefore to gather names by the 'snowball' technique in which each student and tutor in the scheme selected for interview would be asked if they knew of anyone who met the criteria. This did not prove fruitful: for various (probably very sound) reasons, no names were volunteered. The only alternative appeared to be a 'convenience' sample collected in an ad hoc way through contacts and welfare agencies. After various approaches, Family First, mainly involved in housing projects, suggested some possibilities and one interview resulted. Nottingham Inter-Community Trust, a voluntary agency whose activities embraced running employment schemes for the Manpower Services Commission, arranged three group interviews with a total of eleven youths, sixteen-eighteen years old, on a one-year job experience programme. According to the rather rough and ready estimates of teachers and supervisors, their literacy ranged from 'average' down to a reading ability restricted to sightwords. The haphazard character of this sub-group's selection severely restricted the uses to which the resulting information could be put.

With two exceptions, all the students were interviewed separately from their tutors at times and places they had decided together. (In one case, a student asked if the tutor could be present, in the other the tutor (whose house it was) simply 'hung about' on the edge of the conversation, volunteering occasional comments and interpretations.) In all cases a tape-recorder was used and full transcripts were eventually produced from the tapes.

The student interview schedule wȧs divided into four main sections dealing with contact with the literacy scheme and experiences in it, schooling, work, and finally family situation, leisure activities and miscellaneous attitudinal questions concerned with literacy. The duration of the average student interview was about fifty minutes. No direct attempt was made to measure or assess reading or writing abilities. Although the schedule was detailed, the nature of the topic and the variations between students necessitated adjustments to the sequence of questions and occasional omissions. Complete interview schedules and further details of research procedures can be found in Levine (1982).

Table A1.1: *Details of interviews conducted*

Type	*Number Conducted*	*Index Card Level at 1.5.78*
Low-contact Male	7	83
Low-contact Female	4	40
High-contact Male	5	172
High-contact Female	2	93
Total Students	18	388
No-contact Male*	11	
No-contact Female	1	
Tutors**	12	
Employment Interviews	11	
Overall total	53	

* 2 group interviews.

** Several tutors/class organisers were interviewed about more than one student

Appendix 2

Chart A2.1: *English historical literacy rates, selected studies*
All published figures have been converted to rates of literacy. Because of overlapping periods of coverage, the sequence of studies cannot be strictly chronological.

Published source	Primary source	Period covered	Area/ locality	Sex	% literate (or with literacy attribute)	Number of cases	Notes
Thrupp, 1948, 156	Consistory court witness registers – signers versus markers	1467–76		M	40	116	A similar proportion for smaller groups of witnesses in 1373 and 1466
Laqueur, 1976a, 264 and 266	Inventories of the possessions of deceased persons:						
	Books	1531–1699	Devon	Both	22	266	
	Legal documents				55		
	Books	1617–19	Beds.	Both	14	166	
	Legal documents				22		
	Books	1635–1741	Mid. Essex	Both	21	241	
	Legal documents				28		
Stone, 1964, 43	Successful pleas for benefit of clergy by men sentenced to death by Middx. justices	1612–14	London	M	47	204	Derived from W. Le Hardy *Calendar of Middlesex Quarter Sessions Records*, New Series i, 1935, 168
Stone, 1964, 43	Protestation Oath, signers versus markers	1642	S.E. Surrey	M	33	1265	Source as previous entry. Apparently all males 18+ in Reigate and Tandridge
Unwin, 1983,	Testators signing or marking wills	1660–88	Yorks. W. Riding	Both	33	156	Spofforth Region
Vann, 1974–5, 287–93	Hearth tax returns, signers versus markers	1662	Yorks.	M	61	190	
				F	42	19	
			Berks. and Oxon.	M	59	234	
				F	25	24	

Chart A2.1: (contd.)

Published source	Primary source	Period covered	Area/ locality	Sex	% literate (or with literacy attribute)	Number of cases	Notes
Houston, 1982, 204	Assize depositions, signers versus markers	1640–9	Northern Circuit Assizes	M	35	154	Embraces Yorks., Lancs., Durham, Northumb., Westmorland and Cumbria
				F	7	5	
		1660–9		M	46	410	
				F	9	15	
		1680–9		M	55	508	
				F	13	14	
		1720–9		M	58	245	
				F	36	37	
		1740–9		M	70	534	
				F	32	36	
Cressy, 1980, 100	Association oath, signers versus markers	1696	Essex		46	1789	36 parishes
			Herts.	M	64	655	3 parishes
			Suffolk		47	10056	215 parishes
Harrop, 1983, 39	Marriage registers, signers versus markers amongst brides and grooms	1754–96	N.E. Cheshire	M	61	–	Mottram-in-Longlendale parish, selected five-year running averages
				F	24	–	
		1764–8		M	73	–	
				F	27	–	
		1774–8		M	76	–	
				F	26	–	
		1784–8		M	73	–	
				F	25	–	
		1792–6		M	71	–	
				F	31	–	
Grayson, 1983, 55	Parish marriage registers, signers versus markers	1754–1850	Worcestershire				St Clement, St Nicholas and St Martin for Worcester
		1754–60	Worcester	M	59	–	
				F	38	–	

			Rural parishes	M	53	–	Leigh, Edington, Evenlode, Broome and Holt for rural parishes
				F	34	–	
		1771–80	Worcester	M	66	–	
				F	43	–	
			Rural parishes	M	50	–	
				F	32	–	
		1811–20	Worcester	M	64	–	
				F	38	–	
			Rural parishes	M	43	–	
				F	35	–	
		1841–50	Worcester	M	72	–	
				F	59	–	
			Rural parishes	M	53	–	
				F	44	–	
J. Campbell, 1983, 23	Parish marriage registers, signers versus markers	1755	Gloucestershire	M	55	136	Study covers the period 1755–1865, selected years only
				F	29	72	
		1795		M	54	315	
				F	34	199	
		1835		M	53	804	
				F	37	561	
		1865		M	77	902	
				F	80	937	
Sargant, 1867, 127–8	Parish marriage registers, signers versus markers	1754–62	Includes Halifax	Both	51 (42)	c.	Figures in brackets relate to rural parishes taken alone
		1799–1804	Bristol, Lynn and rural areas in Yorks. Dorset and Northants	Both	54 (54)	15000	
Schofield, 1973, 445	Parish marriage registers, signers versus markers	1755	Random sample of 274 English parish registers	M	60 (67)	(1529)	English estimates entail a ± 2% standard error at 95% level of confidence. Number of cases rises steadily from c.1,300 in 1755 to c.2,900 in 1835
				F	46 (26)	(589)	

Chart A2.1: (contd.)

Published source	Primary source	Period covered	Area/ locality	Sex	% literate (or with literacy attribute)	Number of cases	Notes
Laqueur, 1974, 98	Parish marriage registers, signers versus markers	1765	Industrial Lancashire	M	61 (64)	(2189)	Laqueur's figures (in brackets) are decadal averages and incorporate the data in Sanderson, 1972, 83. Standard error = ± 3% at 95% level of confidence
				F	36 (25)	(851)	
		1775		M	60 (60)	(2633)	
				F	37 (20)	(872)	
		1785		M	62 (55)	(3296)	
				F	37 (19)	(1154)	
		1795		M	63 (62)	(6901)	
				F	42 (26)	(2957)	
		1805		M	62 (53)	(4963)	
				F	43 (21)	(1949)	
		1815		M	62 (43)	(4848)	
				F	44 (18)	(2016)	
		1825		M	63 (51)	(6530)	
				F	48 (21)	(2672)	
		1835		M	65 (57)	(5915)	
				F	50 (20)	(2889)	
D. Levine, 1980, 29	Parish marriage registers	1754–1824	Shepshed (Leics.)	M	57	135	
				F	31		
		1825–44		M	59	589	
				F	31		
Bradshaw, 1983, 8	Parish marriage registers	1760–1879	Erewash Valley Coalfield				Nottinghamshire/Derbyshire boundary. Selected decadal averages
		1760–9		M	60	436	
				F	39	562	
		1790–9		M	54	832	
				F	34	916	

		1820–9		M	49	1612	
				F	35	1719	
		1850–9		M	52	2281	
				F	41	2399	
		1870–9		M	69	2744	
				F	66	2974	
Baker, 1961, 12	Parish marriage registers	1754–60	Yorks. E. Riding	M	64	215	17 parishes
				F	39	133	
		1771–80		M	65	329	
				F	36	181	
		1791–1800		M	67	365	
				F	48	157	
		1811–20		M	67	445	
				F	50	337	
		1831–40		M	70	541	
				F	54	423	
		1851–60		M	76	576	
				F	63	477	
		1861–70		M	79	561	
				F	74	512	
W.B. Stevens, 1976, 3	Parish marriage registers	1754–1844	Devon	M	74	–	6 parishes – Eggesford,
		1754–64		F	32	–	St Paul, Exeter,
		1785–94		M	54	–	Kentisbeare, Ottery St
				F	34	–	Mary, Plymstock, Wembury
		1815–24		M	59	–	Selected periods
				F	47	–	
		1835–44		M	59	–	
				F	46	–	
West, 1975, p. 130	Minutes of the Committee of Council of Education (1840–1), Appendix III, p. 138	1840	Northumb. and Durham miners	M	79	843	Data collected from 5 collieries

Chart A2.1: (contd.)

Published source	Primary source	Period covered	Area/ locality	Sex	% literate (or with literacy attribute)	Number of cases	Notes
Altick, 1957, p. 171	Registrar General's returns – the number of persons signing marriage registers	1841	England and Wales	M	67	–	
				F	51	–	
		1851		M	69	–	
				F	55	–	
		1861		M	75	–	
				F	65	–	
		1871		M	81	–	
				F	73	–	
		1881		M	86	–	
				F	82	–	
		1891		M	94	–	
				F	93	–	
		1900		M	97	–	
				F	97	–	

Notes

1 Approaching literacy

1 A note on labels. Minority groups and individuals who possess what are judged by their peers to be discreditable characteristics fight constantly to resist intended insults and more subtle verbal abuse. Familiar terminological battles ensue ('nigger' and 'coloured' versus 'negro' and 'black', 'queer' versus 'gay', 'looney' versus 'mentally ill'). In the course of these prolonged campaigns, the middle ground disappears as more and more labels are appropriated by the protagonists (or, more frequently, by the pressure groups and professionals that do much of the in-fighting in their capacity as volunteers, conscripts or mercenaries). In the present case, there is well-founded resistance to both of the terms most commonly used to denote an incapacity to handle the written word. 'Illiterate' is hyperbolic since very few of the people to whom it is customarily applied are, in fact, totally incapable of reading or writing. 'Sub-literate' is an attempt to meet this objection by employing a comparative rather than an absolute standard of disability (in much the same way as 'visually handicapped' is preferred to 'blind'). The problem then becomes the implication of a definite, fixed threshold of competence, and this notion, as we shall see, is seriously misleading. A recent introduction from the United States, unlikely to achieve wide currency, is 'literacy difference'. Its protective and euphemistic intentions are too blatant; would anyone seriously want to describe notable authors, for example, as possessing a 'literacy difference'? The absence of suitable substitutes and the need for variety results in the use throughout this book of both of the first two terms.

2 As the use of French might suggest, the *histoire du livre* is a continental enterprise for which no strict Anglophone equivalent exists (though the works of Altick and H.S. Bennett bear

some resemblance). For characteristic contributions, see Escarpit (1965) and Febvre and Martin (1976).

3 There are innumerable general introductions to the structuralist interpretation of literature. See, for instance, David Robey (ed.), *Structuralism: An Introduction*, Oxford University Press, 1973; Jonathan Culler, *Structuralist Poetics: Structuralism, Linguistics and the Study of Literature*, Ithaca, Cornell University Press, 1975; Terence Hawkes, *Structuralism and Semiotics*, Berkeley, University of California Press, 1977.

4 Accounts of reception theory are given by Roman Ingarden, *The Literary Work of Art: An Investigation on the Borderlines of Ontology, Logic, and Theory of Literature*, trans. and introduced by George G. Grabowicz, Evanston, Ill., Northwestern University Press, 1973; Wolfgang Iser, *The Act of Reading: A Theory of Aesthetic Response*, Baltimore, Johns Hopkins University Press, 1978; Hans Robert Jauss, 'Literary history as a challenge to literary theory', in Ralph Cohen (ed.), *New Directions in Literary History*, London, Routledge & Kegan Paul, 1974.

5 Discourse analysis entails the linguistic examination of spoken or written exchanges, either as complete conversations and whole texts, or in terms of units larger than the statement/sentence. See Michael Stubbs, *Discourse Analysis: The Sociolinguistic Analysis of Natural Language*, Oxford, Blackwell, 1983.

6 The following remarks, for instance, are taken from Jacquetta Hawkes and Leonard Woolley, *History of Mankind*, Vol. 1, London, Allen & Unwin (for UNESCO), 1963, 359 and 631: 'the most convenient and easily recognizable criterion of civilization is the knowledge of the art of writing. . . . In no part of the world has civilization at any time advanced to any considerable height or achieved any permanence unless by the aid of writing.'

7 There are, however, brief allusions to literacy in *The Evolution of Societies*, edited by Toby Jackson, Englewood Cliffs, N.J., Prentice-Hall, 1977.

8 For literacy in the context of the classroom, see Caroline and David Moseley, *Language and Reading Among Underachievers; A Review of Research*, Windsor, NFER, 1977; E.A. Lunzer and K. Gardner, *The Effective Use of Reading*, London, Heinemann, 1981; Margaret Meek, *Achieving Literacy:*

Longitudinal Studies of Adolescents Learning to Read, London, Routledge & Kegan Paul, 1983.

9 See the references to Strumilin (1964) and Blaug (1966) in the bibliography.

10 See, for example, Daniel Lerner (1963). Lipset (1959) refers to Lerner and four other sources as evidence for his general proposition that 'the higher one's education, the more likely one is to believe in democratic values and support democratic parties'. As far as literacy itself is concerned, Lipset provides a table (76) which compares the 'stable European democracies', calculated to have an average literacy rate of 96 per cent, with (among other categories) 'stable Latin American dictatorships' which average only 46 per cent literate. Exactly what can be inferred from his comparison is not clear as Lipset himself concedes that literacy is both an initial condition associated with the emergence of political democracies, and also the product of enduring democratic government.

11 Paulo Freire is perhaps the best-known, explicitly 'political' writer on literacy, but see also C. and L. Berggren (1975) and the rather miscellaneous collection edited by Hoyles (1977).

12 Psychologists, in particular, have usefully explored the cognitive impact of different forms of the institutionalisation of literacy. See, in particular, L.S. Vygotsky, *Mind in Society: The Development of Higher Psychological Processes*, edited by M. Cole, V. John-Steiner, S. Scribner and E. Souberman, Cambridge, Mass., Harvard University Press, 1978; P.M. Greenfield, 'Oral and written language: the consequences for cognitive development in Africa, the United States, and England', *Language and Speech* 15, 1972, 169–78; J.S. Bruner and D.R. Olson, 'Symbols and texts as the tools of intellect', *Interchange* 8 (4), 1977–8, 1–15; S. Scribner and M. Cole, *The Psychology of Literacy*, Cambridge, Mass., Harvard University Press, 1981; A.R. Luria (1976).

13 Bilingualism is a speaker or community's general capacity to use two languages. Diglossia is a particular situation that occurs when two languages (or major variants of the same language) are employed by a community to serve very distinct functions, with the common consequence that one form comes to be regarded as more formal or prestigious than the other. Pidgins are the hybrid languages that arise out of contact between two communities that are initially unable to communi-

cate with each other, but which gradually import and adopt substantial features from each other's language.

14 For a brief overview of the development of the technology of writing, see Michael Clapham (1957).

15 The following have been selected more or less at random: Magdalen D. Vernon, *Backwardness in Reading: A Study of its Nature and Origins*, Cambridge University Press, 1957; F. Schonell, *The Psychology and Teaching of Reading*, 4th edn, Edinburgh, Oliver and Boyd, 1961; Mildred C. Robeck and John A.R. Wilson, *Psychology of Reading: Foundations of Instruction*, New York, Wiley, 1974; Eleanor J. Gibson and Harry Levin, *The Psychology of Reading*, Cambridge, Mass., MIT Press, 1975; James R. Layton, *The Psychology of Learning to Read*, New York, Academic Press, 1979; Keith Rayner (ed.), *Eye Movements in Reading: Perceptual and Language Processes*, New York, Academic Press, 1983.

16 The *Guardian* of 14 April 1983 carried a report from Bucharest that President Ceausescu had signed a decree prohibiting the possession or use of typewriters by people with criminal records and those who posed 'a danger to public order or state security'. Private citizens are required to register with the police any typewriters they own or intend to purchase. The private ownership of reprographic equipment is already banned. The report suggested that the legislation was designed to suppress publications critical of the regime issued by dissident ethnic groups.

17 On one specific aspect of consumer literacy, see Adult Literacy Support Services Fund, *Understanding Labels: Problems for Poor Readers*, 2nd edn, London, 1980.

2 Defining and measuring literacy and illiteracy

1 For an exploration of 'political literacy' in the context of secondary schooling, see Bernard Crick and A. Porter (eds), *Political Education and Political Literacy*, Harlow, Longman, 1978. For a series of interpretations of 'scientific literacy', see the Spring 1983 issue of *Daedalus*. There is a discussion of the relations between computer and ordinary literacy in Chapter 7.

2 Gray cited, Ministry of Education, *Reading Ability: Some Suggestions for Helping the Backward*, London, HMSO, 1950; J. Duncan, *Backwardness in Reading: Remedies and Preven-*

tion, London, Harrap, 1953. Neither source establishes a clear justification for a strict equivalence between reading ages and functional literacy.

3 Norm-referenced tests (such as conventional intelligence tests) compare an individual's score or rating to an average derived from some appropriate comparison group. A criterion-referenced test (such as the driving test) establishes whether or not an individual can achieve a specified standard of performance.

4 Dale-Chall and FORCAST are measures of the readability of text based on calculations of word difficulty and sentence length expressed in terms of reading age. See Gilliland (1976).

5 The absence of a truly general concept of information that covers meaning/content is a major deficiency in the tools for understanding literacy and illiteracy. The major influences on thinking on this topic have been signalling theories designed for radio and electronic applications (deriving from a pioneering contribution from R.V.L. Hartley in 1928), and the mathematical/statistical tradition of information theory developed mainly by Claude Shannon and Norbert Weiner after World War II. Both of these approaches treat 'messages' as sub-sets of arbitrary symbols or codes selected from much larger collections of predefined symbols. The core of successful communication becomes the transmission of a coded message, the contents of which could not have been predicted in advance, to a recipient which (or who), by decoding it, is able to make a choice or decision in a condition of reduced uncertainty. Assisted by powerful probability measures, this approach has aided the design of complex communication systems, but it has not lent itself to such questions as the significance of messages for the sender or recipient, or the ways in which the use the recipient actually makes of a specific transmission diverges from the sender's intentions. The classical sources mentioned above are: R.V.L. Hartley, 'Transmission of information', *Bell System Technical Journal* 7, 1928, 535–63; Claude Shannon, 'The mathematical theory of communication' in C.E. Shannon and W. Weaver (eds), *The Mathematical Theory of Communication*, University of Illinois Press, 1962 (first published in the *Bell System Technical Journal* in 1948); Norbert Wiener, *Cybernetics*, MIT Press, 1962 [1948].

3 The historical perspective

1 For the development of the Greek alphabet, see the essays collected in E.A. Havelock, *The Literate Revolution in Greece and its Cultural Consequences*, Princeton University Press, 1982.

2 Roman literacy has attracted less attention than Greek, but see T. Haarhoff, *Schools of Gaul*, Oxford, Clarendon, 1920; Kenyon (1932); R.P.V.D. Balsdon, *Life and Leisure in Ancient Rome*, London, Bodley Head, 1969.

3 One example of an oral cultural survival in the era of print are the elaborate systems for memorising information, some of which became the basis of occult philosophies. See Frances Yates, *The Art of Memory*, London, Routledge & Kegan Paul, 1966; W.J. Ong, *Ramus, Method, and the Decay of Dialogue*, Harvard University Press, 1958. Magical systems of belief represent another major survival, dealt with at length in Keith Thomas, *Religion and the Decline of Magic*, Peregrine Books, 1978. Thomas suggests (778) that improved literacy and communications were among the constellation of factors leading to the gradual collapse of the mainly oral systems of magic that included divination, charms, folk medicine, witchcraft and sorcery. E.P. Thompson argues in a review article (*Midland History*, 13, 1972, 41–55) that the decline was much more evident in polite (literate?) culture, and that there are ample signs of the persistence of such beliefs in eighteenth-century popular (oral?) culture. Thompson interprets Wesleyanism as a 'movement of counter-enlightenment' (54), attempting to bridge the sensibilities of the two cultures.

4 The idea that the titled aristocracy should receive, as a preparation for high office, a thorough grounding in the heritage of Latinate culture gained considerable ground during this period. Latin was obviously 'functional' for those dealing with legal or administrative matters only as long as the documents they had to handle contained extensive Latinisms; long after this ceased to be the case, and certainly up until the end of the eighteenth century, the context of classical allusion and literary reference survived as an effective medium for signalling intellectual and social standing. The durability of Latin as a status symbol was partly due to the continuing relative exclusivity of access to this competence, but partly also to the fact that

literacy in Latin never became completely assimilated within specific occupational or technical roles.

5 Cressy's sources on the literacy and illiteracy of women are mainly the signatures of lay deponents to ecclesiastical courts, and other autograph records such as the acknowledgments of the discharge of children from Christ's Hospital for 1637–9, 1667–70, and 1687–9. For details of archival sources see Cressy, 1980, 223, notes 18, 20 and 21.

6 The power of a principled, religiously inspired and socially unselective literacy drive can be seen in late seventeenth-century Sweden where the Lutheran Church, supported by the state, made holy communion and marriage dependent on a test of reading ability (Johansson, 1977). Work by Lockridge (1974) on the immigrants to Colonial New England reveals similar intense pressure to ensure near universal male literacy within the puritan communities by means of compulsory elementary schools.

7 Autobiography, diaries, personal correspondence and jottings, written without formal publication in mind and free from external editing, make up a corpus of evidence on historical literacy that has only recently begun to be fruitfully exploited, but which promises to complement research based on parish register signature rates. See, in particular, Spufford (1979) and Vincent (1981).

8 Some of the research on this point is quoted in Blaug, 1966, 416–17; A.M. Nalla Gounden, *A Study in Human Capital Formation and its Role in Economic Development in India, 1951–1961*, Ph.D. dissertation, Kurushetra University, 1965, 70 and 97; C. and R. Sofer, *Jinja Transformed: A Social Survey of a Multi-racial Township*, Kampala, Uganda, East African Institute of Social Research, 1955, 46–8; V.G. Pons, N. Xydias and P. Clement, *Social Implications of Industrialisation and Urbanisation in Africa South of the Sahara*, Paris, UNESCO, 1956, 269 and 641.

4 Tutors and students

1 Office of Population Census and Surveys, *Health District Data*.

2 DHSS Local Authority Personal Social Services, *Summary of Planning Returns 1977–78 to 1980–81*.

3 *Report of the Chief Constable of Nottinghamshire*, 1979.

4 One example is Robert A. Scott's study of the American system of rehabilitation for the blind and partially sighted, published in 1969 by the Russell Sage Foundation as *The Making of Blind Men*. Scott pointed out that a major disparity existed between the characteristics of the blind population of the United States and the character of welfare provision by private and public agencies. Adults under retirement age and children represented under a third of the total blind population, yet attracted 60 per cent of all economic resources at the expense of the much more numerous aged blind. Scott went on to show that, having recruited selectively, rehabilitation organisations taught their recruits how to behave as stereotypically blind people, emphasising types of training and aids that prolonged dependency. While, for instance, the majority of their clients possessed some residual sight, the agencies insisted on highlighting techniques like braille and the long cane that cannot exploit it but coincide with popular conceptions of appropriate blind behaviour.

5 Illiteracy and work

1 Vertical job mobility implies an increase in job status or seniority, while horizontal shifts are between different jobs at the same status level.

2 Labour economists often treat the major, established manufacturers in oligopolistic markets as 'primary employers', offering premium wage levels and conditions for particular skills, and generally able to be highly selective hirers of labour. The secondary market consists of financially less secure firms functioning on smaller profit margins and able to attract less skilled and experienced personnel. Among the secondary firms, there are usually 'cowboy' operators who survive by cutting corners and sailing close to the wind in respect of the various legal obligations on employers.

3 'Lower grade' work is derived from Amitai Etzioni's (1961) notion of 'lower participants' in organisations who occupy subordinate roles within the organisational authority structure. No judgement about the social value of the work is intended.

6 Dealing with illiteracy

1 An interesting account of the spread of arithmetic and statistical skills among American colonial settlers is provided in Patricia Cline Cohen, *A Calculating People: The Spread of Numeracy in Early America*, University of Chicago Press, 1982.

2 The classical source (in translation) is *Economy and Society: An Outline of Interpretive Sociology*, edited by G. Roth and C. Wittich. 3 Vols, New York, Bedminster, 1968, Vol. 3, Chap. 3.

3 For instance, Hilda H. Golden (1957); Daniel Lerner (1958); K.W. Deutsch, 'Social mobilization and political development', *American Political Science Review* 55, 1961, 493–514; W. Schramm, 'Communication and change', L.W. Pye, 'Communication, institution building, and the research of authority', Ithiel de Sola Pool, 'The mass media and politics in the modernization process', and Daniel Lerner, 'Toward a communication theory of modernization', all in Lucien W. Pye (ed.), (1963); T.W. Schultz, *Transforming Traditional Agriculture*, New York, Arno Press, 1973; S.G. Strumilin (1964); Bert F. Hoselitz, 'Investment in education and its political impact', in J.S. Coleman (ed.), *Education and Political Development*, Princeton University Press, 1965; C.A. Anderson (1966); Samuel Huntington, *Political Order in Changing Societies*, Yale University Press, 1968; Carlo M. Cipolla (1969).

4 One of the traditional objections to inferences to adults from school-based research is the problem of regression of skills and possible relapse into illiteracy. For a view which doubts the significance of regression, see Bryan Rodgers in the *Times Educational Supplement*, 1 July 1983.

5 On the clarity of legal English, see the correspondence in *The Law Society's Gazette* during 1983 (12 January, 67; 2 March, 524; 8 June, 1484). See also Patricia Wright (1981).

6 For analysis and critiques of Freire's political thinking, see J. Demaine, *Contemporary Theories in the Sociology of Education*, London, Macmillan, 1981, 85–91, and several of the contributions to Mackie (1980).

7 The future of literacy and literacies of the future

1 D. Subotic, *Yugoslav Popular Ballads: Their Origin and Development*, Cambridge University Press, 1932; A.B. Lord

(1968); R. Finnegan, *Oral Literature in Africa*, Oxford, Clarendon Press, 1970.

2 McLuhan's *The Gutenberg Galaxy* (1962) and *Understanding Media* (1964) both contain versions of the ideas referred to, as do Ong's works *The Presence of the Word* (1970) and *Interfaces of the Word* (1977), which preceded *Orality and Literacy* (1982), and also the detailed study of printing by Eisenstein cited in the bibliography. See also, Walter Benjamin, 'The storyteller: reflections on the work of Nicolai Leskov' in *Illuminations*, London, Fontana, 1973.

3 For an analysis of the development of Egyptian hieroglyphics which emphasised the importance of ritual applications see Carleton T. Hodge, 'Ritual and writing: an inquiry into the origin of Egyptian script', in M.D. Kinkade, K.L. Hale and O. Werner (eds), *Linguistics and Anthropology: In Honour of C.F. Voegelin*, Peter De Ridder, Lisse, 1975.

4 Deborah Tannen, 'A comparative analysis of oral narrative strategies: Athenian Greek and American English', in Wallace L. Chafe (ed.), *The Pear Stories: Cultural, Cognitive and Linguistic Aspects of Narrative Production*, Norwood, N.J., Ablex, 1980.

5 Although Basil Bernstein's work appears to have a general bearing on these matters, he has stated explicitly (1971, 56, note 4) that: 'The distinction between public and formal language use is not simply a question of an oral and a written language.' Neither of the other major conceptual distinctions that he has employed (restricted versus elaborated codes, classification versus frame) have corresponded in any direct way to the oral/written dichotomy.

6 One social category left out of account in this section are immigrants who may be obliged to rely especially heavily on oral modes of communication. How the adult members of immigrant communities, whose first language is not the one of the host society in which they are living, handle the process of becoming literate in a second language (sometimes, of course, literate for the first time) can be a major determinant of the extent and character of the group's long-term relationship with the native population. While it is among immigrant groups that full illiteracy is likely to be most heavily concentrated, the severe problems of assisting such groups with appropriate programmes and materials fall outside our present concerns.

7 Figures from *An International Survey of Book Production During the Last Decades*, Statistical Reports and Papers, No. 26, Paris, UNESCO, 1982, 10 and 23.

8 Figures from *Benn's Press Directory*, 1984.

9 Derek Price, 'The science of science', in John R. Platt (ed.), *New Views of the Nature of Man*, Chicago, 1965, quoted in Bell (1973).

10 The Letter-Writing Bureau, *The Letter-Writing Report*, London, 1984, 6.

11 D. Butler and A. Sloman, *British Political Facts*, fifth edn, London, 1980, 318; Post Office Briefing Service, *Brief 3*, 1982.

12 Quoted in *Report of the Committee on Data Protection*, (Chairman, Sir Norman Lindop), HMSO, 1978, 325.

13 James L. Hall and Marjorie J. Brown, *On-Line Databases: An International Directory*, second edn, ASLIB, 1981, xvii.

14 Bell's work was one of a series on the same theme. The other influential titles include, Fritz Machlup, *The Production and Distribution of Knowledge in the United States*, Princeton University Press, 1962; Amitai Etzioni, *The Active Society*, New York, Free Press, 1976; Marc Porat, *The Information Economy*, Stanford, Calif., Center for Interdisciplinary Research, 1976; Simon Nora, *L'Informatisation de la Société*, Paris, Documentation Française, 1978, translated as S. Nora and A. Minc. *The Computerization of Society*, Cambridge, Mass., MIT Press, 1980.

15 The designers of a 'high-level' computer language (such as Basic) generally place a high priority on keeping the vocabulary and syntax as intelligible as possible within the user's natural language. In 'low-level' languages (such as any assembly language) immediate intelligibility is sacrificed in order to preserve a close correspondence between each statement in assembly code and one of the instructions in the 'set' that a particular variety of a microprocessor can recognise and execute.

Bibliography

Adamson, J.W. (1929), 'The extent of literacy in England in the fifteenth and sixteenth centuries: notes and conjectures', *The Library*, 10, 2, 163–93.

Adamson, J.W. (1946), *The Illiterate Anglo-Saxon and Other Essays on Education, Medieval and Modern*, Cambridge University Press.

Ahmed, Mustaq (1958), *Materials for New Literates*, New Delhi, Research Training and Production Centre.

ALBSU (1981), *Adult Literacy Unit Development Projects, 1978–80*, Adult Literacy and Basic Skills Unit.

ALBSU (1983), *Literacy and Numeracy: Evidence from the National Child Development Study*, Adult Literacy and Basic Skills Unit.

ALRA (1977), *An Approach to Functional Literacy*, Adult Literacy Resource Agency.

Altick, Richard D. (1957), *The English Common Reader: A Social History of the Mass Reading Public 1800–1900*, University of Chicago Press.

Amsden, Alice H. (ed.) (1980), *The Economics of Women and Work*, Harmondsworth, Penguin.

Anderson, C.A. (1966), 'Literacy and schooling on the development threshold: some historical cases', in C.A. Anderson and M.J. Bowman (eds), *Education and Economic Development*.

Anderson, C.A. and Bowman, M.J. (eds) (1966), *Education and Economic Development*, London, Cass.

Anderson, C.A. and Bowman, M.J. (1976), 'Education and economic modernization in historical perspective', in L. Stone (ed.), *Schooling and Society*.

Anon. (1975), *We Made A Go of It: Twelve People who Learned to Read and Write: by their Tutors*, Pinner, Middx., The Grail.

Arrow, Kenneth J. (1972), 'Models of Job discrimination', in A.H. Pascal (ed.), *Racial Discrimination in Economic Life*, Lexington, Mass., D.C. Heath.

Arrow, Kenneth J. (1973a), 'The theory of discrimination', in O. Ashenfelter and A. Rees (eds), *Discrimination in Labour Markets*, Princeton University Press.

Arrow, Kenneth, J. (1973b), 'Higher education as a filter', *Journal of Public Economics*, 2, 193–216.

Baker, W.P. (1961), *Parish Registers and Illiteracy in East Yorkshire*, East Yorkshire Local History Society.

Bataille, Leon (ed.) (1976), *A Turning Point for Literacy*, Oxford, Pergamon Press.

Bauml, Franz H. (1980), 'Varieties and consequences of medieval literacy and illiteracy', *Speculum*, 55, 237–65.

BBC (1975), *BBC Adult Literacy Handbook*, first edn, London, BBC Publications.

Becker, Gary S. (1971), *The Economics of Discrimination*, second edn, University of Chicago Press.

Becker, Gary S. (1975), *Human Capital*, second edn, Columbia University Press.

Bell, Daniel (1973), *The Coming of the Post-Industrial Society: A Venture in Social Forecasting*, New York, Basic Books.

Bell, Daniel (1979), *The Cultural Contradictions of Capitalism*, second edn, London, Heinemann.

Bell, Daniel (1980), 'The social framework of the information society', in Tom Forester (ed.), *The Microelectronics Revolution*.

Bell, H.E. (1936–7), 'The price of books in medieval England', *The Library*, fourth series, 17, 312–32.

Belville, Margaret (1978), 'Break-in to literacy', *Probation Journal*, 25, 128–33.

Bennett, H.S. (1943), 'Caxton and his public', *The Review of English Studies*, 19, 113–19.

Bennett, H.S. (1946–7), 'The production and dissemination of vernacular manuscripts in the fifteenth century', *The Library*, fifth series, 1, 167–78.

Bennett, H.S. (1965), *English Books and Readers, 1558–1603*, Cambridge University Press.

Bennett, H.S. (1969), *English Books and Readers, 1475–1557*, second edn, Cambridge University Press.

Bennett, H.S. (1970), *English Books and Readers, 1603–1640*, Cambridge University Press.

Bentovim, Margaret and Kedney, R.J. (eds) (1974), *Aspects of Adult Literacy*, Merseyside and District Institute of Adult Education.

Berg, Ivar (1970), *Education and Jobs: The Great Training Robbery*, New York, Praeger.

Berger, Peter L. and Luckmann, Thomas (1971), *The Social Construction of Reality*, Harmondsworth, Penguin.

Berggren, Carol and Lars (1975), *The Literacy Process: A Practice in Domestication or Liberation*, London, Writers and Readers Publishing Cooperative.

Bernstein, Basil (ed.) (1971), *Class, Codes and Control. Vol. 1: Theoretical Studies towards a Sociology of Language*, London, Routledge & Kegan Paul.

Bernstein, Basil (ed.) (1973), *Class, Codes and Control. Vol.2: Applied Studies towards a Sociology of Language*, London, Routledge & Kegan Paul.

Bernstein, Basil (ed.) (1975), *Class, Codes and Control. Vol. 3: Towards a Theory of Educational Transmissions*, London, Routledge & Kegan Paul.

Bhola, H.S. (n.d.), *Functional Literacy – the Concept and the Program*, Indiana University Occasional Paper in Reading (1969?).
Bigsby, C.W.E. (1976), 'The politics of popular culture', in C.W.E. Bigsby (ed.), *Approaches to Popular Culture*.
Bigsby, C.W.E. (ed.) (1976), *Approaches to Popular Culture*, London, Edward Arnold.
Birnbaum, Pierre, Lively, Jack and Parry, Geraint (eds) (1978), *Democracy, Consensus and Social Contract*, London, Sage.
Black, M.H. (1963), 'The printed Bible', in S.L. Greenslade (ed.), *Cambridge History of the Bible, Vol.3: the West from the Reformation to the Present Day*, Cambridge University Press.
Blackburn, R.M. and Mann, Michael (1979), *The Working Class in the Labour Market*, London, Macmillan.
Blaug, Mark (1966), 'Literacy and economic development', *The School Review*, 74, 4, 393–418.
Blaug, Mark (1969), 'The evaluation of functional literacy: an economist's view', in F. Wood (ed.), *The Evaluation of Functional Literacy Projects*.
Blaug, Mark (1970), *An Introduction to the Economics of Education*, London, Allen Lane, The Penguin Press.
Blaug, Mark (1978), 'The empirical status of human capital theory: a slightly jaundiced survey', *Journal of Economic Literature*, 16, 827–55.
Blaxter, Mildred (1975), ' "Disability" and rehabilitation: some questions of definition', in C. Cox and A. Mead (eds), *A Sociology of Medical Practice*.
Bloomfield, Leonard (1964), 'Literate and illiterate speech', in Dell Hymes (ed.), *Language in Culture and Society*, New York, Harper and Row.
Boring, Terrence A. (1979), 'Literacy in Ancient Sparta', *Mnemosyne, Bibliotheca Classica Batava*, Supplementum 54.
Bormuth, John R. (1973), 'Reading literacy: its definition and assessment', *Reading Research Quarterly*, 9, 7–66.
Bormuth, John R. (1978), 'Value and volume of literacy', *Visible Language*, 12, 118–62.
Bowers, John (1969), 'Functional literacy: definition and evaluation', in F. Wood (ed.), *The Evaluation of Functional Literacy Projects*.
Bowman, Mary Jean and Anderson, C. Arnold (1963), 'Concerning the role of education in development', in C. Geertz (ed.), *Old Societies and New States*, New York, Free Press.
Bowren, Fay R. and Zintz, Miles V. (1977), *Teaching Reading in Adult Basic Education*, Dubuque, Iowa, William C. Brown.
Bradshaw, John (1983), 'Occupation and literacy in the Erewash Valley coalfield, 1760–1880', in W.B. Stephens (ed.), *Studies in the History of Literacy*.
Braverman, Harry (1974), *Labour and Monopoly Capital: The Degradation of Work in the Twentieth Century*, New York, Monthly Review Press.
British Association of Settlements (1974), *A Right to Read*, BAS.
British Association of Settlements (1977), *Adult Literacy: A Continuing Need*, BAS.
Bromage, A.W. (1930), 'Literacy and the electorate', *American Political Science Review*, 24, 4, 946–62.

Brown, Rexford (1981), 'National assessments of writing ability', in Carl F. Frederiksen and Joseph F. Dominic (eds), *Writing*.

Brownhill, J.R. (1978), 'Polanyi's philosophy and adult reading problems', *Adult Education*, 50, 289–93.

Bruneau, William A. (1973), 'Literacy, urbanization and education in three ancient cultures', *Journal of Education*, 19, 9–22.

Burns, Alfred (1981), 'Athenian literacy in the fifth century BC', *Journal of the History of Ideas*, 42, 371–88.

Burt, Cyril (1945), 'The education of illiterate adults', *British Journal of Educational Psychology*, 15, 20–7.

Campbell, John (1983), 'Occupation and literacy in Bristol and Gloucestershire, 1755–1870', in W.B. Stephens (ed.), *Studies in the History of Literacy*.

Campbell, M.J. (1980), 'The development of literacy in Bristol and Gloucestershire 1755–1870', Ph.D. thesis, University of Bath.

Capp, Bernard (1979), *Astrology and the Popular Press: English Almanacs 1500–1800*, London, Faber and Faber.

Carroll, John B. and Chall, Jeanne S. (eds) (1975), *Toward a Literate Society: The Report of the Committee on Reading of the National Academy of Education*, New York, McGraw-Hill.

Cashdan, Asher (ed.) (1976), *The Content of Reading*, London, Ward Lock.

Chandler, George (1973), 'Research on books and reading in society in the United Kingdom', *International Library Review*, 5, 277–82.

Charnley, A.H. (1978), 'Aims and achievements of adults in remedial literacy schemes: with special reference to Cambridgeshire', Ph.D. thesis, University of Leicester.

Charnley, A.H. and Jones H.A. (1979), *The Concept of Success in Adult Literacy*, Cambridge, Huntingdon Publishers.

Chaytor, H.J. (1945), *From Script to Print*, Cambridge University Press.

Chiplin, Brian and Sloane, Peter J. (1974), 'Sexual discrimination in the labour market', *British Journal of Industrial Relations*, 12, 371–402.

Cipolla, Carlo M. (1969), *Literacy and Development in the West*, Harmondsworth, Penguin.

Clanchy, M.T. (1979), *From Memory to Written Record: England 1066–1307*, London, Edward Arnold.

Clapham, Michael (1957), 'Printing', in Charles Singer, E.J. Holmyard, A.R. Hall and Trevor Williams (eds), *A History of Technology*, Vol. III, Oxford University Press.

Clark, Peter (1976), 'The ownership of books in England, 1560–1640: the example of some Kentish townsfolk', in Lawrence Stone (ed.), *Schooling and Society*.

Clyne, P. (1972), *The Disadvantaged Adult: Educational and Social Needs of Minority Groups*, Harlow, Longman.

Coates, Ken and Silburn, Richard (1968), *Poverty: the Forgotten Englishmen*, Harmondsworth, Penguin.

Coates, Ken and Silburn, Richard (1980), *Beyond the Bulldozer*, Department of Adult Education, University of Nottingham.

Collinson, P. (1981), *Times Literary Supplement*, 9 Jan.
Collison, Robert (1973), *The Story of Street Literature*, London, Dent.
Committee on Plan Projects of the Government of India, (1963), *Report on Social Education*, New Delhi, Government Printing Office.
Cook, Wanda Dauksza (1977), *Adult Literacy Education in the United States*, Newark, Del., International Reading Association.
Cook-Gumperz, Jenny and John J. (1981), 'From oral to written culture: the transition to literacy', in Marcia Farr Whiteman (ed.), *Writing*, Vol.I.
Cooper, Thomas W. (1981), 'McLuhan and Innis: the Canadian theme of boundless exploration', *Journal of Communication*, 31, 153–61.
Cornish, W.R. (1981), *Intellectual Property: Patents, Copyright, Trade Marks and Allied Rights*, London, Sweet and Maxwell.
Corrigan, Philip and Gillespie, Val (1978), *Class Struggle, Social Literacy and Idle Time: The Provision of Public Libraries in England as a Case Study in 'The Organisation of Leisure with Indirect Educational Results'*, Brighton, John L. Noyce.
Couvert, R. (1979), *The Evaluation of Literacy Programmes: A Practical Guide*, Paris, UNESCO.
Cox, C. and Mead, A. (eds) (1975), *A Sociology of Medical Practice*, West Drayton, Middx., Collier Macmillan.
Cressy, David A. (1972), 'Education and literacy in London and East Anglia 1580–1700', Ph.D. dissertation, Cambridge University.
Cressy, David (1977a), 'Levels of illiteracy in England 1530–1730', *Historical Journal*, 20, 1–23.
Cressy, David (1977b), 'Literacy in seventeenth-century England: more evidence', *Journal of Interdisciplinary History*, 8, 141–50.
Cressy, David (1980), *Literacy and the Social Order: Reading and Writing in Tudor and Stuart England*, Cambridge University Press.
Crosby, Ruth (1939), 'Oral delivery in the middle ages', *Speculum*, 11, 88–110.
Daniel, W.W. (1974), *A National Survey of the Unemployed*, P.E.P. (Policy Studies Institute).
Dank, Barry M. (1971), 'Coming out in the gay world', *Psychiatry*, 34, 180–97.
Davies, W.J.F. (1973), *Teaching Reading in Early England*, London, Pitman.
Davis, Fred (1961), 'Deviance disavowal: the management of strained interaction by the visibly handicapped', *Social Problems*, 9, 120–32.
Davis, Natalie Zemon (1975), *Society and Culture in Early Modern France*, Stanford University Press.
Davison, Alice and Kantor, Robert N. (1982), 'On the failure of readability formulas to define readable texts: a case study from adaptions', *Reading Research Quarterly*, 2, 187–209.
Deanesly, M. (1920), 'Vernacular books in England in the fourteenth and fifteenth centuries', *Modern Language Review*, 15, 349–58.
Dearden, R.F., Hirst, P.H. and Peters, R.S. (eds) (1972), *Education and the Development of Reason*, London, Routledge & Kegan Paul.
Department of Education and Science (1972), *Children with Special Reading Difficulties: Report of the Advisory Committee on Handicapped*

Children, (Prof. J. Tizzard, Chairman), London, HMSO.
Department of Education and Science (1973), *Adult Education: A Plan for Development*, (Sir Lionel Russell, Chairman), London, HMSO.
Department of Education and Science (1975) *A Language of Life*, (Sir Alan Bullock, Chairman), London, HMSO.
Department of Education and Science (1977), *Adult Literacy: Developments in 1976/77*, London, HMSO.
Department of Education and Science (1978a), *Adult Literacy in 1977/78: A Remarkable Educational Advance*, London, HMSO.
Department of Education and Science (1978b), *Statistics of Education: Schools*, Vol.1, London, HMSO.
Department of Education and Science and Scottish Education Department, *Adult Literacy: Progress in 1975/76*, London, HMSO.
Department of Employment (1981), *Review of Administrative Forms*, London, DOE.
Derksen, J.B.D. (1957), 'Illiteracy and national income', in UNESCO, *World Illiteracy at Mid-Century*.
Destrez, J. (1935), *La 'Pecia' dans les Manuscrits Universitaires du XIIIe et du XIVe Siècle*, Paris, n.p.
DeYoung, John E. and Hunt, Chester L. (1962), 'Communication channels and functional literacy in the Philippine Bario', *Journal of Asian Studies*, 22, 67–77.
Diringer, David (1947), *The Alphabet: A Key to the History of Mankind*, London, Hutchinson.
Disch, Robert (ed.) (1973), *The Future of Literacy*, Englewood Cliffs, N.J., Prentice-Hall.
Division of Extension (1975), *Adult Functional Competency: A Summary*, Division of Extension, University of Texas, Austin.
Doeringer, Peter B. and Piore, Michael J. (1971), *Internal Labour Markets and Manpower Analysis*, Lexington, Mass., D.C. Heath.
Doob, L.W. (1961), *Communication in Africa: A Search for Boundaries*, Yale University Press.
Douglas, Jack D. (ed.) (1970), *Deviance and Respectability*, New York, Basic Books.
Dow, Sterling, (1973), 'Minoan and Mycenaean literacy', in I.E.S. Edwards, C.J. Gadd, N.G.L. Hammond and E. Sollberger (eds), *The Cambridge Ancient History*, third edn, Vol.II, Part 1, Cambridge University Press.
Downing, John (ed.) (1964), *The First International Reading Symposium*, Oxford, Cassell.
Downing, John (1973), 'Cultural priorities and the acquisition of literacy', *International Review of Education*, 19, 345–54.
Eagleton, Terry (1983), *Literary Theory: An Introduction*, Oxford, Blackwell.
Eisenstein, Elizabeth L. (1968), 'Some conjectures about the impact of printing on western society and thought: a preliminary report', *Journal of Modern History*, 40, 1–56.
Eisenstein, Elizabeth L. (1979), *The Printing Press as an Agent of Social Change: Communications and Cultural Transformations in Early Mod-*

ern Europe, 2 Vols, Cambridge University Press.

Elliott, Philip (1982), 'Intellectuals, the "information society" and the disappearance of the public sphere', *Media, Culture and Society*, 4, 243–53.

Escarpit, Robert (1965), *The Book Revolution*, Paris, UNESCO.

Etzioni, Amitai (1961), *A Comparative Analysis of Complex Organizations*, New York, Free Press.

Evans, N.R. (1980), 'Testators, literacy, education and religious belief', *Local Population Studies*, 25, 42–50.

Febvre, Lucien and Martin, Henri-Jean (1976), *The Coming of the Book*, trans. by David Gerard, London, New Left Books.

Figurel, J. Allen (ed.) (1970), *Reading Goals for the Disadvantaged*, Newark, Del., International Reading Association.

Finnegan, Ruth (1981), 'Literacy and literature', in Barbara Lloyd and John Gay (eds), *Universals of Human Thought*, Cambridge University Press.

Firth, C.B. (1917), 'Benefit of clergy in the time of Edward IV', *English Historical Review*, 32, 175–83.

Fisher, Donald L. (1981), 'Functional literacy tests: a model of question-answering and an analysis of errors', *Reading Research Quarterly*, 3, 418–48.

Forester, Tom (1980), *The Microelectronics Revolution*, Oxford, Blackwell.

Frawley, William (ed.) (1982), *Linguistics and Literacy*, New York, Plenum.

Frazer, James George (1951), *The Golden Bough: A Study in Magic and Religion*, third edn, 12 Vols, London, Macmillan [1907–15].

Frederiksen, Carl F. and Dominic, Joseph F. (eds) (1981), *Writing: The Nature, Development and Teaching of Written Communication*, Vol. 2, Hillsdale, N.J., Lawrence Erlbaum.

Freeman, Howard E. and Kassebaum, Gene G. (1956), 'The illiterate in American society', *Social Forces*, 34, 371–5.

Freidson, Eliot (1966), 'Disability as social deviance', in Marvin B. Sussman (ed.), *Sociology and Rehabilitation*.

Freire, Paulo (1972a), *Pedagogy of the Oppressed*, Harmondsworth, Penguin.

Freire, Paulo (1972b), *Cultural Action for Freedom*, Harmondsworth, Penguin.

Freire, Paulo (1973), *Education for Critical Consciousness*, New York, Seabury Press.

Furet, François and Sachs, Wladimir (1974), 'La croissance de l'alphabétisation en France: XVIIIe–XIXe siècle', *Annales: Economies, Sociétés, Civilisations*, 29, 3, 714–37.

Furet, François and Ozouf, Jacques (1982), *Reading and Writing: Literacy in France from Calvin to Jules Ferry*, Cambridge University Press.

Gabel, Leona C. (1969), *Benefit of Clergy in England in the Later Middle Ages*, New York, Octagon Books, [1929].

Galenson, David W. (1981), 'Literacy and age in preindustrial England: quantitative evidence and implications', *Economic Development and Cultural Change*, 29, 813–30.

Gellner, Ernest (1964), *Thought and Change*, London, Weidenfeld and Nicolson.

Gellner, Ernest (1981) 'Setting the zeal on the Muslim state', *Times Higher Education Supplement*, 20 Nov., 12–13.

Ghazzali, A. and Harris, J. (eds) (1976) *Literacy and the Adult*, Dept. of Adult Education, University of Manchester.

Gilliland, John (1976), *Readability*, London, Hodder and Stoughton.

Girouard, Mark (1980), *Life in the English Country House*, Harmondsworth, Penguin.

Goffman, Erving (1968), *Stigma: Notes on the Management of Spoiled Identity*, Harmondsworth, Penguin.

Gold, Patricia C. and Horn, Pamela L. (1983), 'Intelligence and achievement of adult illiterates in a tutorial project', *Journal of Clinical Psychology*, 39, 1, 107–13.

Golden, Hilda H. (1955), 'Literacy and social change in underdeveloped countries', *Rural Society*, 20, 1–7.

Golden, Hilda H. (1957), 'Illiteracy and urban industrialization', in UNESCO, *World Illiteracy at Mid-Century*.

Goldschmidt, E.P. (1943), *Medieval Texts and their First Appearance in Print*, Bibliographical Society of London.

Goldschmidt, E.P. (1950), *The Printed Book of the Renaissance: Type, Illustration, Ornament*, Cambridge University Press.

Goody, Jack (ed.) (1968), *Literacy in Traditional Societies*, Cambridge University Press.

Goody, Jack (1977a), *The Domestication of the Savage Mind*, Cambridge University Press.

Goody, Jack (1977b), 'Literacy, criticism and the growth of knowledge', in Joseph Ben-David and Terry Nichols Clark (eds), *Culture and its Creators: Essays in Honour of Edward Shils*, University of Chicago Press.

Goody, Jack, Cole, Michael and Scribner, Sylvia (1977), 'Writing and formal operations: a case study among the Vai', *Africa*, 47, 289–304.

Goody, Jack and Watt, Ian (1968), 'The consequences of literacy' in Jack Goody (ed.), *Literacy in Traditional Societies*.

Gorman, T.P. (1981), 'A survey of attainment and progress of learners in adult literacy schemes', *Educational Research*, 23, 190–8.

Gough, Kathleen (1968), 'Implications of literacy in traditional China and India', in Jack Goody (ed.), *Literacy in Traditional Societies*.

Gove, Walter R. (ed.) (1975), *The Labelling of Deviance*, New York, Sage.

Graff, Harvey J. (1975), 'Literacy and history', *History of Education Quarterly*, 15, 467–74.

Graff, Harvey J. (1976), *Literacy in History: An Interdisciplinary Research Bibliography*, Chicago, Ill., The Newberry Library.

Graff, Harvey J. (1978a), 'Literacy past and present: critical approaches in the literacy/society relationship', *Interchange*, 9, 1, 1–21.

Graff, Harvey J. (1978b), 'The reality behind the rhetoric: the social and economic meanings of literacy in the mid-nineteenth century: the example of literacy and criminality', in N. McDonald and A. Chaiton (eds), *Egerton Ryerson and his Times*, Toronto, Macmillan.

Graff, Harvey J. (1979), *The Literacy Myth: Literacy and Social Structure in the Nineteenth Century City*, New York, Academic Press.
Graff, Harvey J. (ed.) (1981), *Literacy and Social Development in the West: A Reader*, Cambridge University Press.
Gray, W.S. (1956), *The Teaching of Reading and Writing*, Paris, UNESCO.
Grayson, Jacky (1983), 'Literacy, schooling and industrialization; Worcestershire 1760–1850' in W.B. Stephens (ed.), *Studies in the History of Literacy*.
Greenleigh Associates (1966), *Field Test and Evaluation of Selected Adult Basic Education Systems*, New York, Greenleigh Associates.
Hammond, J.L. and Hammond, Barbara (1930), *The Rise of Modern Industry*, fourth edn, London, Methuen.
Hampson, Roger (1978), 'A study of D.H.S.S. leaflets: the language of bureaucracy', M.A. thesis, University of Bristol.
Hampson, Roger (1979), 'D.H.S.S.'s private language', *New Society*, 4 Jan.
Harding, D.W. (1972), 'The role of the onlooker', in A. Cashdan and E. Grugeon (eds), *Language in Education*, London, Routledge & Kegan Paul with the Open University Press.
Hargreaves, David Harold (1980), *Adult Literacy and Broadcasting, The BBC's Experience*, London, Pinter.
Harman, David (1970), 'Illiteracy: an overview', *Harvard Educational Review*, 40, 226–43.
Harman, David (1974), *Community Fundamental Education*, Lexington, Mass., D.C. Heath.
Harris, Louis and Associates (1970), *Survival Literacy Study* (No. 2036), New York, L. Harris and Associates.
Harris, Louis and Associates (1971), *The 1971 National Reading Difficulty Index*, New York, L. Harris and Associates.
Harrison, Bennett and Sum, Andrew (1979), 'The theory of "dual" or segmented labour markets', *Journal of Economic Issues*, 13, 687–706.
Harrop, Sylvia, A. (1983), 'Literacy and educational attitudes as factors in the industrialization of North-East Cheshire, 1760–1830', in W.B. Stephens (ed.), *Studies in the History of Literacy*.
Harvey, F.D. (1966), 'Literacy in the Athenian democracy', *Revue des Etudes Grecques*, 79, 585–635.
Hatley, Victor A. (1966), 'Literacy at Northampton, 1761–1900', *Northamptonshire Past and Present*, 4, 379–81.
Havelock, Eric A. (1973), 'Prologue to Greek literacy', in *Lectures in Memory of Louise Taft Semple*, University of Cincinnati Classical Studies, Vol.2, University of Oklahoma Press.
Havelock, Eric A. (1976), *Origins of Western Literacy*, Toronto, Ontario Institute for Studies in Education.
Havelock, E.A. (1982), *The Literate Revolution in Greece and its Cultural Consequences*, Princeton University Press.
Haviland, R.M. (1973), *Provision for Adult Literacy in England*, Reading, University of Reading, School of Education Centre for the Teaching of Reading.

Hawkes, Jacquetta and Woolley, Leonard (1963), *History of Mankind: Cultural and Scientific Development*, Vol. I, London, Allen and Unwin (for UNESCO).

Hay, Denys (1957), 'Introduction', to G.R. Potter (ed.), *The New Cambridge Modern History*, Vol. I., Cambridge University Press.

Hay, Denys (1958), 'Literature, the printed book', in G.R. Elton (ed.), *The New Cambridge Modern History*, Vol. 2, Cambridge University Press.

Hay, Denys (1967), 'Fiat lux', in John Carter and Percy H. Muir (eds), *Printing and the Mind of Man*, London, Cassell.

Hay, Wendy (1978), *Adult Literacy in Britain: An Annotated Bibliography*, London, The Library Association.

Heath, Shirley Brice (1981), 'Toward an ethnohistory of writing in American education', in Marcia Farr Whiteman (ed.), *Writing*, Vol.I.

Heath, Shirley Brice (1983), *Ways with Words*, Cambridge University Press.

Herder, Johann Gottfried von (1959), *Über den Ursprung der Sprache*, Berlin, Akademie-Verlag [1772].

Hertzler, Joyce Oramel (1965), *A Sociology of Language*, New York, Random House.

Hill, Christopher (1967), 'Review of Peter Laslett, *The World we Have Lost*', *History and Theory*, 6, 117–27.

Hill, Christopher (1980), *Some Intellectual Consequences of the English Revolution*, London, Weidenfeld and Nicolson.

Hill, M.J., Harrison, R.M., Sargeant, A.V. and Talbot, V. (1973), *Men out of work*, Cambridge University Press.

Hills, Philip (ed.) (1980), *The Future of the Printed Word*, London, Frances Pinter.

Hirsch, Fred (1977), *Social Limits to Growth*, London, Routledge & Kegan Paul.

Hollis, Patricia (1970), *The Pauper Press: A Study in Working Class Radicalism of the 1830's*, Oxford University Press.

Home Office (1979), *Criminal Statistics, 1978*, London, HMSO.

Houston, R.A. (1982), 'The development of literacy: Northern England, 1640–1750', *Economic History Review*, second series, 35, 199–216.

Hoyles, Martin (ed.) (1977), *The Politics of Literacy*, London, Writers and Readers Publishing Cooperative.

Hughes, Everett C. (1937), 'Institutional office and the person' in *The Sociological Eye: Selected Papers*, Chicago, Aldine, 1971. (Originally published in the *American Journal of Sociology* 43, 1937.)

Hunter, C. St John with Harman D. (1979) *Adult Illiteracy in the United States: A Report to the Ford Foundation*, New York, McGraw-Hill.

Hurt, John (1971), *Education in Evolution: Church, State, Society and Popular Education 1800–1870*, London, Hart-Davis.

Hurt, John (1975), 'Education and the working class', *Society for the Study of Labour History*, Nos 30 and 31.

Innis, Harold A. (1951), *The Bias of Communication*, Toronto University Press.

Innis, Harold A. (1972), *Empire and Communications*, 2nd edn, rev. by M.Q. Innis, Toronto University Press.

Jeffrey, Jane and Maginn, Chris (1978), *The Failure of Literacy Provision in Manchester*, mimeo.

Jeffries, Charles (1967), *Illiteracy: A World Problem*, Pall Mall Press.

Johansson, Egil (1977), 'The history of literacy in Sweden in comparison with some other countries', *Educational Reports Umea*, 12.

Jones, H.A. (1977), 'Education and disadvantage', *Vaughan Paper*, No. 22, Department of Adult Education, University of Leicester.

Jones, H.A. and Charnley, A.H. (1978), *Adult Literacy: A Study of its Impact*, National Institute of Adult Education.

Jordan, W.K. (1961), *The Charities of Rural England, 1480–1660*, London, Allen and Unwin.

Kahan, A. (1966), 'Determinants of the incidence of literacy in rural nineteenth century Russia', in C.A. Anderson and M.J. Bowman (eds), *Education and Economic Development.*

Karabel, Jerome and Halsey, A.H. (eds) (1977), *Power and Ideology in Education*, Oxford University Press.

Kedney, R.J. (ed.) (1975), *The Adult Illiterate in the Community*, Bolton College of Education.

Kemeny, John G. (1983), 'The case for computer literacy', *Daedalus*, Spring, 211–30.

Kenyon, Frederick G. (1932), *Books and Readers in Ancient Greece and Rome*, Oxford, Clarendon Press.

King, Donald W. (1980), 'Electronic alternatives to paper-based publishing in science and technology', in P. Hills (ed.), *The Future of the Printed Word.*

Kohl, Herbert (1974), *Reading, How to*, Harmondsworth, Penguin Education.

Kozol, Jonathan (1978), 'A new look at the literacy campaign in Cuba', *Harvard Educational Review*, 48, No.3, 341–77.

Lacy, Dan (1983), 'Reading in an audiovisual and electronic era', *Daedalus*, Winter, 117–28.

Lampe, G.W.H. (ed.) (1969), *The Cambridge History of the Bible*, Vol.2, Cambridge University Press.

Laqueur, Thomas W. (1974), 'Literacy and social mobility in the industrial revolution in England', *Past and Present*, 64, 96–112.

Laqueur, Thomas W. (1976a), 'The cultural origins of popular literacy in England 1800–1850', *Oxford Review of Education*, 2, No. 3, 255–75.

Laqueur, Thomas W. (1976b), 'Working-class demand and the growth of English elementary education 1750–1850', in Lawrence Stone (ed.), *Schooling and Society.*

Laqueur, Thomas W. (1976c), *Religion and Respectability: Sunday Schools and Working Class Culture 1780–1850*, Yale University Press.

Laslett, Peter (1971), *The World We Have Lost*, London, Methuen.

Lawson, John and Silver, Harold (1973), *A Social History of Education in England*, London, Methuen.

Leach, Edmund (1977), 'Literacy be damned!', *Observer*, 19 March.

Leach, Edmund (1978), Address, Loughborough University of Technology, unpublished mimeo.

Leavis, Q.D. (1932), *Fiction and the Reading Public*, London, Chatto and Windus.

Leed, Eric (1980), 'Voice and Print', in Kathleen Woodward (ed.), *The Myths of Information*.

Leith, Dick (1983), *A Social History of English*, London, Routledge & Kegan Paul.

Lerner, Daniel (1958), *The Passing of Traditional Society*, Glencoe, Ill., Free Press.

Levine, David (1980), 'Illiteracy and family life during the first industrial revolution', *Journal of Social History*, 14, 25–44.

Levine, Kenneth (1980), *Becoming Literate*, SSRC research report, Department of Sociology, University of Nottingham.

Levine, Kenneth (1982), 'Functional literacy: fond illusions and false economies', *Harvard Educational Review*, 52, 3, 249–66.

Lewis, Naphtali (1974), *Papyrus in Classical Antiquity*, Oxford, Clarendon Press.

Limage, Leslie J. (1980), 'Illiteracy in industrialized countries: a sociological commentary', *Prospects*, 10, 2, 141–58.

Lipset, Seymour Martin (1959), 'Some social requisites of democracy: economic development and political legitimacy', *American Political Science Review*, 53, 69–105.

Lockridge, Kenneth A. (1974), *Literacy in Colonial New England*, New York, W.W. Norton.

Lockwood, David (1966), *The Blackcoated Workers: A Study in Class Consciousness*, Unwin University Books [1958].

Lord, Albert Bates (1968), *The Singer of Tales*, Harvard University Press.

Luria, A.R. (1976), *Cognitive Development: Its Cultural and Social Foundation*, trans. by M. Lopez-Morillas and L. Solotaroff, ed. Michael Cole, Harvard University Press.

MacFarlane, Tom (1976a), *Teaching Adults to Read*, London, Adult Literacy Resource Agency.

MacFarlane, Tom (1976b), 'The adult literacy curriculum: the content must be the goal', in Asher Cashdan (ed.), *The Content of Teaching*.

Mackie, Robert (ed.) (1980), *Literacy and Revolution: The pedagogy of Paulo Freire*, London, Pluto Press.

McCall, Daniel F. (1971), 'Literacy and Social structure: essay review', *History of Education Quarterly*, 11, 85–91.

McCann, Philip (ed.) (1977a), *Popular Education and Socialization in the Nineteenth Century*, London, Methuen.

McCann, Philip (1977b), 'Popular education, socialization and social control: Spitalfields 1812–1824', in Philip McCann (ed.), *Popular Education and Socialization in the Nineteenth Century*.

McKinlay, John B. (1975), 'Clients and organizations', in John B. McKinlay (ed.), *Processing People: Case Studies in Organizational Behaviour*, New York, Holt Rinehart & Winston.

McLuhan, H.M. (1962), *The Gutenberg Galaxy: The Making of Typographic Man*, London, Routledge & Kegan Paul.

McLuhan, H.M. (1964), *Understanding Media: The Extensions of Man*, London, Routledge & Kegan Paul.

Mace, Jane (1979), *Working with Words: Literacy beyond School*, London, Writers and Readers Publishing Cooperative.

Madge, Charles (1955), 'Some aspects of mass literacy', *British Journal of Educational Studies*, 4, 3–14.

Mandeville, Bernard (1970), *The Fable of the Bees*, ed. Phillip Harth, Harmondsworth, Penguin [1723].

Marshall, T.H. (1950), *Citizenship and Social Class and Other Essays*, Cambridge University Press.

Meadows, A.J. (1980), 'The future of the printed word: economic and social factors', in Philip Hills (ed.), *The Future of the Printed Word*.

Midwinter, Eric (1970), *Nineteenth Century Education*, Harlow, Longman.

Milroy, Lesley (1980), *Language and Social Networks*, Oxford, Blackwell.

Miner, John Nelson (1962), 'Schools and literacy in later medieval England', *British Journal of Educational Studies*, 11, 16–27.

More, Hannah (1830), *The Works of Hannah More*, Vol.III, *Stories for the Middle Ranks of Society and Tales for the Common People*, London, T. Cadell.

Moyle, Donald (ed.) (n.d.), *Perspectives on Adult Illiteracy*, United Kingdom Reading Association, Occasional Publication.

Mumford, Lewis (1963), *Technics and Civilization*, New York, Harcourt, Brace and World [1934].

Musgrove, Frank (1977), *Margins of the Mind*, London, Methuen.

Nafziger, Dean, Thompson, R., Brent, Hiscox, Michael D. and Owen, Thomas R. (1975), *Tests of Functional Adult Literacy: An Evaluation of Currently Available Instruments*, Portland, Oregon, Northwest Regional Educational Laboratory.

National Association for Remedial Education (1972), *Adult Illiteracy*, Kingston upon Hull, NARE.

Neuburg, V.E. (1967), 'Popular education and the beginnings of mass literacy in eighteenth century England, with particular reference to the influence of chapbooks', M. Ed. thesis, University of Leicester.

Neuburg, V.E. (1968), *The Penny Histories: A Study of Chapbooks for Young Readers over Two Centuries*, Oxford University Press.

Neuburg, V.E. (1969), 'Literacy in eighteenth century England: a caveat', *Local Population Studies*, 2, 44–6.

Neuburg, V.E. (1970), 'Popular education and literacy', *Local Population Studies*, 4, 51–5.

Neuburg, Victor E. (1973), 'The literature of the streets', in H.J. Dyos and Michael Wolff (eds), *The Victorian City: Images and Realities*, Vol.I, London, Routledge & Kegan Paul.

Neuburg, V.E. (1977a), *Popular Education in 18th Century England: A Study in the Origins of the Mass Reading Public*, London, Woburn.

Neuburg, V.E. (1977b), *Popular Literature: A History and Guide*, Harmondsworth, Penguin.

Northcutt, N., Kelso, C. and Barron, W.E. (1975), *Adult Functional Competency in Texas*, University of Texas Press.

Olson, David R. (1981), 'McLuhan: preface to literacy', *Journal of Communication*, 31, 136–43.

Ong, Walter J. (1970), *The Presence of the Word*, New York, Simon and Schuster.
Ong, Walter J. (1977), *Interfaces of the Word*, Cornell University Press.
Ong, Walter J. (1982), *Orality and Literacy: The Technologizing of the Word*, London, Methuen.
Open University (1973), *Resources for Reading*, Unit 17, Reading Development Course PE261, Milton Keynes, Open University Press.
Open University (1975), *Communication*, Social Sciences Foundation Course D101, Block 3, Unit 8, Milton Keynes, Open University Press.
Open University (1979), *Adults and Education*, Educational Studies Course E222, 'The Control of Education', Unit 14, Milton Keynes, Open University Press.
Opie, Iona and Peter (1972), *The Lore and Language of Schoolchildren*, Oxford, Clarendon Press [1959].
Orme, Nicholas (1973), *English Schools in the Middle Ages*, London, Methuen.
Oxenham, John (1980), *Literacy: Writing, Reading and Social Organisation*, London, Routledge & Kegan Paul.
Papert, Seymour (1980), *Mindstorms: Children, Computers and Powerful Ideas*, Brighton, Harvester Press.
Parkes, M.B. (1973), 'The literacy of the laity', in D. Daiches and A. Thorlby (eds), *The Medieval World*, Aldus Books.
Parry, Geraint (1978), 'Citizenship and knowledge', in P. Birnbaum, J. Lively and G. Parry (eds), *Democracy, Consensus and Social Contract*.
Parry, Milman (1971), *The Making of Homeric Verse*, London, Clarendon.
Parry, Milman and Lord, Albert Bates (eds) (1953), *Serbocroatian Heroic Songs*, 2 Vols, Harvard University Press.
Parsons, Talcott (1966), *Societies: Evolutionary and Comparative Perspectives*, Englewood Cliffs, N.J., Prentice-Hall.
Parsons, Talcott (1977), *The Evolution of Societies*, ed. Toby Jackson, Englewood Cliffs, N.J., Prentice-Hall.
Patten, T.H. and Clark, G.E. (1968), 'Literacy training and job placement of hard-core unemployed negroes in Detroit', *Journal of Human Resource* 3, 1, 25–46.
Paz, D.G. (1976), 'Working class education and the state 1839–1849: the sources of government policy', *Journal of British Studies*, 16 (1), 129–52.
Phelps, E.S. (1972), 'The statistical theory of racism and sexism', *American Economic Review* 62, 4, 659–61.
Phillips, H.M. (ed.) (1964), *Economic and Social Aspects of Educational Planning*, Paris, UNESCO.
Phillips, H.M. (1970), *Literacy and Development*, Paris, UNESCO.
Pollard, Graham (1937), 'The company of stationers before 1557', *The Library*, fourth series, 18, 1–38.
Postman, Neil (1970), 'The politics of reading', *Harvard Educational Review*, 40, 244–52.
Powell, William R. (n.d.), 'Levels of literacy', in Donald Moyle (ed.), *Perspectives on Adult Illiteracy*.
Pye, Lucien W. (ed.) (1963), *Communications and Political Development*, Princeton University Press.

Rein, Martin (1970), 'Problems in the definition and measurement of poverty', in Peter Townsend (ed.), *The Concept of Poverty*, London, Heinemann.

Resnick, D.P. and L.B. (1977), 'The nature of literacy: an historical exploration', *Harvard Educational Review*, 47, 370–85.

Resnick, D.P. (ed.) (1983), *Literacy in Historical Perspective*, Washington D.C., Library of Congress.

Richardson, H.G. (1941), 'Business training in medieval Oxford', *American Historical Review*, 46, 259–80.

Ricoeur, Paul (1973), 'The model of the text: meaningful action considered as a text', *New Literary History*, V, 91–117.

Riesman, David (1956), *The Oral Tradition, The Written Word, and The Screen Image*, Antioch University Press.

Riesman, David (1970), 'The oral and written traditions', in Edward Carpenter and M. McLuhan (eds), *Explorations in Communication: An Anthology*, London, Cape.

Robins, Kevin and Webster, Frank (1983), 'The mis-information society', *Universities Quarterly*, Autumn, 344–55.

Safilios-Rothschild, Constantina (1970), *The Sociology and Social Psychology of Disability and Rehabilitation*, New York, Random House.

Sanderson, Michael (1972), 'Literacy and social mobility in the industrial revolution in England', *Past and Present*, 56, 75–104.

Sanderson, Michael (1974), 'A rejoinder (to Laqueur)', *Past and Present*, 64, 108–12.

Sargant, W.L. (1867), 'On the progress of elementary education', *Journal of the Royal Statistical Society*, 30, 125–8.

Scheff, Thomas J. (1966), *Being Mentally Ill: A Sociological Theory*, Chicago, Aldine.

Schofield, R.S. (1968), 'The measurement of literacy in pre-industrial England', in J. Goody (ed.), *Literacy in Traditional Societies*.

Schofield, R.S. (1973), 'Dimensions of illiteracy, 1750–1850', *Explorations in Economic History*, 10, 437–54.

Schultz, T.W. (1963), *The Economic Value of Education*, Columbia University Press.

Schultz, T.W. (1971), *Investment in Human Capital: The Role of Education and Research*, Glencoe, Ill., Free Press.

Schultz, T.W. (1976), *Transforming Traditional Agriculture*, New York, Arno Press [1964].

Schuman, Howard, Inkeles, Alex and Smith, David H. (1967), 'Some social psychological effects and non-effects of literacy in a new nation', *Economic Development and Cultural Change*, 16, 1–14.

Scott, Robert A. (1969), *The Making of Blind Men: A Study of Adult Socialization*, New York, Russell Sage Foundation.

Scott, Robert A. (1970), 'The construction of conceptions of stigma by professional experts', in Jack D. Douglas (ed.), *Deviance and Respectability*.

Scribner, Sylvia and Cole, Michael (1973), 'Cognitive consequences of formal and informal education', *Science*, 182, 553–9.

Scribner, Sylvia and Cole, Michael (1978), 'Unpackaging literacy', *Social Science Information*, 17, 19–40.
Sheldon, William D. (1970), 'Literacy: a world problem', in J. Allen Figurel (ed.), *Reading Goals for the Disadvantaged.*
Shils, Edwards (1960), 'Mass society and its culture', *Daedalus*, 89, No.2, 287–314.
Shils, Edward (1972), *The Intellectuals and the Powers and Other Essays*, University of Chicago Press.
Shuy, Roger W. (1970), 'Language variation and literacy', in J. Allen Figurel (ed.), *Reading Goals for the Disadvantaged.*
Silver, Harold (1965), *The Concept of Popular Education*, London, MacGibbon and Kee.
Silver, Harold (1983), *Education as History: Interpreting Nineteenth and Twentieth Century Education*, London, Methuen.
Simon, Brian (1960), *Studies in the History of Education 1780–1870*, London, Lawrence and Wishart.
Smith, Anthony (1982), 'Information technology and the myth of abundance', *Daedalus*, No.4, 1–16.
Smith, Frank (1982), *Writing and the Writer*, London, Heinemann.
Smith, Roger (1967), 'Education, society and literacy: Nottinghamshire in the mid-nineteenth century', *University of Birmingham Historical Journal*, 12, 42–56.
De Sola Pool, Ithiel (1982), 'The culture of electronic print', *Daedalus*, No.4, 17–31.
De Sola Pool, Ithiel (1983), *Technologies of Freedom*, Harvard University Press.
Spence, A. Michael (1974), *Market Signalling: Informational Transfer in Hiring and Related Screening Processes*, Harvard University Press.
Spufford, Margaret (1979), 'First steps in literacy: the reading and writing experiences of the humblest seventeenth century spiritual autobiographers', *Social History*, 4, 407–35.
Starr, Paul (1983), 'The electronic reader', *Daedalus*, Winter, 143–56.
Start, K.B. and Wells, B.K. (1972), *The Trend of Reading Standards*, Windsor, National Foundation for Educational Research.
Stedman Jones, Gareth (1977), 'Class expression or social control?', *History Workshop*, 4, Autumn, 162–70.
Steinberg, S.H. (1979), *Five Hundred Years of Printing*, Harmondsworth, Penguin [1955].
Steiner, George (1971), 'Tomorrow', in *In Bluebeard's Castle: Some Notes towards the Redefinition of Culture*, London, Faber and Faber.
Steiner, George (1975), *Why English?*, Presidential Address, The English Association.
Steiner, George (1978a), 'Text and context', in *On Difficulty and Other Essays*, Oxford University Press [1976].
Steiner, George (1978b), 'After the book?', in *On Difficulty and Other Essays*, Oxford University Press [1972].
Stephens, W.B. (1976), 'Illiteracy in Devon and Cornwall during the industrial revolution 1754–1844', *Journal of Educational Administration and History*, 8, 1, 1–5.

Stephens, W.B. (1977a), 'Illiteracy and schooling in the provincial towns, 1640–1870: a comparative approach', in D.A. Reeder (ed.), *Urban Education in the Nineteenth Century*, London, Taylor and Francis.

Stephens, W.B. (1977b), 'Male and female illiteracy in seventeenth-century Cornwall', *Journal of Educational Administration and History*, 9, 1, 1–7.

Stephens, W.B. (ed.) (1983), *Studies in the History of Literacy: England and North America*, Museum of the History of Education, University of Leeds.

Stevens, Jenny (1974), 'A right to read', *Personnel Management*, 6, August, 26–9.

Stewart, Peter (1978), *Literacy Skills: Standards and Demands in Further Education*, Bolton Technical College.

Sticht, T.G. (1977), 'Comprehending reading at work', in M.A. Just and P.A. Carpenter (eds), *Cognitive Processes in Comprehension*, Hillsdale, N.J., Lawrence Erlbaum.

Sticht, T.G., Taylor, J.S., Kern, R.P. and Fox L.C. (1972), 'Project REALISTIC: determination of adult functional literacy levels', *Reading Research Quarterly*, 7, 424–65.

Stock, Arthur (1982), 'The United Kingdom: becoming and staying literate', *Prospects*, XII, No.2, 221–32.

Stone, Lawrence (1964), 'The educational Revolution in England, 1560–1640', *Past and Present*, 28, 41–80.

Stone, Lawrence (1965), *The Crisis of the Aristocracy 1558–1641*, Oxford University Press.

Stone, Lawrence (1969), 'Literacy and education in England, 1640–1900', *Past and Present*, 42, 69–139.

Stone, Lawrence (ed.) (1976), *Schooling and Society: Studies in the History of Education*, Johns Hopkins University Press.

Storch, Robert D. (ed.) (1982), *Popular Culture and Custom in Nineteenth Century England*, Beckenham, Croom Helm.

Strumilin, S.G. (1964), 'The economics of education in the USSR', in H.M. Phillips (ed.), *Economic and Social Aspects of Educational Planning*.

Stubbs, Michael (1976), *Language, Schools and Classrooms*, London, Methuen.

Stubbs, Michael (1980), *Language and Literacy*, London, Routledge & Kegan Paul.

Sussman, Marvin B. (ed.) (1966), *Sociology and Rehabilitation*, Washington D.C., American Sociological Association.

Tannen, Deborah (ed.) (1982a), *Spoken and Written Language: Exploring Orality and Literacy*, Norwood, N.J., Ablex.

Tannen, Deborah (1982b), 'The myth of orality and literacy', in W. Frawley (ed.), *Linguistics and Literacy*.

Thomas, Hendrik (1974), 'Literacy without formal education: a case study in Pakistan', *Economic Development and Cultural Change*, 22, 489–95.

Thompson, E.P. (1967), 'Time, work-discipline and industrial capitalism', *Past and Present*, 38, 56–97.

Thompson, E.P. (1968), *The Making of the English Working Class*, Harmondsworth, Penguin.

Thompson, James Westfall (1960), *The Literacy of the Laity in the Middle Ages*, New York, Burt Franklin [1939].

Thrupp, Sylvia L. (1948), *The Merchant Class of Medieval London*, University of Chicago Press.

Tipps, Dean C. (1973), 'Modernization theory and the comparative study of societies: a critical perspective', *Comparative Studies in Society and History*, 15, 199–226.

Townsend, Peter (1962), 'The meaning of poverty', *British Journal of Sociology*, 13, 210–27.

Townsend, Peter (1979), *Poverty in the United Kingdom*, Harmondsworth, Penguin.

Tyack, David (1966), 'The kingdom of God and the common school', *Harvard Educational Review*, 36, 447–69.

Tyler, William (1980), 'Credentialism and work organization: a neo-Durkheimian perspective', unpublished paper, University of Kent.

UNESCO (1947), *Fundamental Education: Common Ground for all Peoples*, New York, Macmillan.

UNESCO (1949), *Fundamental Education: A Description and Programme Monographs on Fundamental Education No. 1*, Paris, UNESCO.

UNESCO (1951), *Learn and Live: A Way Out of Ignorance for 1,200,000,000 People*, Paris, UNESCO.

UNESCO (1956), *Literacy Teaching: A Selected Bibliography*, ESD/18/A, Paris, UNESCO.

UNESCO (1957), *World Illiteracy at Mid-Century*, Paris, UNESCO.

UNESCO (1964), *World Literacy Programme*, 13/PRG/4, Paris, UNESCO.

UNESCO (1965a), *World Conference of Ministers of Education on the Eradication of Illiteracy*, Final Report, Paris, UNESCO.

UNESCO (1965b), *Literacy as a Factor in Development*, Minedlit/3, Paris, UNESCO.

UNESCO (1965c), *Provisional for the Preparation of Pilot Experimental Work-Oriented Literacy Projects*, LIT/EX/65/7, Paris, UNESCO.

UNESCO (1966), *An Asian Model of Educational Development: Perspectives for 1965–80*, Paris, UNESCO.

UNESCO (1970a), *Functional Literacy: Why and How*, Paris, UNESCO.

UNESCO (1970b), 'The concept of functional literacy and its application', ED/WS/170, Turin Literacy Round Table, unpublished mimeo.

UNESCO (1973), *Practical Guide to Functional Literacy: A Method of Training for Development*, Paris, UNESCO.

UNESCO (1976), *The Experimental World Literacy Programme: A Critical Assessment*, Paris, UNESCO.

UNESCO (1978a), *Statistical Yearbook*, 1977, Paris, UNESCO.

UNESCO (1978b), *Estimates and Projections of Illiteracy*, CSR–E–29, Paris, UNESCO Division of Statistics on Education.

University of Nottingham (1978a), 'Literacy' (Bibliography), University Library.

University of Nottingham (1978b), 'Basic education and the disadvantaged adult' (Bibliography), University Library.

University of Reading (1972–), *Literacy Documents*, Series D (Bibliography) Literacy Documentation Service, Agricultural Extension and Rural Development.

Unwin, Robert W. (1983), 'Literacy patterns in rural communities in the Vale of York, 1660–1840', in W.B. Stephens (ed.), *Studies in the History of Literacy*.

Vanderpool, Eugene (1973), 'Ostracism at Athens', in *Lectures in Memory of Louise Taft Semple*, University of Cincinnati Classical Studies, Vol. 2, University of Oklahoma Press.

Vann, Richard, T. (1974–5), 'Literacy in seventeenth-century England: some hearth-tax evidence', *Journal of Interdisciplinary History*, 5, 287–93.

Versluys, J.D.N. (1977), *Research on Adult Literacy: A Bibliography*, Tehran, International Institute for Adult Literacy Methods.

Vincent, David (1981), *Bread, Knowledge and Freedom*, London, Europa.

Vincent, David (1982), 'The decline of the oral tradition in popular culture', in Robert D. Storch (ed.), *Popular Culture and Custom in Nineteenth Century England*.

Voysey, Margaret (1972), 'Official agents and the legitimation of suffering', *The Sociological Review*, 20, 533–51.

Webb, R.K. (1950), 'Working class readers in early Victorian England', *English Historical Review*, 65, 333–51.

Webb, R.K. (1954), 'Literacy among the working classes in nineteenth century Scotland', *Scottish Historical Review*, 33, 100–14.

Webb, R.K. (1955), *The British Working Class Reader, 1790–1848: Literacy and Social Tension*, London, Allen and Unwin.

West, E.G. (1965), *Education and the State: A Study in Political Economy*, Institute of Economic Affairs.

West, E.G. (1975), *Education and the Industrial Revolution*, London, Batsford.

West, E.G. (1978), 'Literacy and the industrial revolution', *Economic History Review*, second series, 31, 369–83.

Wharton, C.R. (1966), 'Education and agricultural growth', in C.A. Anderson and M.J. Bowman (eds.), *Education and Economic Development*.

Whitelock, Dorothy (ed.) (1955), *English Historical Documents c.500–1042*, London, Eyre and Spottiswoode.

Whiteman, Marcia Farr (ed.) (1981), *Writing: The Nature, Development, and Teaching of Written Communication*, Vol.1, Variation in Writing, Hillsdale, N.J., Lawrence Erlbaum.

Wickwar, W.H. (1928), *The Struggle for the Freedom of the Press, 1819–1832*, London, Allen and Unwin.

Wiener, Joel H. (1969), *The War of the Unstamped: The Movement to Repeal the British Newspaper Tax 1830–1836*, Cornell University Press.

Wilks, Ivor (1968), 'The transmission of Islamic learning in the Western Sudan', in J. Goody (ed.), *Literacy in Traditional Societies*.

Williams, Raymond (1976), 'Communications as cultural science', in C.W.E. Bigsby (ed.), *Approaches to Popular Culture*.

Willis, Paul E. (1977), *Learning to Labour: How Working Class Kids get Working Class Jobs*, Farnborough, Hants., Saxon House.

Wood, F. (ed.) (1969), *The Evaluation of Functional Literacy Projects*, UNESCO Workshop, University of London Institute of Education.

Woodbury, Stephen A. (1979), 'Methodological controversy in labour economics', *Journal of Economic Issues*, 13, 933–55.

Woodward, Kathleen (ed.) (1980), *The Myths of Information: Technology and Postindustrial Culture*, London, Routledge & Kegan Paul.

Wormald, C.P. (1977), 'The uses of literacy in Anglo-Saxon England and its neighbours', *Transactions of the Royal Historical Society*, fifth series, 27, 95–114.

Wormald, F. and Wright C.E. (eds) (1958), *The English Library before 1700: Studies in its History*, London, Athlone.

Wright, Louis B. (1935), *Middle-Class Culture in Elizabethan England*, University of North Carolina Press.

Wright, Patricia (1981), 'Is legal jargon a restrictive practice?', in Sally M.A. Lloyd-Bostock (ed.), *Psychology in Legal Contexts: Applications and Limitations*, London, Macmillan.

Wrightson, Keith (1982), *English Society, 1580–1680*, London, Hutchinson.

Zinovyev, M. and Pleshakova, A. (1962), *How Illiteracy was Wiped Out in the USSR*, Moscow, Foreign Languages Publishing House.

Index

Index